MY AUTOBIOGRAPHY

MY AUTOBIOGRAPHY

by James Last
with Thomas Macho

Translated from German by Caterina Last

metro

Published by Metro Publishing
an imprint of John Blake Publishing Ltd,
3 Bramber Court, 2 Bramber Road,
London W14 9PB, England

www.blake.co.uk

First published in hardback in 2007

ISBN 978 1 84454 434 9

British Library Cataloguing-in-Publication Data:

A catalogue record for this book is available from the British Library.

Design by www.envydesign.co.uk

Printed and bound in Great Britain by William Clowes Ltd, Beccles, Suffolk

1 3 5 7 9 10 8 6 4 2

Original Title: Mein Leben by James Last, with Thomas Macho.
First published by Wilhelm Heyne Verlag.
© 2006 by Wilhelm Heyne Verlag, a division of Verlagsgruppe Random
House GmbH, München, Germany

All images reproduced by kind permission of Jurgen Mehl with the exception
of: section one, p4, below, p6, above, section two pages 2 and 3 © Gerd Tratz;
section two, p7, above and p8 © hgm-press; section two, p7, below
© Peter Boosey section one, p8 from James Last's personal collection.

Every attempt has been made to contact the relevant copyright-holders,
but some were unobtainable. We would be grateful if the appropriate
people could contact us.

contents

prologue:
In Palm Beach

Today is 16 April 2006, the night before my 77th birthday. I've come a long way and every day my past stretches further into the distance while the future grows shorter. Looking around my room, I see gold records, piles of scores, sheet music and more documents... photos, letters, concert programmes, mountains of CDs – the essence of a life. My life.

And images too... my parents in Bremen. My brothers, Werner and Robert. Waltraud, my first wife. The children, Ron and Caterina. Next summer Caterina will visit me with her husband and their two sons, Lenny and Jeremy. The boys are my dearest friends and best critics: if I play a new tune for them and they look at me with blank faces, I know I've got to do better. On the other hand, if they start really getting into it, I know I'm on the right track. For them, a summer holiday in Florida is paradise: the pool, the golf course, the terrific climate – and Grandpa, who finally has lots of time for them.

For more than 30 years, I have been drawn to this sunny, relaxed land. Our house is built right on a gorgeous golf course, at the 11th hole – a par four, dogleg left, 380 yards long, partly over marshland. The whole area used to be a gigantic swamp until it was drained years ago. There are still many exotic animals on the golf course: sand hill cranes, grey herons, wagtails, lynxes, and vultures – even Florida panthers appear every now and then. Sometimes an alligator will sunbathe lazily at the first tee.

Thanks to Christine, my second wife, I lead a remarkably healthy life at my age. We get up at seven in the morning. Before we have breakfast, we exercise: Christine jogs, and I do fitness walking. Afterwards, we swim a few laps in our pool and then have muesli with yoghurt for breakfast. I spend the morning in my study composing, arranging or preparing for the next tour or a TV appearance. That is my life: music is the air that I breathe.

Today, I work as many hours as I did when I was younger, but now I spend much more time on each arrangement, sometimes months. There always needs to be one more figure in the strings here, another crescendo there... If you work without lyrics, you need some other way of getting emotions across. If you don't succeed, the music is like an empty room. Furnishing this room in such a way that an audience feels at home in it is a beautiful task, albeit sometimes difficult and laborious. Anyone who thinks the computer makes work easier is mistaken. It merely allows you to come closer to perfection because you have countless possibilities at hand.

Then there's the light show for the performance. A full lighting concept has been in my head for months, more than a year before the next tour's starting date. In the past, many things were left to chance and sometimes the light show only worked well towards the end of the tour. Now I demand that everything is perfectly coordinated from the first beat, because I want to thrill my audience right from the start.

Our opening number, our prologue, is very important and it will be really tremendous this time. I've chosen the song 'Somewhere over the Rainbow' from the movie *The Wizard of Oz*, which Judy Garland sang in 1939. That makes the tune just about ten years younger than me but we will use the sound of 2006: a swirl of strings in a minor key, accompanied by the sound of rain. Then, as a rainbow appears across the auditorium, the mood changes to major. Two trumpets, to the left and right of the drums, play the melody. It has to be absolutely electrifying. It has to send a shiver down the spine of the whole audience – just like it did to me while writing the score. Is that kitsch?

Later in the show we might add 'You Are so Beautiful' – the Joe Cocker hit – for Bob Findley, who plays a muted trumpet so beautifully. I can hear exactly how it will sound. Or Joe Dorff, our new pianist, might sing a tune, like he often does when we all relax in the hotel bar after a concert and there's a piano around. Joe's got a great voice. I am moved every time he sings R. Kelly's 'I Believe I Can Fly'. The song will signal the end of a long night; we know it's time to hit the hay.

This afternoon, I will play a round of golf with Christine. Afterwards, we'll cook for a friend from Vienna who is staying with us, so our evening might finish a little later than usual. We'll sit on our porch and enjoy the balmy Florida night with a bottle of fine red wine.

At 6pm sharp, the phone will ring. It will be midnight in Europe, so over there it's already my birthday. Peter from Switzerland, one of my most loyal fans, will be on the phone. The first well-wisher. The phone could go on ringing for the next couple of hours: maybe the evening on the porch won't be so peaceful after all.

Memories of past birthday parties go through my mind. My 50th birthday in London, with thousands of fans singing 'Happy Birthday' at the sold-out Royal Albert Hall. My 60th birthday in Bremen, where we gave an open-air concert in the market square and 5,000 people came to congratulate me. My 70th birthday in Hamburg, when my musicians presented me with a memorial tablet at St Michael's, Hamburg's landmark church… Have seven years really passed since then?

This year, I won't have a large celebration. I'll go out to dinner at a nice restaurant with Christine and my family, we'll toast my birthday with a glass of champagne – and I will realise to my disbelief that my 78th year has begun…

part one:
A Bremen Town Musician

Little Hans

In 1929, the year of my birth, a ship named after my home city won the Blue Riband for the fastest crossing of the Atlantic. The *Bremen* was a magnificent passenger ship and the dance band for its well-heeled passengers would have played pieces like 'Ich küsse ihre Hand, Madam' (I Kiss Your Hand, Milady), 'Siboney' and probably the great hit of that year, 'Happy Days Are Here Again'. Although considering that Black Friday was about to hit the New York Stock Exchange and bring on the Great Depression, they would hardly turn out to be 'Happy Days'.

When I was born on 17 April, our house at 33 Helmholtz Street in the suburb of Sebaldsbrück, was not yet finished. The stairs to the first floor were still being built, so every night my dad had to carry me up a rickety ladder to bed. This sensation of floating in my father's arms is my earliest childhood memory – although it is hard to believe it could be real since I was less than a year old.

The Lasts, my father's side of the family, were notorious in Bremen. There were twelve children, ten of them boys, and almost all of them boxed for sport. They had been a bit wild as lads. When the gang descended on a pub, it was a case of, 'Watch out, the Lasts are coming!' The boys would saunter in through the front door, knock back a beer and then exit through the back. None of them paid. A bunch of madmen.

I was the youngest child in a large family. My father's first wife had died young, and he brought three children into his second marriage, Bernhard, Fred and Minna, who hated her name so much she would only respond to Gitta. Bernhard was 15 years older than me, and to me he was always just 'The Brother'. In fact, once in school I was supposed to write a composition about my family and in all seriousness I wrote, 'My oldest brother is called Brother.' He in turn called me his 'Boy' and would order me about. I was proud of being allowed to tidy up his room for him.

It was surely not easy for my mother, Martha, to receive a dowry like that, but she had a giant heart. In her opinion, there was plenty of room for more children in our family, so along came we three: Robert, Werner and I, the baby of the family.

My father was a minor official at the Bremen Department of Works. Since our family was so blessed with children, it was clear we couldn't enjoy much luxury. During the week we would usually eat reheated stew for days on end out of the same pot. On Friday my mother would set off to the Department of Works, taking me with her, to collect my father's pay packet. Then she would go from shop to shop buying up the leftovers: ends of sausage, cake leftovers and anything at which our 'betters' turned their noses up. For us, sausage on bread at the weekend was a real feast. It wasn't until I was a bit older that we even got chops every now and then.

We would always eat together. My father would arrive home at five on the dot, the family would gather around the table and then we'd start. Needless to say, we would always eat every last crumb on our plates.

In those days, Sebaldsbrück still lay on the outskirts of Bremen. Our street was full of semi-detached houses, except for ours which stood on its own. My parents had scrimped and saved for every last brick. On the ground floor there was the kitchen and two rooms, and on the first floor were three bedrooms. As the youngest, I was allowed to sleep in my parents' bedroom.

Built on to the house was a laundry, and there was an extension to this extension – the toilet with a pit for the waste water. This, of course, had to be emptied every so often, a task my father, rather crassly, used to describe as 'fishing for eels'.

The garden in front of the house was a paradise for me and my friends. We could romp around and make noise to our hearts' content. For a long time, my favourite place was the sandbox my father built for us.

When I turned ten, I was overjoyed to get a Schuco model car for my birthday. From then on, the street was my playground. In those days it had still to be tarred over, and most of the traffic was me and my little tin car. It had a proper gear stick and I felt just like a grown-up. In winter I would carry out my tyre tests. There was no central heating in our house, just an oven in the living room and the kitchen stove, on which my mother would warm her feet when she was cold. During the night the stove would go out, so the kitchen would cool down and the condensation that ran down the windows during the day would form little patches of ice on the floor. It was on these that my Schuco car had to undergo curve and acceleration tests. The wheels would spin and I was able to establish quite clearly that winter tyres were required when the temperature outside was below seven degrees.

Even at Christmas expensive toys like an electric train set – the greatest of all my wishes – remained just a dream. But we always had a giant Christmas tree that reached to the ceiling. Every year my dad would decorate it with old iron baubles from his first marriage, much to the disapproval of my mother. But he knew no mercy: the awful things had to be hung right at the front. And every Christmas he played a shellac record of his favourite piece: the interlude from the opera *Notre Dame* by Franz Schmidt. Many years later I recorded it for him on one of my classical LPs.

As soon as my father came home from work he was there for us kids. In summer, weather permitting, we would pack the cold leftovers of the previous evening's meal and some soft drinks and ride down to the Weser river to go swimming – it was wonderful! But my father's greatest passion was music. Every weekend he would head off to play at some wedding or baptism or village festival. He had a bicycle trailer for his accordion and drums, and thus equipped he'd set off on his way. Quite often he'd turn up an hour early because he could barely wait for it to start. Sometimes he played two instruments at once: his hi-hat and bass drum at his feet and the accordion in his hands. He had perfect pitch, too, and he was the first person to teach me tricks that I could use later – when arranging music, for instance. 'When you change key, you have to go up a minor third...' He usually played from memory, although we had masses of sheet music at home.

These events were known as *Muggen* – music nights – and for just four marks he put heart and soul into playing all night. Sometimes he would play little improvisations of his own, just off the top of his head. He called them his 'Delmenhorst pieces' – I still don't know why he named them after that particular town. At about three or four in the morning my father would arrive home, dead tired, put his head down on the kitchen table and sleep for a while. At six he had to leave for work at the power station.

These music evenings were an important part of my father's life – in more ways than one. Since he never even took a penny from his pay packet, his performances were a way of earning pocket money for himself – and even then he would give some of it to us kids. If my older brothers were short of cash, they only had to say, 'Dad, can you spare a mark?' and he'd always whip out his ancient wallet and come up with something for them. He didn't need much for himself. If he went to the pub for a beer, someone would usually pay for it because he was the best storyteller around. As a young lad he had gone to sea and he had so many stories to tell that he never ran out of things to say. He could entertain his mates for hours on end.

When he was out reading the gas meters, I would often see him standing in someone's front garden with a cup of coffee in his hand: he'd be chatting and laughing with the housewife whose meter he had just read. He'd tease her and have a bit of fun with everyone: such light-heartedness perhaps compensated for the nature of his work.

If he went shopping, he would take hours to get home. 'Other people have made a trip around the world in the time you take to go shopping!' he'd be told.

'Life is for living!' was his motto, something I adopted for my own life. Once when I was in hospital – as an adult – my father was supposed to visit me. He was due during the doctor's rounds, but neither he nor the doctor turned up. It turned out the two of them had been sitting next door and my father had been telling stories. When they finally turned up at my bedside, the doctor was really impressed. 'Your father is a great man!' He was someone who felt a need to give everything he had, to share everything. It seems I have inherited that from him.

My relationship with my brothers was wonderful. I was the baby of the family, so they were never really my playmates, as the age difference was too great. But our family liked to clown around and even my father would join in. Werner was the most talented comic of us all. He would make such fun of our good-hearted mother that she really had to put up with a lot. All three of us inherited our father's love of music, in contrast to my half-brothers and half-sister, who were not at all musical. Werner practised trombone, our father would drum on his kit in the overcrowded kitchen, and Robert always had his saxophone within reach. Once he had arranged to meet a pretty girl at the bus stop, but just continued blowing on his sax. When we pointed out he was late for his rendezvous, he just said, 'Oh, she can wait. Practice is more important!'

Our home was just like a music school – you could say I just needed to put all the notes together. There was a piano in the living room – it used to be an electric pianino but we had taken out the cylinder – and I plinked out my first scales on that. Our mother put up with this circus with great patience, especially as her family had not been particularly musical – except for her uncle Leo, a dreamy person who had played the violin.

My mother was always there for us, although such a large household meant a lot of work – especially since the house-hold appliances then were completely inadequate compared to today. I can still see myself standing with her at the big mangle in the laundry, helping her to wring out a giant pile of washing. Afterwards, we used the water out of the wash tub as bath water, so the laundry was also the bathroom. In winter that was a very short-lived pleasure! Once the oven that heated the tub had cooled down, you could almost go ice-skating in the laundry.

From time to time I'd hear my mother say, 'With so many children, I hardly have a life!' But, even if she did complain now and again, she was very happy in the depths of her heart – if she hadn't wanted such a big family, she certainly wouldn't have married a man who already had three children. Our father often teased her, although usually she might not quite get his good-natured joke straight away.

She never kept a tight rein on us children. 'If you hit me,' I would say cheekily, 'I'll pinch your varicose veins!' That was about the height of our differences. Despite the closeness of our living arrangements, there was never really any exchange of angry words, either between my parents or between us children. When I think back to my family, I only ever see smiling faces.

Later, my relationship with my mother became very deep. After I'd been in Florida for a while, my parents would come and visit from time to time and we would catch up on the holidays they'd never been able to afford in the past. Twice I flew from the USA to Germany for one day, just to celebrate my mother's birthday. I wanted to give her a surprise, so I got out of the taxi a couple of doors down from 33 Helmholtz Street. I could see her leaning on the windowsill, looking down the street. Who could that be? Her expression grew more and more incredulous, her eyes growing bigger, until she finally burst out: 'Hansi! Is it really you? What are you doing here?!'

My mother remained living in our house in Sebaldsbrück, the house of my childhood, until the day she passed away...

Schooldays in the Shadow of the Swastika

I spent my entire schooldays – from the beginning of primary school till the end of music college – in Nazi Germany. I was four years old when Hitler seized power, so the swastika, the marching troops and the uniforms were everywhere and therefore didn't seem out of the ordinary. But to me and my friends in our little world on Helmholtz Street they held no special meaning.

I wasn't particularly good at school. I was actually rather shy and one of the 'good' kids. I did occasionally get a clip around the ear, but these were all the more memorable for being so unjust. Once a teacher slapped my face during school choir because he claimed I had been talking. I was completely innocent, but the clout was so hard that I ended up getting an ear infection. Another time it was a cloakroom incident. I sat in the last row of class and behind me were the coat racks. A schoolmate had sat on my seat and used his feet to bend all the cloak hooks. The teacher stormed towards me with a face like thunder.

'What have you done!?' he demanded angrily.

'It wasn't me,' I replied meekly.

'That's what they all say!' he said, drawing himself up in front of me and clipping me on the ear.

But I never saw any of these people wearing a party badge. If I stop to think about it, some of my teachers could well have been Nazis, but my school time in Bremen was essentially free of ideology.

Despite the distances and the passage of time, I still keep in contact with some of my early school friends. They would often turn up when I was in Bremen with my band for TV recordings. One of them, Günter Boschen, lived in our street. He was an orphan and lived with his adoptive parents. Once I gave him my old accordion for his birthday, and later on, when I celebrated my 16th birthday, he turned up with this old thing – now almost an antique – and gave it back to me.

There was a strong bond between us kids in our little street. For instance, when Günter caught scarlet fever and was taken to hospital in an ambulance, we all stood around it waving goodbye and shouting, 'Come back soon!'

a bremen town musician

One day I was playing in the street with my beloved Schuco car when I heard Hitler's voice from the radio at the kitchen window: 'We have been returning fire since 4.45...' It was 1 September 1939, and he was announcing to the Reichstag in Berlin the Reich's staged declaration of war against Poland. Naturally I had no idea what was really going on but later, when I was ten and heard about shooting and war, it seemed obvious to me that 'we' would win, come what may. After all, 'we' had Max Schmeling and Max Schmeling was the strongest boxer in the world, so 'they' wouldn't stand a chance.

When I think back to it, they were more the naïve thoughts of a six-year-old. I was a 'late bloomer' – and, as you will see, this applied in many respects. How could I have even suspected that I would only survive the Second World War unscathed because I had been born 'too late'? For me, the inconceivable catastrophe of this war was something completely abstract. It was something that was happening far, far away and had nothing whatever to do with my life.

We didn't talk about politics at home. However, we did listen to the foreign news from the BBC in London, which very soon took on a different tone to what the Reich propaganda would have us believe. 'Dum dum dum dummmm, dum dum dum dummmm – hier ist die BBC mit ihrem deutschsprachigem Service...' You could hear it every evening from the kitchen window, and a neighbour would call out, in broad Low German, 'Mr Last, whad'd 'e say?'

Listening to this programme was strictly forbidden and one day there was a loud knock at the door. But it wasn't the police, just a well-meaning neighbour. 'Good grief, Mr Last! Turn the radio down – everyone in the street can hear it!'

There were no dyed-in-the-wool Nazis in our immediate neighbourhood, otherwise the reaction would have been different. But one day, Mr Haupt, who lived on the other side of the street, was arrested in his home – for political reasons, it was rumoured. He was apparently in a concentration camp, which fortunately he survived, and after the war he joined the Social Democratic Party (SDP), which was then still rooted in the workers' movement and had been banned by the Nazis.

Even in the worst years of the war we didn't really suffer any personal hardship. We had always lived very modestly even in times of peace, so there wasn't much difference. Now and again I'd help out at the baker's or the butcher's in our street to bring in some additional food for us. I'd count up the ration coupons or put bread in the oven and in return I would maybe get a bread roll or a piece of sausage. I didn't really see it as work: it was fun.

Yet slowly but surely the thundering of the big guns drew closer and suddenly the horror was at our door, too. My brothers, who had been working in the Borgward and Focke-Wulf arms factories, were called up to join the Wehrmacht. Suddenly it was quiet in our house. Instead of eight of us, there were only four: my parents, my sister Minna and I. Both Focke-Wulf and Borgward manufactured in Bremen – Borgward was even in our suburb – so from 1941 onwards the city had become an important target for the bombing raids of the Royal Air Force. My father was in the civil air defence and I was his messenger. I received a helmet with a big 'M' for *Melder* – messenger – on it, and at night, when the planes flew over and the bombs fell, I had to run out of the bunker through shrapnel, defence fire and falling houses to report to the command points.

I was far too excited to feel fear during these hazardous runs. Someone must have been holding a protective hand over me, since I never suffered even the slightest scratch.

Later, in 1943, the true horrors of war were brought home to us in all their clarity. One July evening we could see a bright fire on the horizon from our balcony. It was Hamburg, burning from a hail of Allied bombs. But there was worse to come. The same year the doorbell rang and I went to open the door. There stood the mayor of Sebaldsbrück, and he had never been to our house before.

He asked if my parents were home, but my mother was already right behind me.

He only managed to say, 'Your son Bernhard...' but he didn't need to go on. We ran out to my father, who was trimming his beloved fruit trees in the garden.

'Dad, Bernhard's been killed in action!'

My father crumpled: he fell to the ground and cried like a small child. My world crashed down, too. Bernhard, my beloved big brother. Bernhard, my hero in so many things. Bernhard, of whom the family was so proud, dead. It was incomprehensible. I pictured Bernhard, a tailor, standing at his sewing machine tapping out the rhythm of the music on the radio. I thought of the last evening we'd spent together, when he was home on leave from the front. He had invited some girls over and I, proud as punch, was permitted to put on the records for 'the grown-ups'. Helmut Zacharias played 'Sweet and Lovely' while they bopped along to it. Then he said, 'Boy, into bed!' and my evening was over, although for him it was just beginning. Perhaps it was the last moment of happiness in his all-too-short life.

Not so long ago I found a letter from one of Bernhard's comrades among some old documents, describing the tragic circumstances of his death. My brother had been in a foxhole during the Wehrmacht's 'glorious' Russian campaign and a tank had crushed him.

His premature death left me with an indelible loathing for war of any kind, but at the same time I also realised something else. You have to get on with life when everything around you falls to pieces.

Our parents never tried to push any of us into a particular profession. They never said, 'You have to do this or that!' Everything I have done in life has arisen from my own inner drive. Being compelled to do something gives rise to dissent and aggression. Not having to, on the other hand, creates freedom. My father always said, 'Nothing is worse than a profession that brings you no joy and that is torture for decades on end. It's better to have less money but be happy!' I think he knew exactly what he was talking about. Without his weekly excursions into the world of entertainment and music, he probably never would have been such a contented person.

There was no doubt that music would also play an important role for us younger children. Robert and Werner, eight and six years older than me respectively, both had private music lessons. They had earned the money for this themselves from their jobs at the arms factories. When I was 14 and had to face the matter of getting a qualification, they both supported my wish to take up music, too. 'Whatever you do, don't work in the arms factory,' they said. 'Make sure you get to a decent music school.'

But I was not a child prodigy by any stretch of the imagination. I didn't even have my first piano lesson until I was 12. My teacher thought herself a lady, rather than a woman. When I played my etudes for her, she would get bored and gaze out the window at the occasional passing traffic. She was a typical teacher of the old school and constantly let me know all the things I could not do. After a year she declared, with complete conviction, 'My dear boy, nothing will come of you. Music is not your path. Look for something more sensible...'

Despite this devastating verdict, I didn't give up. My next piano teacher was called Ernst Wellen, and he was like a father to me. He was calm and competent and had the right feeling for my sense of music. He would put his coffee cup down on the piano – but in such a way that it didn't rattle – and then we would discuss every detail of the notation, the melody phrasing and the right expression. He gave me back my joy for music. Today it is taken for granted that talent should be encouraged and supported. Thank God that Ernst Wellen knew that back then, too.

But in the dramatically worsening situation of the German Reich in 1943, all the private music schools had long since closed. The only remaining way to further my musical education was the *Heeresmusikschule*, the army music school. After a year of lessons with Mr Wellen, I felt ready to risk reporting for the entrance exam in Frankfurt. There they sat, the honourable gentlemen – not in uniform but in suits and ties – and listened carefully with stern faces and ears pricked to my performance of a piece by Bach. I am not an exam person at all – skinny little Hans was trembling from top to toe – but I got over the first hurdle.

Then we had the sports test. Although I was actually quite good at sport, I could never really throw a ball very well – and now I had to report for ball-throwing! I only managed a weak throw and thought I'd blown my chance. Evidently, however, they didn't attach too much importance to it, because they still accepted me at the school.

Originally I had wanted to study the clarinet, but the powers-that-be had already decided I should study the bassoon. But, before I had even reported for my first day, the school in Frankfurt was bombed, so I was posted instead to the romantic little town of Bückeburg, near Hanover.

When I entered the school, I – and the 50 other newcomers – had to stand along in front of the entire troop of teachers. The first on the right was Mr Rieb, who was to be my teacher. He only held the low rank of private, so I said to myself, if he's only a private he must be a good person and an even better musician, otherwise he'd be a staff sergeant or – even more unmusical – a second lieutenant!

Private Rieb was a congenial admirer of all sorts of music and I liked him on the spot because he reminded me of Mr Wellen. As well as being responsible for the instrument room, he was in charge of double-bass lessons. I had already been thinking about making dance music with Robert and Werner, so the double bass interested me a lot because it fitted in so well with drums and accordion, the instruments my brothers played. Up until then, they had been content with simply imitating the bass vocally every now and then, much in the style of Flying Pickets.

'And which wind instrument do you want to play?' asked Private Rieb.

Again, I declared my wish to learn clarinet, thinking of Benny Goodman, about whom I had known for some time. Whenever I'd gone with my mum to pick up Dad's pay packet at the gas works, I'd seen a big poster of a clarinettist in the office. 'Criminal hands fingering an A,' it declared. The clarinettist was Benny Goodman, designated 'the swing-Jew Benni Gutmann from Neu York' by Reich propaganda. That was what really caught my attention, so clarinet it was going to be.

'I'm afraid that's not possible. You can only take tuba with bass,' said Private Rieb, and instantly I had a giant E-flat tuba in my hands. Oh well, better than a bassoon. The mouthpiece was so big that it slipped back and forth across my little mouth when we were marching, but I must admit I hardly ever practised since I found it so easy to play.

The music school demanded a lot from us. Besides our music lessons, we had to complete normal military training, as well as finishing our O-levels. Since it was an army school we obviously had to wear uniforms – my first pair of long trousers, by the way – and had to report in a military fashion: 'Cadet Private Last, reporting for practice duty, sir.'

I was given a small homework book with notes like: 8hrs, PP, R32, which meant 8am, piano practice, room 32. After this was TP – tuba practice – in a different room. At times the rooms were so far apart that you had to go through several courtyards to get from one to the other, but you couldn't dawdle on the way. The teachers had calculated the times required to a T, and anyone who overstepped the allotted time had a double pile of sheet music slapped on them. There was a small peephole in the door of every practice room, just like in a prison. Every now and then, the peephole would open and a stern pair of eyes would check whether the students were working diligently.

One of the first pieces I had to play on the bass with a bow was the overture to *The Thieving Magpie* by Rossini. Even now I can see myself as a young lad standing in that music room, sweat pouring down my face as I scraped out endless series of semi- and demisemiquavers.

In contrast to my old days with Mr Wellen, our lessons were very dry. We were always getting new pieces of music, which we had to study endlessly, and free interpretation was just as frowned on as light entertainment. In my class, incidentally, was Horst Fischer, who later became a well-known soloist in popular music with his 'Golden Trumpet'.

In the evenings we played jazz on the side, with me usually playing drums. We didn't have the sheet music, of course, but we knew the songs from the illegal radio stations. Jazz had been declared 'degenerate music' by the Nazis and was consequently forbidden. Our ploy was to have various bits of meaningless scores lying around, with German names. 'Mosquito' was the name we gave 'Perdido', a piece that I eventually recorded with my band more than 40 years later.

So, if the staff sergeant stormed into the room – 'Enough of that! We won't have that music being played here!' – we would feign innocence. 'Permission to speak, sir! But look, sir, that is a German tune!'

Little did I know that this trick would serve me just as well decades later, on a tour through the realm of an entirely different totalitarian regime.

Apart from this contemptuous, deprecating attitude towards anything to do with Jews or blacks, our everyday school life was largely free of the Third Reich and its atrocities, despite our uniforms.

One summer day in 1944, we all had to muster because something important and outrageous had happened. We were told that an attempt had been made on the life of the Führer, a heinous crime, but that 'providence had saved our beloved Führer' etc etc. I stopped listening. Only music counted for us students, nothing else had anything to do with us – or so we thought. One day one of our teachers took us to a labour camp in Minden, though I don't know why. We didn't go in, but it brought home to us much more clearly conditions in the Third Reich. We saw the prisoners, both Germans and foreigners, and what a dreadful state they were in. We realised these people were in direst need and later we returned, without our teacher, and threw bread to them over the fence.

My schooling at Bückeburg would normally have led to me becoming an opera conductor or something similar. I must say the thought did appeal to me, but the final collapse of Nazi Germany put an end to any such ambitions: the school was closed in April 1945. As strange as it may seem, up to that point we boys had never touched on the topic of war among ourselves. We were young and so busy with our etudes and circles of five that we barely took note of the drama playing itself out around us. Perhaps we just blotted it out to protect ourselves.

In the last weeks of the war, though, its tragic reality struck us full blast. All my friends and classmates born before 1 April 1929 had to march off with the last contingent of the Nazi regime into a senseless battle that had been long since lost. I was extraordinarily lucky. I had entered this world 17 days 'too late', and that probably saved my life. I was allowed to go home.

Radio Days

The war was still raging, so getting the 110 kilometres from Bückeburg to Bremen was not easy. The nearest train station was about ten kilometres away in Minden, where most of the boys from my school year had been deployed. Minden, however, was a launch base for the V1 rockets so dreaded by the Allies, so it was an important target for the approaching British troops. Many thousands of people were fleeing. The trains were completely overcrowded, with every space being bitterly fought for – and I don't mean in the sense of a seat. Passenger trains had long since ceased running and we had to make do with freight trains.

To make matters worse, I had sprained my ankle in the midst of all this chaos, so I was in a panic that I wouldn't manage to get home. Finally, I succeeded in catching a train from Minden to Hanover, more or less as the last person on board. With my sprained ankle, I was hanging on to the outside of one of the wagons and the journey was truly harrowing. Although I wore a uniform, we had received an ID card that declared: 'Cadet privates are not soldiers within the meaning of the Defence Act.'

That turned out to be very helpful when dealing with the American and British troops.

When I finally arrived back in Bremen, exhausted and covered in soot, I found a completely bombed-out city: ruined houses, rubble and frightened, emaciated people crawling out of their cellars. The horror in their expressions told of the nightmare of the nights of bombing, many deaths, fear and hunger and the loss of their existence. On my way through the expanse of rubble to Helmholtzstrasse I ran into neighbours, who told me, 'A bomb has just exploded in your garden. It doesn't look good.' In shock and fearing the worst, I ran home as quickly as I could. Luckily, the house was still standing – only part of one wall was missing. The fruit trees my father had so carefully nurtured 'for hard times' had all been destroyed, but my parents were alive.

We used the hole that the bomb had blown in our garden to bury a few things that we, in our naivety, believed had better be hidden underground: my school uniform, my father's hunting rifle and my mother's costume jewellery – the last thing she wanted was for strange soldiers to make off with it. They arrived a few days later: a handful of British soldiers were temporarily billeted on us. Months later, when the British and American soldiers had left our house, we had to make an excavation of almost archaeological proportions to retrieve our treasures.

In the last days of the war, Bremen was put under American administration. The US soldiers wanted to have a bit of atmosphere in their bars, and somehow they'd heard that the Last family could play music. Shortly after my return, a giant black GI in uniform turned up at our door and bellowed, 'Do you play music?' He was probably looking for my brothers, but neither of them had returned from captivity so I was the only one there.

I had to get into a jeep with him and drive to an improvised dance club, where I stumbled through a couple of numbers on the piano. I had no idea what the latest US hits were, but the good thing was that I got sheet music – so-called hit kits – and suddenly discovered a fascinating new musical world. There were some fantastic songs among them, such as 'Nancy (With the Laughing Face)', 'Always', 'Don't Fence Me In' and 'Rum and Coca Cola'. Over the years I have recorded many of them with my orchestra.

My pay was in cigarettes and chocolate. I shared out the chocolate among the children in our street but the cigarettes were as valuable as cash. My father exchanged them for butter and once even for a baby pig from a farmer. There was a shortage of food and even in the cities there wasn't much that was edible to be found. He brought the pig home in a rucksack on his bicycle after nightfall, which was risky since we weren't allowed out after dark. Consequently, he couldn't put his lights on, and the pig grunted the whole way home. My father and I slaughtered the poor animal in our laundry – a true feast in those lean times.

But the cigarettes I got from the Americans held another meaning for me. They were my first real payment – and thus I irrevocably became a professional musician. I have never earned money with anything but music.

It was at this time, immediately after the war, that I did something for the first time that was to make me famous: I arranged music. It was the background music for an American documentary entitled *The Hunters*. I received a few musical sketches and had to make an enormously long score out of them. I don't think I knew that what I was doing was called 'arranging', but I set to work and tried to do my best. I had only just turned 16.

One by one my brothers' musician friends returned home from their war service. It seemed obvious that they should form a dance band and play in the GI clubs. Robert and Werner were still in captivity, but I could play the bass so I was one of the crew. The only problem was that I didn't have an instrument. What was

I to do? Finally, I made a beeline for my old teacher and, with feigned despair, begged him for help. I desperately wanted to practise the bass – would he perhaps let me borrow his? The good man actually let me have his bass, so now I could perform.

The club in which I now played my fingers to the bone for several nights was called Malepatus. But I had been used to using a bow for classical music, and at 16 my skin was still too soft to withstand plucking for hours on end. I had blood blisters on my forefinger, middle finger, little finger – everywhere.

The behaviour in these clubs was anything but civilised and the GIs were none too gentle. They fired their revolvers at the ceiling Wild West style, the whisky flowed copiously, the atmosphere grew more heated and finally one of these roughnecks kicked my bass so hard with his big soldier's boots that the instrument broke. With a guilty conscience I trotted back to my poor teacher and made my confession.

I didn't have to wheedle to get my next instrument: the American military government simply confiscated one for me. We played at these club evenings till curfew, but, while the soldiers cheerfully went back to their quarters, we had to pack up our instruments and somehow get home in the dark. I had a particularly hard time with my cumbersome instrument. But it was worth it. We got butter and cigarettes as pay – and, when the GIs were gone, we searched the empty bar for cigarette butts to make into 'new' ones.

One evening, one of the musicians told me about a great drummer he had met in a prisoner-of-war camp in Bad Kreuznach. He was German but wore a British uniform and was allowed to play music for the British soldiers – highly unusual at this camp, which was well known for its strictness. 'When this smashing musician gets home,' my friend said, 'it'd be great to have him in our little combo!'

Sure enough, when this 'smashing musician' was released from captivity, he joined us straight away on the drums – it was none other than my brother Robert! A short time later, Werner returned home as well, but neither of them ever breathed a word of their experiences in the war.

Still, we three were a team again. The only disadvantage was that I had to give them back their suits, which by now fitted me quite well.

Around this time a cardboard sign at Bremen station opened up a very interesting field of activity for me. MUSICIAN WANTED, it read. The notice was signed by Hans-Günther Oesterreich, now recognised as the founder of Radio Bremen. 'Hänschen' Oesterreich was a remarkable man. During the war he had run the Nazis' European broadcasting station from occupied Belgrade. Although this was part of their propaganda machine, he used his remote post to broadcast forbidden music, such as jazz or tunes by Jewish composers, thus cleverly countering official policy. Towards the end of the war, he applied to the US military government for a licence to set up his own broadcasting station, which was granted at the end of 1945. Now he was looking for musicians.

I knew nothing of that, of course, when I went to his 'office', which consisted of a desk under a fruit tree in a small garden. I introduced myself and my luck was in: he didn't have a double-bass player yet. My fellow musicians were Friedrich Meyer, who later married the film actress and singer Margot Hielscher, on the piano and Adalbert Luczkowski, who we called Albert Lollipop, on the violin.

The first broadcast took place on 23 December 1945 from a little villa in Schwachhauser Heerstrasse – live, of course. A melodic identity signal was created using three tuned water glasses, and Hänschen made the following announcement: 'If you hear a scratching noise, it isn't because the record is damaged, but because it is raining outside.' The station couldn't get away without canned sound completely, however, so requests were made in the *Weser-Kurier* newspaper for people to donate records. Within a few days countless shellac records, collected by the enthusiastic citizens of Bremen, had piled up in the radio station.

In the first few months of 1946, more and more musicians returned home from captivity, and so the first dance orchestra of Radio Bremen was formed under the direction of Friedrich Meyer. It played hits and American dance music, and we were particularly inspired by the unmistakable sound of Glenn Miller. Our favourites were 'American Patrol', 'In the Mood' and the romantic 'Moonlight Serenade'. In the mid-1970s, I produced an album that reminded me of these times: it was called *In the Mood for Trumpets* and was a kind of homage to Glenn Miller.

Soon we got a new studio. The Bremen Radio Theatre was an old cinema that had been converted in a makeshift fashion to fill the acoustic requirements. They put in a thick, sound-dampening carpet, a few long panels of fabric to separate the rhythm section acoustically from the rest of the orchestra, and a large, fine-spray flower-sprinkler to make sure the air didn't get too dry in the improvised studio.

Our live radio concerts gave us our first experience with a concert audience. It wasn't enough to simply play an instrument, however – you also had to act the part. I went swinging through the programme, bent apparently breathlessly over my bass with an ecstatic expression on my face. And what do you know? My efforts even got my name its first mention in a review! The writer, for the *Weser-Kurier* in May 1947, used railways metaphors to describe the concert. 'The brilliant, rhythmically precise orchestra under the direction of Hans Rehmstedt was a slow train, a passenger train, a fast train and an express train, with diverse stations from Cornelis op den Zieken at the piano, Günther Schnittjer, vocals, and Hans Last on bass.' That was it. Not exactly a heady hymn of praise, but it was a start.

Apart from the big dance band, there was also supposed to be a smaller combo for lighter music. So we founded the Last-Becker Ensemble, consisting of Karl Heinz Becker on trumpet, Alfred Andre on saxophone, my brothers Werner and Robert on accordion and drums, and me on double bass. Apart from the radio, we also played small clubs and pubs in the area with varying line-ups, and performed at a variety of dance events. On one occasion, Cornelis op den Zieken, a Dutchman who sometimes played piano for us, had agreed we'd play a gig in the small town of Cloppenburg, but unfortunately Robert fell ill so we didn't have a drummer.

I suggested my father as a replacement.

'What?! Your father?!'

Dad had been born in 1889, so he was almost 60, a veritable Methuselah for us 20-year-olds. However, when I told him what the problem was, he was immediately as keen as mustard. He set up his drums in the kitchen, I sang the songs and he practised. One song was 'Cumana', a pacy number in a samba rhythm, and Old Man Louis flew into it like a madman. After a few days' practice, he was fitted for a black suit and a red bow tie. Freshly shaved, he looked as rosy as a suckling pig.

As we were on our way to Cloppenburg, Dad discovered there were little posters announcing our performance on the trees: NORTH GERMANY'S LEADING DANCE BAND, they boasted. That excited him even more. Once at our destination, we set up and began to play straight away. The people of Cloppenburg were thrilled. His eyes brightly lit, Dad played with wild enthusiasm – and then came that samba piece he had practised for so long. He got faster and faster until the samba was flying along. 'You're getting faster!' I whispered to him from my position on bass.

'What? Faster? All right then!' and he stepped it up a notch, giving it his all. At the end he was completely out of breath – but he'd had such fun, and so did we.

We also had the number 'Cherry Pink' in our programme, in which the trumpet plays a brief introductory solo – a long, drawn-out note that rises and falls, and which is followed by the entry of the drums. It was up to the trumpeter how long he took until he had finished his little solo and Dad always sat on tenterhooks, waiting with drumsticks raised, ready for his cue. We must have played that song at least ten times and each time the trumpeter took longer and longer, just to tease my dad.

We received 200 marks each for the evening, and my father felt like a king on the drive back home. He thought things would continue like that but he was, after all, just a replacement, so it turned out to be only a brief pleasure for him.

A little later, Cornelis op den Zieken and I were invited to audition as musicians for Helmut Zacharias, then a noted jazz violinist. We duly caught the train to Hamburg, but, when we arrived, Helmut was not available. He'd just had a fight with his wife, Hella, and a wardrobe stood in front of the door so no one could enter. And with that our first meeting had to be postponed.

All That Jazz

At that time I was still living with my parents, as were Werner, Robert and his young wife, Marianne. Although our house was anything but a palace, my mother's warm-hearted nature created such a good atmosphere in these narrow confines that no disputes worth mentioning ever came up. We laughed a lot together and got on extremely well.

The end of the 1940s saw the beginning of what came to be known as the German 'economic miracle'. People sensed that things were taking a turn for the better, and with it the demand for entertainment grew. Soon the little Last-Becker Ensemble became a 13-man orchestra that played at many evenings of dancing and variety entertainment, which were very popular at that time. Now and then we took the opportunity to improvise some pieces and these were christened – what else! – Delmenhorst pieces.

I didn't only play dance music, however. The world of jazz had fascinated me since my time among the GIs. Immediately after the war, there was a radio programme called *Jazz at the Philharmonic* every Sunday afternoon. Absolute silence had to reign in the house as Robert, Werner and I hung on the radio and listened spellbound to our great heroes: Count Basie, Stan Kenton and Duke Ellington. My inspiration as bass player was Chubby Jackson from the Woody Herman Orchestra. Later I also admired Niels-Henning Orsted-Pedersen, the ingenious young Dane who played with Oscar Peterson.

In those days, jazz was virtually synonymous with a new attitude towards life, for shaking off the ghosts of the past. We wanted to show the world we could do more than just play thudding marching music. In many places, dedicated musicians and music admirers did their best to make jazz more popular. With typical German precision, clubs like the German Jazz Federation now brought this wonderful, free form of music to the people by way of advisers, workshops, business reports and elected presidents.

For a time at the end of the 1940s and beginning of the 1950s Robert and I played in the Andreas Hartmann Trio. Our recordings were broadcast on the radio, so bit by bit I came to the attention of other musicians, like Helmut Zacharias, as already mentioned, or the pianist Paul Kuhn. To my surprise, I became a member of a jazz set that set the tone in Germany: Günther Fuhlisch and Albert Mangelsdorff, both on trombone, Rolf Kühn and Franz von Klenck, both on alto saxophone and clarinet, Hans Podehl on drums, and Max Greger on tenor saxophone.

In 1950 I had the honour of being voted Germany's favourite jazz bass player. The magazine *Gondel* – a popular men's magazine of the time that featured music, high society, entertainment and, of course, beautiful women – had organised a poll for readers, critics and musicians. I won the so-called jazz poll three times in a row.

The first German Jazz Festival took place in Frankfurt on Main in 1953. The following rather pathetic announcement appeared in the magazine of the German Jazz Federation (DJV):

The jazz festival of the DJV takes centre stage for the friends of German jazz and is likely to be the greatest jazz event in post-war Germany. A brilliant array of the best German jazz musicians, the winners of a survey among jazz lovers ... have agreed to appear. ... Last but not least Hans Last, leader of a radio music ensemble, will get on the train in Bremen, and Max Greger ... in Munich, to go to Frankfurt. Any jazz lover who hears these names will be anxious to hear these All Stars, and will be crossing his fingers that he won't miss this once-in-a-lifetime experience...

The featured attraction was the German All Stars, made up of the winners of the poll. The line-up included Paul Kuhn on piano, Max Greger on tenor sax, Günther Fuhlisch on trombone, Fred

Bunge on trumpet, Franz von Klenck on alto sax, Gerhard Hühns on guitar, Teddy Paris on drums and Hans Last on bass. Among the pieces we played were 'How High the Moon', 'Oh Lady Be Good' and … 'Mosquito' – 'Perdito'!

The All Star concert was released as an LP on the Telefunken label – the first German jazz concert to be released on record in its entirety. One newspaper reviewer wrote, 'First of all I will mention the most exquisite aspect: the rhythm. I am not alone in claiming that there has never been a rhythm group in Germany (or indeed perhaps in Europe) such as this one with Paul Kuhn, Gerd Hühns, Teddy Paris and Hans Last … They have everything a good rhythm group should have: they are tight, but at the same time relaxed, they have drive and yet they don't push … They swing as well as the greatest of the greats, and yet they are purely German.'

A few times I was on stage with one of the real greats of jazz, the violinist Stéphane Grappelli. He was giving a concert in Berlin and the MC grandly announced his entrance: 'And here he is, the greatest jazz violinist in the world!' Grappelli, a rather small man, appeared at the top of a classical show staircase and stepped delicately, slowly and carefully down the stairs. The audience immediately adopted a typically cynical Berlin attitude towards these dainty movements: 'Oh, look, the man can walk!' When he finally reached the bottom of the steps, Grappelli calmly took his time to tune his violin. Again there were comments from the audience: 'Ooh! He can tune it, too!' Then he let it rip, playing with passionate intensity at a frenzied tempo. The drummer could hardly keep up with him and was completely out of breath. It was fantastic to experience and even the quick-witted Berliners were left speechless.

I am convinced that my success as a jazz bass player was directly connected to my classical training at Bückeburg. Anyone who has mastered Johann Sebastian Bach and his form of counterpoint is nimble enough to find his way around jazz. I was really proud to be such a fixture in the German jazz scene in the 1950s and I am still proud that my name had such a good reputation in those circles. For a musician that was a kind of knighthood. In Bremen I would never have had access to this universe, but the jazz festival in Frankfurt was really something. It was the emancipation of German jazz.

Waltraud

In those days I was so consumed by music that I hardly had eyes or ears for anything else – not even girls. As I said, I was a late bloomer in many things, even for the rather prim attitudes of those times. In the end, though, I couldn't escape Cupid's arrow – although it did hit me in slow motion, so to speak.

I met Waltraud, who later became my wife, because her father, Hellmuth Wiese, was a violinist and made music with my father. Having been given the task of delivering some sheet music to the Wiese family, I rang the doorbell; she stood in the doorway – and that was it. It didn't exactly feel like love at first sight, and we didn't fall into each other's arms, but somehow I knew she was the one. I kept dropping in at her family's place and she was always there. I was 21 and Waltraud was two years younger, a dental assistant and even a bit musical. Quietly and gently, something more than a mere attraction grew between us. Gradually we found our way to each other. We learned to trust and accept each other and had great mutual respect, which was probably the most important thing for our future together. Perhaps that sounds rather unromantic, but we really did find each other, certain that we belonged together.

a bremen town musician

We both still lived with our parents, so the time we spent together was on our best behaviour. Before I met Waltraud, I had had absolutely no experience with girls. I might have smooched around a bit in darkened entrance halls, but now, when I rode home from her place over the rough cobblestones on my bicycle, I could really feel the saddle. We kissed and cuddled for hours and petted a little, but nothing ever happened, and still…

At the weekend we often went dancing, she wearing her little hooped socks, me in my suit with turned-up cuffs and broad lapels. I was even very slow to notice Waltraud's physical attributes. We had a recording with Vico Torriani in the Bremen Radio Theatre and Waltraud arrived on her bicycle, elegantly dressed in a black cocktail dress with a stunning neckline. It was only then I noticed what lovely breasts she had.

It was a few years before we took the big step and decided to get married, but that was because of my uncertain financial situation. When Waltraud took her mother into her confidence, she threw her hands in the air and cried, 'Good grief! Not a musician!'

But by 1955 the time had come, though I have to admit even this, an unforgettable experience for most people, was nothing like a romantic novel. I didn't even actually ask her to marry me: one day I simply said, 'What do you think? We've known each other for so long now and get on so well, we should probably actually get married.'

Her answer was just as matter-of-fact: 'Yes, sure, why not?'

It was obvious to both of us anyway that we belonged together. And so, without much fuss, we entered the state of marriage in the town hall of Hemelingen (a suburb of Bremen), celebrating just with the family.

Around the same time I joined the North West German Radio (NDR) Orchestra in Hamburg. I had already written arrangements for the Last-Becker Ensemble and the full orchestra in Bremen, so in the first half of the 1950s I was given the task of conducting a string orchestra for Radio Bremen. For this I founded the Hans Last Orchestra and could now experience for the first time what it meant to take on musical responsibility and be able to put my own ideas into practice.

This may have been stimulating, but it wasn't very lucrative. The orchestra was freelance and twice a week we made recordings or performed live on radio for a fee. But because Radio Bremen was the public station of a small federal state, it couldn't afford to pay attractive money, so I had to look around for alternatives.

I had occasionally brought in musicians from Hamburg for my orchestra – an extra trombone here, a trumpet or a saxophone there – and that was how I had made my first contacts with the NDR radio station there. One day a piece by its musical director, the Swiss composer Rolf Liebermann, was due to be performed there, called *Konzert für Jazzband und Sinfonieorchester* (Concert for Jazz Band and Symphony Orchestra). Their bass player had trouble getting it right, so some of the musicians who had played for us suggested the bass player from Bremen. He could do it!

So I went over to Hamburg, played the concert and decided to take up an offer from Liebermann to try my luck in that city. Waltraud agreed to the move immediately. She was a person of action and knew exactly what opportunity was opening up for us. As was customary in those days, she had given in her notice at her job when we got married, so there were no organisational obstacles, and so we set off for our new life in the city on the Elbe. Our first Hamburg address was a small flat at Pension Birken on Heimhuderstrasse. There was an old grand piano in the living room, for which we had to pay extra. The bed in the bedroom sank deeply in the middle, and Waltraud and I often fell into each other's arms there. At last! Living together so closely was wonderful and, for us as newly weds, a completely new and very cosy experience.

However, my new position also meant a small retrograde step, since the move to NDR meant I had to play under someone else's baton. Franz Thon, saxophonist and clarinettist, was the leader of the dance orchestra – a position he held right up until 1980. A born musician, he was a man of extraordinary energy and he conducted his orchestra with extreme dedication. However, it was soon brought home to me that my renewed subordination was not going to be simple.

We were to record a tune called 'Taboo' and in it I had to play a phrase with the trombones. Thon had extremely fine hearing and immediately remarked, 'Bass and trombones are not in synch.'

'You're right,' I retorted cockily. 'The trombones are too slow.'

At that, one of the trombonists, who was also head of the orchestra executive committee, stood up and put me in my place. 'In our orchestra,' he said coolly, 'it has never been the bass player's job to tell the trombonists what to do.'

Typical civil servant! I thought as I dolefully made my way home. Employees in cushy jobs!

Back then I used an acoustic bass most of the time. I was the first bass player in Hamburg to get an electric bass, a Gibson, but for my very first record release of my own I still used my old bass. The single was called 'Tricks in Rhythm' and I recorded it with the drummer from the NDR Dance Orchestra, Siegfried Enderlein. Despite the rather limited options of the recording technology in those days, we still managed to achieve some fairly original sounds by making multiple recordings on one track, adjusting the tape speed and other little tricks.

The piece was played on radio quite often and NDR TV used one of the 'tricks' to accompany its famous seal logo as the interval signal for a long time. Even then I was not granted the pleasure of seeing my own name printed on the record cover – we were just called Mr Bass & Mr. Drums. I later sold my Gibson bass to Ladi Geisler, the bassist for Bert 'Fips' Kaempfert. So the renowned 'crackling bass' sound in Fips's orchestra was made by my old Gibson!

The NDR Orchestra often accompanied the singing stars of that time, such as Vico Torriani, Bibi Johns and Peter Alexander. Peter, who was from Vienna, was then just at the beginning of his career: he would become Austria's most popular entertainer of the 1970s and 1980s, celebrated for his many parodies. His first great success was a song called 'Das Machen nur die Beine von Dolores' (The Legs of Dolores); we recorded a version of it in the 1980s for the album *Deutsche Vita*. That time the clatter of Dolores's heels came from Waltraud, who had to walk back and forth in the studio to create it.

Many years later, Peter visited us in Fort Lauderdale. He had planned to stay just a couple of days but they turned into a week. We spent several enjoyable evenings together, and he entertained us with his wonderful Vienna parodies – oldies but goodies.

Udo Jürgens also came to Hamburg to do some radio recordings, long before he made his breakthrough as a pop singer. He really wanted to sing 'Summertime', but his idea of it was vastly different to that of Franz Thon. It simply wouldn't work and, after several failed attempts, he was a bundle of despair. I felt really sorry for him. It would be a few years yet before Udo managed to find his own style with his song 'Jenny'.

This experience with young singers would turn out to be good experience when, a short time later, I started to work as an arranger and producer for various pop stars.

My Drug

In those days I wrote an extraordinary amount of arrangements for NDR, but none of them was for my own compositions; that was frowned upon because the arrangers would have earned too much in royalties. Instead, I wrote arrangements for others, for Franz Thon and the second-in-command, Alfred Hause. My first arrangement for Hause was 'In the Still of the Night', for which I got all of 80 marks. It was a pauper's fee, but before long the fees were going up to three or four hundred marks a tune.

One man who I learned a great deal from was the pianist and orchestra leader Kurt Wege. He rewrote hit songs as chamber music for strings, piano and harp. I began to arrange string quartets with orchestral accompaniment for him. One of my earliest 'James Last' recordings is based on this technique: my quartet arrangement of the Beatles' 'Yesterday' on the LP *Beat in Sweet*.

I was soon also very active for Helmut Zacharias, who had now turned to the vast field of popular entertainment. Every now and then he'd put his own name under one of my arrangements. In these matters I was young and naive and inexperienced; for me only the music was important. In any case, we made recordings with singing stars like Mona Baptiste (a Trinidadian who was very popular in Germany), Bully Buhlan (a Berlin singer and film actor), Gerhard Wendland (a famous German pop singer) and many others.

For I while I toured with Zacharias through Europe playing bass. He always had a bottle of Steinhäger schnapps at the ready in his big Borgward car – for emergencies, of course. Although Helmut had a large string orchestra, during the concerts he used an additional playback tape to make the sound richer and fuller. Before the tour started I stood alone at night in the Hamburg

Opera House post-synchronising every single title that we had in the programme to boost the bass on these tapes.

On stage I wore headphones in which I could hear the playback so I could play in time. Essentially it was the same principle that we use today in our concerts: a so-called click track dictates the rhythm and the orchestra has to take its cue from that. On one occasion the tape machine – which was clearly visible on the podium – went haywire during 'Wenn der weiße Flieder wieder blüht' (When the White Lilac Blooms Again) and came wobbling to a stop because the electricity failed. But the real violins played on undaunted, so the audience probably didn't notice amid the general confusion.

I had already gained some experience with doubling the strings when I was working with my orchestra in Bremen, by super-imposing a second recording. While my fellow musicians experimented with recording the first, second, third and fourth violins at the same time and then making a second recording, I would record each violin section individually with all of the violins, but four times. Although we only had eight violins, two violas and two cellos, our strings sounded as opulent as those of Mantovani.

I played these recordings for the man who conducted the greatest Hamburg orchestra of the 1950s, Harry Hermann. He had once been a viola player for the Vienna Philharmonic, so his expectations of the optimal orchestra sound were accordingly opulent and he had a reputation for being difficult. His own orchestra consisted of about a hundred musicians, a giant body of sound made up of both the dance and radio orchestras of NDR. Hermann was struck by the way in which I had arranged the strings, and he was amazed I had been able to achieve such a rich sound with so few resources.

'Come and work for me!' he said. It fitted perfectly with my romantic streak.

a bremen town musician

Hermann wanted to sound like the Boston Pops Orchestra and his dream was to create large arrangements in the style of Gershwin. My first job for him was 'The Breeze and I'. I wrote a light, airy introduction – the breeze, as it were, breathing across the stave – then the melody for eight cellos and twelve violas. It sounded so luxurious and full that my scalp began to tingle.

Then there was 'Bess You is My Woman Now' from the opera *Porgy and Bess*. Anneliese Rothenberger and Lawrence Winters, a black baritone from the Hamburg State Opera, sang this piece accompanied by the huge orchestra – and Hansi Last had arranged it! I can hardly describe the feelings the music evoked in me: it was simply fantastic. Turning such a wonderful ensemble of musicians and singers into sound gave me such an incredible high, like a drug. Even today it sends shivers of amazement down my spine when I happen to hear one of these opulent arrangements.

Another star I went on tour with in the mid-1950s was Maximilian Michael Andreas Jarczyk, better known as Michael Jary. He made his big break as a hit composer in 1938 with 'Roter Mohn' (Red Poppy). Two of his greatest evergreens are 'Ich weiss, es wird einmal ein Wunder geschehen' (I Know a Miracle Will Happen Some Day) sung by Zarah Leander, and the Hans Albers song 'Das kann doch einen Seemann nicht erschüttern' (That Won't Surprise a Sailor). In 1955, the film *Wie werde ich Filmstar* – (How to Become a Film Star) starring Nadja Tiller and Theo Lingen – was released. The music was by Michael Jary and the big hit was 'Zwei Herzen im Mai' (Two Hearts in May), sung by the lovely Swedish singer Bibi Johns.

In those days a film wasn't launched in every big city on the same day: there were different premiere days in the most important locations. Consequently, we travelled the country playing in the various premiere cinemas as the supporting programme. Bibi Johns – who was my age – was madly admired, not least by Jary, but the spoiled star composer got the cold shoulder. He was often quite drunk, could swear like a trooper and tended to put on airs: 'I want champagne! A whole tub full!' On the other hand, we musicians were allowed to travel with him in his Mercedes 600, which for me was something special.

Sometimes he would call me at home late at night, saying, 'Hansi, I need another arrangement. We have a recording early tomorrow and I don't have a leader. Can you do something suggesting Hamburg in the mist and the harbour?'

'Yes, of course. Where's the music?'

'Don't have any; you'd have to write it.'

So I'd sit down, with ships in my mind's eye, the harbour, foghorns – and in no time I'd have it done.

Slowly Waltraud and I found a new circle of friends in Hamburg, particularly among my fellow musicians at NDR. Right next to our flat was a small pub, the Moorweiden Casino, where a young man occasionally performed on his accordion. His name was Bert Kaempfert. Fips, as everyone called him, was completely unknown at that time. He was a very relaxed fellow, just like his music. We spent many a lively evening together at that pub. Later, long after the two of us had become famous, the media repeatedly tried to imply that there was some kind of competitive jealousy between us, but that was never the case. We just weren't the type of people for that.

Spare time was already scarce since I was always writing, and by now I was on the road quite a lot with Alfred Hause, Franz Thon or Helmut Zacharias. But Waltraud supported me with her generous equanimity and let me go my way. She knew what music meant to me and what a privilege it was for me to be able to earn our money this way. Perhaps she already suspected this was just the beginning of an increasingly restless life on tour.

a bremen town musician

At the beginning of 1956 I received full tenure as full-time bassist at NDR. Waltraud and I moved to a larger flat in Heinrich-Hertzstrasse in the suburb of Uhlenhorst, and finally dared to consider having offspring. Caterina was born in 1957 and Ron arrived a year later. When Rina was born, the doctor called me at six in the morning to congratulate me on becoming the father of a healthy daughter. When I remained silent, he asked uncertainly, 'Is something wrong?'

'No,' I said, 'it's just... I won't be getting the electric train set after all.' My old childhood dream would just have to wait a little...

Lest I seem a little unfeeling, I should say straight away that the birth of my two children made my personal happiness complete. Often it was me who would get up at night to look after them. Changing nappies, bathing, giving them their bottles – I did all of that gladly. Sometimes I couldn't go back to sleep because musical thoughts would be going through my head, so I'd sit down and commit them to paper. It was always worth it: a few times I neglected to do this and by the morning my ideas had evaporated.

Waltraud was not only a fantastic wife, but also a wonderful mother. She went along with everything – the nights of writing for Harry Hermann, Franz Thon or Alfred Hause – and she was a steady anchor for Rina and Ron. From the beginning we had agreed to bring up our children with as much freedom and ease as possible. When I see the results today, I have the feeling that we did a good job. Despite the fact that I often couldn't be at home for weeks on end, and despite the innumerable studio appointments and later the successes that came pouring over me, Waltraud managed to give Rina and Ron a more or less normal childhood. She navigated around all the hazards that my popularity entailed for the children.

As the youngsters grew older, the question of a more spacious home arose. In 1960 the opportunity arose to purchase a terraced house in Holitzbergstrasse in Hamburg-Langenhorn. We mulled over it for a long time, made calculations, planned meticulously – and decided to do it. Neither of us could sleep the night before signing the sales agreement. The following morning we dressed in our best clothes for the big event – Waltraud wore her fur and I even put on a tie. It was one of the most important signatures I have ever made. We spent many happy years in the house in Langenhorn before we moved to Florida in the 1980s.

When we moved in, my father came to visit. Proud of being a new 'owner', he greeted everyone in the street with 'Hello, neighbour!' He hadn't changed a bit. Even when he came to visit later on, he'd take about two hours to take the rubbish to the bins across the road because he'd chat to everyone he met – just the same as in Bremen.

Our new house had five rooms and was surrounded by a big garden. My study was in the basement, and from there I could see the children playing in the sandbox. We soon developed friendships with our neighbours and a whole new circle of friends grew up. We went on outings with them and had parties together. Holitzbergstrasse was a real party area – everyone was always inviting others over. Someone might have a roast in the oven, someone else would prepare dessert, and a third would see to the drinks. We had the longest table, which we'd set with candles and such like and take to wherever the party was. It was these parties that later inspired me to do the *Non Stop Dancing* LPs.

Alaska and a Sailor

In 1959 Alaska became the 49th state to join the United States of America. On this occasion I received two or three lines of musical notation that I was expected to arrange as a large piece entitled

'Alaska' for the Harry Hermann Orchestra. These few lines of music had been written by Lothar Olias, composer and producer for Freddy Quinn. Freddy had already carved out an impressive career for himself – at this time he was the uncrowned record king of Germany – so working for Olias was certainly an honour.

I was immediately inspired by the theme of Alaska, so I didn't even really need the notes. I imagined sled dogs, vast snow-covered expanses, giant forests, cloudy mountain peaks and abandoned gold-rush towns. The composition I had received from Olias had been no longer than about 16 bars scribbled on a little piece of paper: I turned it into a piece that played for eight or nine minutes with everything that an orchestra had to offer: oboes, flutes, bassoon, horns – a giant array. It was fun and the orchestra enjoyed it, too. They really put themselves into it and I was happy and proud.

Some time later, however, I received some mail from England. Someone had sent me a large arrangement asking me to translate the musical terms into English. The title of the piece was 'Alaska' and the author's name was given as Lothar Olias. Something was wrong here! Olias had given me 16 bars, but it was my large work that had been printed. Yet nowhere was there any mention of Hans Last. As I was shy, I didn't ring Olias for a few days. I pointed out the error – after all, it was obviously my composition – and Olias clearly felt uncomfortable. 'Well, er… what do you think we should do? Do you have time to fit in more work for me?'

'Certainly, but I want to be properly paid for it,' I replied.

We agreed that he would transfer 1,000 marks to me as a belated payment for 'Alaska'. That was a somewhat small sum, since I was handing over the rights to him. I agreed.

Two days later, he called asking whether I would arrange something for Freddy. Olias was a heavy smoker, so his music arrived written on smelly, nicotine-stained paper, but I set to work anyway. I arranged quite a number of songs for Freddy's albums and films, such as *Die Gitarre und das Meer* (The Guitar and the Sea) or *Heimweh nach St. Pauli* (Longing for St Pauli). Then there was his 1962 song which has since become a classic, 'Junge, komm bald wieder' (Come Home Soon, My Son). I can still visualise how the instruments were arranged around the microphone where Freddy stood, every little detail. We all had a little smile on our faces, because we knew that something special was being created. And so it was: the song became one of Freddy's biggest hits.

Word of my part in this success quickly got around and soon I was being flooded with commissions for work. Margot Eskens wanted a new arrangement of the song 'Mama' – 'by tomorrow' naturally, so I worked on it all night. Alfred Hause needed a few tango pieces for his tour of Japan – I wrote them. Then came Caterina Valente, Lolita, Hanne Wieder, Brenda Lee, Fred Bertelmann, Lale Andersen and many more. I was well on the way to becoming a well-paid professional writer.

On top of this NDR offered me a permanent position for life. All of a sudden I could see my life for the next 30 years set out before me as if on a drawing board: going to the radio station every day, going to the canteen every day, the same faces every day – and then retiring. It might sound immodest, but it wasn't enough for me. I didn't want to spend the rest of my life on such a predictable, orderly path. And I certainly didn't want to be the man in the background writing his fingers to the bone for the success of others. A decision had to be made – and fast.

And so it was that I took temporary leave of absence from NDR, and set off to make my own way into the future.

part two:

Non Stop Dancing

The Beatles' New Clothes

Since I had done arrangements for many German pop stars, I'd had quite a lot of involvement with the record company Polydor, whose headquarters were just near the Hamburg radio station. Now, under the aegis of Lothar Olias, I recorded several albums for the company – none of which would make me famous.

First there were two pot pourris of mood music, both called *Die gab's nur einmal* (It Only Happened Once), in 1963 and 1964. These were released under the name Hans Last und die Rosenkavaliere (Hans Last and the Knights of the Rose), and consisted of hits from the 1940s and 1950s played in 'classical' style.

My next foray was as Orlando and called *Musikalische Liebesträume* (Musical Dreams of Love). This time, since I actually wanted to earn some money, I arranged pieces for which the copyright had expired, among them some classical compositions such as Liszt's 'Liebestraum' (Dream of Love) and Toselli's 'Serenade'. These were done in a style that came quite close to my first *Classics up to Date* productions.

The most fun I had was making two cabaret albums. One of them was called *Songs für Mündige* (Songs for Grown-Ups). Lothar Olias wrote some very light-hearted songs and street ballads to lyrics by Fritz Grasshoff, and these were performed by such greats of cabaret and stars of the stage as Ernst Stankowski, Inge Meisel, Gustav Knuth and Hanne Wieder.

> *Let me paint you*
> *My lovely brief liaison*
> *Horizontally*
> *You are like a landscape*
> *Your belly is a hamlet*
> *In the loveliest canton,*
> *The market square with 3 corners*
> *And a tiny wee pension*
> *Or*
> *We kids played pro and punter*
> *Under Mrs Kläre's sheets*
> *For her, the game was blunter*
> *For us … we played for sweets.*

I had the 'last' word on the arrangements: a great pleasure. These albums weren't exactly flops, but they weren't raging successes either. And, even though they were fun, they weren't what I really wanted to create. So I gathered all my courage, marched in to see the head of Polydor, Heinz Voigt, and asked him if I could produce something myself for a change. Something new!

'Have you got something in mind, then?' he asked.

'Yes, I think so.'

The idea was actually very simple. Whenever Waltraud and I were invited to a party, we always encountered the same thing: it took ages for a party atmosphere to get going. If we turned up among the first guests, the atmosphere was generally funereal: 'Good evening, Mr Last. How are you?'

'Fine, thanks... and you?'

'Oh, I'm fine, too. Thanks very much. And your lady wife?'

'Can't complain...'

Once the greeting ritual was over and no one knew what else to say, the only thing to do was to put on, at best, a Trini Lopez or Mantovani album.

It was this rigid formality that I wanted to overcome. If the hosts couldn't provide the party mood, then let it come from the record player. The basic principle was dance music, current chart hits, with party sounds in the background. Clapping, humming along, whistling and a boisterous atmosphere – quite simply, life! It would be non-stop dancing.

It was actually my father who had given me the idea. As the baby of the family I had been allowed to perch on his knee on a Saturday afternoon when he listened to Radio Copenhagen. They would broadcast live music, and in the background you could always hear people chatting, the clatter of cups and glasses, the whole coffeehouse atmosphere.

So *Non Stop Dancing* was what I remembered from the days of my dad's armchair. When I told him that I was giving up my permanent job at NDR for a risky career with Polydor, however, he threw his hands up in the air in horror. 'Why on earth are you giving that up?!' he exclaimed in typical civil-servant mode. 'You could have a secure income there for your whole life!'

The question that now preoccupied me, though, was how to get the party mood into the grooves of an LP as convincingly as possible. Well, the best thing would be to tape a real party! First of all, we recorded the band and choir without any additional sounds. When the recording was done, I had the band roll up again and the six singers gave their best to get party sounds going. At the beginning it sounded a bit thin, more like a bowling-club sing-along. But soon these occasions developed into really great parties. I invited friends to the studio, the choir was there and usually my musicians as well. We served bread rolls, beer and schnapps to loosen people up, and then Peter Klemt, the sound engineer put on the tape – and the party took off. The choir sang along with everything and my guests sang, clapped and danced. Sometimes there was too much of a good thing and I had to edit out certain words that could be heard rather too clearly.

Our recordings were so up to the minute that the tape was often only ready at the last second. The people would be standing in the studio waiting to get going, getting drunk and drunker, while I was still cutting and mixing. Over the years more and more people began coming along to these parties. At first there were only 20 or 30, but then there were 50 and then 150 guests – doctors and lawyers, chic young girls and fine ladies. As time went on it became the in thing to go along to Hans's non-stop parties.

When I had finished mixing the first LP, *Non Stop Dancing '65*, complete with clapping and party noise, some of the people at Polydor listened to it and pronounced, 'What a shame! The music is really good, but what's the point of all that noise on it?' But in the end they got the message, and, since the record was intended for the international market, they also decided to change my name.

A short time later Waltraud and I were about to go to the German pop festival at Baden-Baden. We were just getting into the car when the postman came running towards us, waving a cardboard box containing the first *Non Stop Dancing* record, hot off the pressing plant. Naturally, we could hardly contain ourselves: Waltraud tore open the package, pulled out the LP – and gaped at me in amazement. 'Look, they've put "James Last" on it. Why? Your name is Hans, they all know that, so why have they put James?'

I had no idea. When we got back, I asked Polydor and their answer was, 'The music is so international, James simply sounds better.' The funny thing is, today all my English fans call me Hansi, but in Germany I am still James.

Non Stop Dancing was incredibly successful, but that wasn't just because of the party sounds. It was also because of the choice of tracks. In 1965 the Beatles broke into the German charts for the first time, and those four boys were unmistakably the trendsetters for the development of contemporary music. The so-called jazz musos in the NDR Dance Orchestra only griped about who the heck these Beatles were supposed to be and ignored their music completely. In contrast, I thought to myself, If these lads are so into this music, I'd better find out about it and find a way to arrange it for an instrumental band. I was the first person to do that. That was a real gap in the market.

One of the main reasons older people had a hard time accepting this newfangled music was because they didn't understand the lyrics. The generation gap was much more dramatic in the 1960s than it is today. The younger people were rebellious and wanted to distinguish themselves clearly from the oldies in their looks, their clothes and their whole way of life. One very significant distinguishing feature in all this was the music. I didn't do anything special apart from play it in an instrumental form, suddenly making it acceptable to their parents. The melodies were somehow familiar to them, but they didn't quite realise that these were their children's favourite songs, because there was no English in my arrangements. Our *Non Stop Dancing* choir didn't have any lyrics to begin with: they simply sang 'la la la' to the melody, the same as Ray Conniff did.

The *Non Stop Dancing* LP was decisive for my future. I said goodbye to my secure job at NDR and became a producer and bandleader. A high-speed, breathtaking journey then followed, taking me straight to the top.

Happy Sound

When I joined Polydor I found three very congenial partners, and together we formed the ideal quartet for success. My boss was Heinz Voigt, who had previously been manager of the bandleader Kurt Edelhagen, having met him in an internment camp after the war. In 1953 he came to Polydor's parent company, Deutsche Grammophon, and from the mid-1960s he was head of Polydor Germany. A real 'Gentleman of Music' who knew the music industry inside out, Heinz was both my patron and a fatherly friend. After leaving Polydor he became publishing director at Intersong. He died in 2002 at the age of 83.

Heinz had signed me to my first contract, but it turned out to contain a significant loophole: I had only been signed as a producer, so another company could have come in at any time and signed me as an artist. No one at Polydor had really registered that fact, but one man recognised the error and made sure my contract was changed to an artist's one in 1966. That man was number two of the trio, Ossi Drechsler. An Austrian, Ossi had begun his career as a sales manager for Philips in Vienna, before moving to Polydor in Hamburg in 1965 as an assistant production manager. I was one of his first big successes, so to speak. We met at one of Heinz's mad parties, and Ossi told me he'd first seen me at the Vienna Concert Hall in 1955, playing double bass in Helmut Zacharias's orchestra.

Ossi had a very good nose for new talent. He had discovered the 'master of a thousand voices', Gotthilf Fischer, and the 'Ode to Joy' singer-composer Miguel Rios, and in 1968 he brought the Czech singer Karel Gott out from behind the Iron Curtain. In 1979 Ossi would become managing director of Polydor for three years.

The fourth man in our alliance, Werner Klose, was a qualified printer and typesetter. He'd started out in Deutsche Grammophon's advertising department in 1955, dealing with classical culture from Gustav Gründgens (one of Germany's greatest actors) to the conductor and composer Wilhelm Furtwängler – far removed from the gutters of light enter-tainment! But soon he was promoted to advertising manager at Polydor, at which point he really got down to business – ten hours a day, seven days a week were perfectly normal working hours for him.

Together, we were an invincible team and no one could come between us. Our relationship was unusually warm: Heinz Voigt, Ossi Drechsler, Werner Klose and I were bound in a close friendship that went far above the usual working relationships and included our families. That simplified and even made possible many things that would later become unimaginable under changing company management.

The enormous success of *Non Stop Dancing* whetted our appetite for more, and, shortly afterwards, someone at Polydor announced, 'We need an album with a Hammond organ!'

Now that was a completely different challenge, but OK – I'd do something with organs. In the end I used two of them – one right, one left, to get a real stereo sound – added percussion, double bass, guitar, saxophone and accordion, and arranged two dozen numbers that I had played with my brothers way back in the American clubs. At first I wasn't particularly excited by the Hammond idea, since it wasn't really my taste, but when my wife heard the test pressings she was ablaze with praise. 'What are you on about? That's first-class bar music!'

So, one night I sat down, poured myself a whisky, lit a couple of candles and took my time listening to a few of the recordings. And what do you know! I had to admit that Waltraud was right. In a dim, after-hours bar this music could provide just the right atmosphere. Sure enough, the record sold en masse – every bar played it and I ended up producing four Hammond albums in all.

The album was supposed to be called *In the Hammond Bar – Hans Last and his Combo* but that sounded a bit boring. In those days, it was fashionable in a bar to order a whole bottle of vodka, gin or whisky, give it to the bartender to look after, and next time you were in the bar, you had him bring out your personal bottle. This went on until it was empty and was called 'whisky à gogo'. So one astute advertising fellow came up with the name *Hammond à gogo*, a sort of brand name that we kept up for a whole 'á gogo' series.

On the first *Hammond á gogo*, incidentally, you can find the number that had got my father into such a sweat all those years before, the samba 'Cumana'. We also had a minor mishap with that album. According to the German society for music performing rights, GEMA, a medley was strictly restricted to three titles, each of a maximum length of 1 minute and 45 seconds. That had been agreed with both the publishers and the composers because of their modes of accounting. GEMA kept a close eye on such things, so we had to keep to the rules. Our problem now was that one track was too long – I had miscalculated and, by the time we noticed the mistake, the musicians had long since left the studio which meant we couldn't re-record. In the end we simply took a big pair of scissors and shortened the tape. That's why that particular track has no change of key, no bridge to the next song, no meaningful musical transition at all. But no one has ever noticed, and it didn't diminish the album's success. Over the years I have received six gold records for the first volume of *Hammond á gogo* alone.

Purely out of habit, I happened to also play double bass myself on these albums, with Jochen Ment playing tenor saxophone and accordion, and my brother Robert the drums. On the Hammond organs were Hermann Hausmann, a pianist from NDR, and Günter Platzek, who became an integral part of my band from that point on.

Günter was one of a kind, who used his wit to cover up many of his insecurities. A talented self-taught musician, he was supposed to become a hotel manager, but instead of taking over his parents' hotel in Hanover he decided on a career in the music industry. And just as I'd met Waltraud through my profession, he'd met his Carla through his – after the war, she'd been a dancer in the GI club in Augsburg where he'd been playing.

Gunter was a fantastic jazz musician, but classical music was not one of his strengths. He was a bit too restless for that. Sometimes when he couldn't get a particular classical piece down the way I wanted it in the studio, I simply took over his part, for instance for the 'Pavane' by Ravel. For 'Träumerei' (Reverie) by Schumann, I had to conduct every single beat for him. You have to really breathe this music, otherwise the magic is lost.

Günter was certainly no concert pianist, but he was a man of incredible energy, sensational musically, someone who could captivate the listeners with his playing. When he visited us in Florida many years later, we went to a wonderful, elegant restaurant, a 'black-tie' affair, which had a piano bar. As the night grew long, Günter sat down at the piano with the pianist and played a third hand. The two got talking and at some point the pianist stood up and said, 'Why don't you play for a while?' Typical Günter – he didn't show off at the piano, he played just the way he always did and instantly the atmosphere in the bar improved noticeably. In no time at all there were 20 people gathered around the piano where previously there had been only about four or five.

Günter was also an excellent vibraphone and xylophone player. When we were on holiday with the band in Manzanillo in Mexico, he found an old xylophone with clay pots as resonating bodies, which he could hang from his neck. He was absolutely thrilled and said straight away that he wanted to play it on stage. Once again he had found a new acoustic colour, enriching our sound.

After Günter's more than untimely death of a heart attack in November 1990, it took ages before we found a pianist of a similar calibre – until 2002, to be precise, when our present man at the keyboard, Joe Dorff, joined the band.

After the Hammond LP became a hit, my Polydor trio and I hit upon the idea of recording folk songs. Because of all the arrangements I had made for others over the years, my musical mind had received the best training. Then, as now, if someone throws words at me like 'folk songs' or 'evergreens', songs start shooting through my mind and I can immediately hear what they should sound like. Instantly I start arranging the songs in my head: a simple melody... a choir should hum... the trumpets play alternately from left and right... and in no time I have the introduction to 'The Merry Traveller' in my head. Then it continues with flutes... oboe... and cembalo. I wanted to have the cembalo in my recordings back then because it represented the sound of the new musicians of the time. George Harrison, for instance, created a similar sound on his 12-string guitar.

Even the choice of songs comes to me mostly without prompting. I start with some melody... rhythm... key... atmosphere... structure... Then the transition to a new theme evolves in my head, and finally the whole potpourri. It seems perfectly logical to me that 'Ain't She Sweet' can only be followed by 'Bei mir bist du schön'.

My ideal concept of an LP is that it has to be as compact as a single. It has to play all the way through on one wave of harmonious momentum so no one even contemplates lifting the needle. One song has to flow seamlessly into the other.

Of the many albums I recorded in the early years, the three volumes of *Trumpet à gogo* count among my favourite projects. They have songs on them from the period after the war when I played piano in the American GI clubs, numbers like 'American Patrol', 'Caravan' and 'Begin the Beguine' – all of them fantastic pieces which almost count as classics today. These arrangements, all of them very easy listening and sometimes with a Latin touch, became the epitome of the 'Happy Sound' and a worldwide success. The rhythm section – in particular my brother Robert's drums, but also xylophone, piano, double bass and percussion – gave this sound its essential character. One critic wrote at the time, 'In the background of Last's recording there is such an amazement of peeping, twittering, ringing and rattling that any Caribbean band would go green with envy.'

Another very special production for me was our recording of *Hair* in 1969. At that time the Vietnam War was *the* big talking point. The anti-war protests in America were becoming more vocal, magnified intensely by the burgeoning Flower Power movement. The joyful flower children and their easy attitude towards sex and drugs stood in stark contrast to the puritanical establishment under Richard Nixon and Lyndon B. Johnson.

Then a musical swept through Broadway that turned previous ideas of morality completely upside down: *Hair*, by Galt McDermot (music) and Gerome Ragni/James Rado (lyrics). It was all about conscientious objection and free love. On stage they dropped fairly obscene words like 'masturbation' and 'cunnilingus' and eventually even their clothes. Naked people on stage! For many upright citizens that was a scandal.

But within a very short time this brilliant show had taken the world by storm – and to me the music was simply wonderful! So there was no doubt about it: we had to do it! And not only the big hits like 'Let the Sunshine In' or 'Aquarius' – no, we would record a whole LP. I set to work with ardour. I didn't want to produce this vibrant music in our familiar *Non Stop Dancing* sound. I wanted it to be something new – arrangements unlike any we had played before – so we experimented in the studio. We let tape recorders run backwards, and we covered microphones with glass bottles to achieve special sound effects. Instead of human voices, I used flutes. I distorted brass instruments with a phaser, and I varied the rhythm and tempo in parts quite considerably from the original. The result was an LP that made me happy from start to finish – and it represented an important step in our musical development.

Maestro up to Date

In the spring of 1968 I was sitting with a few musicians in the canteen of NDR, my former place of work, when Harald Vock came over to our table. Vock was not only a well-known author of crime stories, but also the head of entertainment at NDR.

'How would you like to try something new?' he asked me. 'What do you say to us recording *The Threepenny Opera* together?'

I was always interested in doing something new, but, to be perfectly honest, *The Threepenny Opera* was not exactly something I'd always wanted to do. I would have to think my way into it from a completely new angle. But he had hardly finished talking when the notes began dancing in my head, and soon the idea took a grip on me. Eventually I said yes, and, thus, for a short time, I became an opera conductor.

There are many self-professed music connoisseurs who believe that this work by Brecht and Weill is something more than special. I see it in a much more relaxed manner. I never felt the urge to fall on my knees in awe. Without wanting to offend anyone, there are many things in music that are predictable and one of them is *The Threepenny Opera*. I'd much rather listen to 'Mack the Knife' in some of its jazzier versions than in the original Brecht/Weill version.

Working on this piece was a new challenge for me and above all an interesting technical assignment. I dipped in here and there, carefully reorchestrating some parts. That almost turned out to be bad move, since Lotte Lenya, Kurt Weill's widow and his successor in legal title, wanted to prevent the recording from being released because she didn't think it was right that I should use an electric bass instead of an acoustic double bass. Eventually I was able to convince Ms Lenya that her husband's work would not suffer from my adaptation.

The actors and singers engaged for this recording were fantastic: Hannes Messemer as Macheath, Helmut Qualtinger as Peachum, Karin Baal as Polly, Martin Held as the London Chief of Police, Hanne Wieder as Jenny Diver, Hans Clarin as Beggar – a spectacular cast! Until now, I hadn't had anything to do with most of them but working with these artists was tremendous fun, though I found the songwriter Franz Josef Degenhardt, who played the Ballad Singer, an offbeat character. Although he was known for being critical of society, he spent a lot of the work breaks talking about his chauffeur and his gardener.

The recording was awarded the Deutsche Schallplattenpreis, roughly the German equivalent of the Grammy, in 1968. That came as a great surprise to me and meant very special recognition of our work. I would actually have preferred the record company to have released the album – which was an elaborate, three-record set – on the Deutsche Grammophon yellow label for classics. But Deutsche Grammophon refused, giving the flimsy excuse that James Last was a popular entertainer and not a 'serious' artist, so he didn't belong in the higher realms of classical music.

This differentiation is mere window dressing, if only because of the fact that many of the most significant classical works were originally composed as entertainment. The success of my classical LPs shows up how ludicrous this artificial division into 'popular' and 'serious' music is.

The question then became: if current chart hits and folk songs could become interesting to new audiences through my arrangements, why not classical music as well? The idea for the *Classics up to Date* series originally came from Polydor International, and the notion of rearranging the famous works of great composers was just what an old romantic like myself was waiting for. My classical training in Bückeburg had left its mark, and I had always felt particularly attracted to analysing the scores of the great masters. Whether Bach or Mozart, Bartók, Debussy or Shostakovich, my life could never be dull, because I simply love to rummage around in notes, seeing how old Ludwig van Beethoven had put together his sound or how he had achieved one effect or another.

For *Classics* I pared down the main theme of a symphony, an aria or a piano concerto, reducing the piece to its musical kernel. At the same time it was very important to me to only change the original as scrupulously as possible. I set my sights on a leaner instrumentation; here and there perhaps I'd rewrite the strings a little, and finally I'd underlay the arrangement with a gentle rhythm. In this way I would serve up the immortal works in small, easily digestible portions – and suddenly people who would never have bought a classical LP became interested in Schubert sonatas and Bizet suites.

In the 1960s, classical music was still a very starchy affair, celebrated with grim rigour. Classical compilations in the vein of *Chill out mit Mahler* (Chill Out With Mahler) or *Brahms für unterwegs* (Brahms for the Road) were just as unthinkable as classical radio stations with 'Best of Classics' programmes.

So I can say in all honesty that I was a true pioneer in this area. One critic once commented, 'What Karajan achieved for a greater popularity of classical music through his excellent PR work and his glamorous personality, James Last achieved through his classical arrangements.' That made me truly proud and, tellingly, a James Last classical music sampler even made it into the British classical music charts in 2003.

It has always given me enormous pleasure to track down new titles for the *Classics* productions and to arrange pieces that aren't quite so well known, such as 'The Enchanted Lake' by Lyapunov on *Classics from Russia*. I can spend hours in the Steinway store in Hamburg, rummaging around in piles of musical scores and gaining inspiration. Or I dig around for buried treasure in my study in Florida, where there are piles of piano arrangements and complete concert scores of all musical styles. There are cantatas by Bach, waltzes by Strauss, symphonies from Haydn to Bruckner, songs by Schubert and Hugo Wolf, concerts by Tchaikovsky, operettas, operas – works by wonderful artists who have made my life infinitely richer.

The choice is almost unlimited… and yet I remember a situation in which I once genuinely could not think of a single thing. While I was preparing for my first *Classics* album, I was sitting in my study at two in the morning. I was dog tired but I desperately needed one more number for the recording the following morning. But my brain was empty – the flash of inspiration refused to come. Waltraud came to see if I was all right.

'It's time you went to bed. You've got the recording tomorrow.'

'But I need another piece! I have to think of something.'

Waltraud thought for less than two seconds, and then said, 'Why don't you take the "Toreador Song" from *Carmen* and do it a bit like the "River Kwai March"?'

That was all I needed – everything fell into place and suddenly it was all so simple: the theme would be whistled, and then the choir would join in humming, then four horns, a flute... The arrangement was finished at six, and we recorded it almost exactly as I had imagined it after Waltraud's suggestion.

A significant feature of my classical arrangements was the Bergedorf Chamber Choir, conducted by Hellmut Wormsbächer, whom I had met when I was recording a Christmas album with Freddy Quinn. The choir consisted of 40 singers, who backed up our violas and cellos with their voices – they doubled the strings, so to speak, and added the necessary warmth to the sound. Many listeners may never have even noticed that a choir was humming in the background, as there were no lyrics. But the singers created a unique atmosphere, and I owe a lot to Hellmut Wormsbächer and his choir. They were all amateurs, but their voices were an integral part of our sound.

Over the years, my classical arrangements became more and more sophisticated and the pieces more demanding. When I finally ended up with really challenging ones like *Symphonie Fantastique* by Berlioz, I could not produce them with such a small crew. At times we even had a whole symphony orchestra in the studio.

The *Classics* albums were far and away the bestsellers among my productions. Almost every recording sold over a million copies. We even reached the singles charts in Italy with Beethoven's 'Romance in F' – the Beatles were number one, we were number two and the Rolling Stones number three. That really was an incredible feeling!

Studio Hamburg

Two innovative technological developments contributed very significantly to the success of my music. First was the long-playing record, which had just begun to take the world by storm. This fledgling medium was only a few years old and offered a whole new potential for composition because of its longer playing time. More important, though, was the invention of stereophony, which became widely popular at the beginning of the 1960s. Record buyers were completely rapt at the new sound – suddenly the music had a spatial dimension and the living room transformed itself into a concert hall.

All our recordings at the time were made in Studio Hamburg in Rahlstedt. Deutsche Grammophon, Polydor's parent company, had set up a large hall there as a music studio, and both classical and popular music recordings were supposed to be made there. However, the studio was too 'dry' for the classical musicians and too echoey for us, so it was decided to adapt the rooms exclusively for popular music. Large resonance boxes were attached to the walls to vary the reverberation interval, and there were flexible walls to separate the different instruments from each other acoustically. From the word go I was thrilled with the rich variety made possible by this technique.

To begin with, we recorded mostly with a single stereo

microphone, so I noted on the score where the instruments should be seated to achieve the sound effect that I had in mind. The choir stood right at the back; the strings were arranged in a semicircle in front of them, and the drums, bass speakers and guitars were placed in the middle under the microphone. Front left was the oboe, opposite was the flute and one or two trumpets on each side, left and right, for the echo effect. The trumpets on the left would begin a phrase, and then those on the right would repeat it in a slightly modified form, giving that familiar stereo sound that we were known for. That was how our 'classical' concert formation arose, what today might be called the corporate identity of the James Last Band. This arrangement of the instruments has remained unchanged, even today.

Towards the end of the 1960s, recording technology evolved more and more, offering yet more potential. Double-track tapes were followed by four-, eight- and finally sixteen-track machines, so we could record the instruments in groups, first the rhythm section, then the wind instruments and finally the strings and solos. We could also play around with different ideas to achieve unusual sound effects through distortion. For instance, in the studio we incorporated standard lamps into our tape-threading paths. We would arrange them at different distances depending on the piece's tempo, sometimes metres apart. We would then let the tape run around the lamps between the recording head and the playback head, achieving spectacular reverberation and echo effects.

One huge advantage of the studio was its size. The room was almost as large as Hamburg main railway station: 50 metres long, 25 metres wide and 15 metres high. In a space this big, 16 musicians could spread themselves out so they were sitting at different distances to the microphone. This created a magnificent spatial sound. In addition, there was also a very large, tiled echo room which contained a loudspeaker and a microphone. This is where the recordings of different instruments were played, re-recorded and mixed in with the existing material to add a particular expanse to the sound. Today these effects are all artificially created because the large studio halls no longer exist, and there is always the risk that the sound will have too technical a feeling.

Crucial for the sound of the orchestra were the efforts of my work companion of many years, our sound engineer Peter Klemt. He had an excellent instinct for sound and his talent certainly played an important part in our success. With any other sound engineer vital little differences to our sound would probably have been missing.

The studio in Rahlstedt was at our disposal almost 24 hours a day. Since it belonged to the company, we didn't have to pay hire charges, so we could try out new ideas at any time, even if it was just for a few hours. It was during one of these spontaneous experiments that a really great story evolved, and the result has never been published anywhere, 'The Ballad of...'

But first things first. We were recording one of our *Sing mit* (Sing Along) LPs and for one short number, 'Ein Bett im Kornfeld' (A Bed in the Cornfield), an actor was supposed to read the words. We were having a break, so I went over to the canteen and there was my old friend Heinz Reincke, magnificent as the 'Hauptmann von Köpenick' (a notorious German military impostor who had become the focus of a famous play). He was already somewhat sozzled and in the merriest of moods. Reincke, although famed for being Germany's showpiece Prussian, was actually an actor at the Vienna Burgtheater, and in perfect Burgtheater German he was reciting a poem at the top of his voice, 'Die Scheißhaus-Ballade' (The Ballad of the Shitehouse)!

As the title no doubt conveys, it was a rather hefty piece, not for general consumption, and particularly contentious because people round about were trying to eat. Once he had finished his performance, I asked him if he would do our 'Cornfield' number.

'I can, but I have to catch my train to Vienna in time, for a Burgtheater actor is not permitted to fly!' he boomed throughout the whole canteen.

'No problem. Just come over when you're ready and we'll soon have it in the bag.'

So Heinz came over to our huge studio, by now empty of musicians and with only two lamps on, and opened a can of caviar and a bottle of vodka.

'This is better than my own parties!' he bellowed.

After he'd had his caviar on toast and followed it with vodka, he said, 'So, start the tape!' He recited his text and 'Ein Bett im Kornfeld' became 'Ein Korn im Feldbett' (A Schnapps in the Camp Bed) and in 15 minutes we were done. 'Heinz, we still have time,' I said. 'Couldn't you do that poem you recited this afternoon?'

'Oh, you mean that crap about the Black Knight? Of course I can! Do you know where I heard that the first time? It was in the middle of the war and I was walking along in the cold Russian night with a subaltern doctor. It was so damned cold that the snot froze in our noses. We were terribly afraid, and to keep our mind off it this bloke told me the "Shitehouse Ballad"! I laughed out loud. Man, I laughed so loud that the Russians didn't attack us because they thought we were a whole company!' Heinz Reincke, as he lives and breathes.

And that is how we recorded 'The Ballad of the Shitehouse' – with nary a Russian in sight, but with caviar and vodka in the warmth of a studio.

Back at home I sat down, listened to the tape and wrote a gentle melody for the strings as a counterpoint to Heinz's bawdy recitation. We recorded this melody the following day and finally we had the Bergedorf Chamber Choir come into the studio.

Naturally, we couldn't inflict this frivolous ballad on these good people, so we left out Reincke's voice and the choir merely hummed along with the string section – magnificent! Helmut Wormsbächer was thrilled. Finally I called everyone into the production room and played them the finished piece – including Reincke's recitation. Peter Klemt started the tape, you could hear the strings, and the choir sounded like it was in a cathedral – and then came the words. Wormsbächer's face grew redder and redder – the poor man was absolutely horrified.

We only ever made a single pressing of this recording, which we sent to Heinz Reincke, asking him if we could release it. 'You can do what you like with it,' was his reply, 'as long as you put on it: BURGTHEATER ACTOR HEINZ REINCKE!'

Jukebox a gogo

Whether it was classics, folk songs, or the *à gogo* series, whatever I produced in those years turned to gold. I received 12 gold records for the first volume of *Trumpet à gogo* in Australia alone. The folk-song album *Ännchen von Tharau* was in the German charts for six months, and between 250,000 and 400,000 copies of every volume of *Non Stop Dancing* were sold in Germany, apparently without effort. It was simply unbelievable. No one had reckoned with a success of these dimensions, least of all myself. After all, I wasn't some glittering pop star, just one of many bandleaders in the early years of their career. But the most incredible part was that I only had to do what I loved to do anyway – spend every day of my life with music. I simply had the great fortune to strike the right note with millions of people without ever consciously striving to do so.

Right from the beginning I also produced albums aimed at the international market. *That's Life* or *Instrumentals for Ever* were primarily intended to make me known in the English-speaking world. My breakthrough in Britain came when Polydor started a huge advertising campaign there. After an initial knock-back from Polydor in London, who feared this 'kraut' music would leave the British public cold, the company brought out a compilation called *This is James Last* and sold it at a rock-bottom price. The album promptly shot into the charts and was an enormous hit, catapulting me to fame there.

The result was more and more specific requests from different Polydor divisions around the world. The first country I had to record a special album for was Japan, where German orchestras had always been well received. Werner Müller and Alfred Hause, for instance, had enjoyed great success there for many years. Someone particularly astute at Polydor Japan recognised that I could be at least as strong an attraction and suggested we produce an LP with the romantic title *Sekai Wa Futari No Tameni* (The World Belongs to Lovers). And that's how I came to busy myself with Japanese pop songs. I'd never heard of the original artists – names such as Naomi Sagara, Yukari Ito, Youichi Sugawara or Akira Fuse – but their music immediately struck a chord with me. Better still, I already knew the type of arrangements the Japanese preferred – an opulent, mellow string sound – because I'd discovered it a few years before when arranging tangos in Far Eastern style for Alfred Hause. The record was released only in Japan and is regarded by collectors as the rarest and most coveted trophy of all. It became my 'Penny Black' in black vinyl.

The next Polydor division to ask about a special production was the Netherlands. Despite the fact that my records claimed an unbelievable 15 per cent of Dutch Polydor sales at the time, the company was initially cautious. The Dutch market seemed too small for its own album. A meeting was arranged, at which the head of Polydor Holland, Everett Garretsen, briskly stated he could guarantee sales of at least 20,000 copies. That seemed to be sufficiently profitable for my bosses, so I set to work arranging Dutch folk songs in the style of *Ännchen von Tharau*. The LP was called *James Last Op Klompen*.

It turned out that good old Everett had miscalculated badly. The album went gold inside three months and Garretsen sent the following telegram to Hamburg: 'Today we sold 100,000th Op Klompen record – stop – thrilled – stop – congratulations – stop – preparing official press conference.' All in all, 250,000 copies of *Op Klompen* were sold, and requests for it were suddenly coming in from Germany – even though no one knew the songs there! *Op Klompen* was eventually released in Germany too.

In 1969 we appeared live in Holland for the first time, receiving thundering applause for our excerpts from *Op Klompen* on the TV show *Grand Gala du Disque* in Amsterdam. This popular show was to become a regular platform for us over the years: our appearances on it contributed a great deal to my continuing popularity in Holland. I ended up making four more LPs for the Dutch, all of which reached gold or platinum.

In the wake of this mega-seller came orders from other Polydor branches for similar productions for the Scandinavian market (*In Scandinavia*) and for Great Britain (*Last of Old England*) – which also went gold.

Everything just worked. I had something like an inner jukebox and it seemed to work well with every idea. Title followed title, album followed album. In very short order I produced a record of rock 'n' roll numbers (*Rock Around With Me*), one of melodies from the 1940s and 1950s (*Non Stop Evergreens*), a Christmas LP (*Christmas Dancing*), a sprinkling of operetta (*Happy Lehar*), a few drinking songs (*Humba Humba à gogo*) and – since we were in Hamburg – sea shanties (*Käpt'n James bittet zum Tanz* – Cap'n James Requests this Dance). Whatever was required, I wrote and recorded and wrote and recorded…

At this point I was working around the clock. A long and strenuous day in the studio would be followed by an equally long night in my study at home. That's where all my arrangements came into being, note for note, for every single instrument, for hundreds of numbers. Only rarely did I crawl, dog tired, into bed with Waltraud before four in the morning. Usually the telephone would start ringing again at eight, because someone at the record company wanted to advise me of new deadlines and appointments. But by then I would have been awake for a while, preparing for the next recording.

As soon as I finished an arrangement, it was our trombonist Detlef Surmann's turn. Up until about 1990 he was also my music copyist, which meant he received a finished score from me with the voices of all the instruments and from that he had to copy out all the notes for the individual musicians and the singing voices. That meant a lot of stress for Detlef, especially when it came to the string instruments in classical pieces. If they only had semiquavers or demisemiquavers to play, that went on for page after page of sheet music. At the beginning Waltraud used to take the music to Detlef, but as time passed it became too much, so I sent the papers over in a taxi. With all that driving back and forth, a taxi company could have financed its own upkeep.

Often the deadlines were so tight I hadn't completely finished arranging all the instruments – perhaps only the rhythm group, because the strings were only due to be recorded a week later. In the meantime, I could quickly write something else… The amount of music we produced on paper was unbelievable: it would fill a large room. You only need to work it out: two pages per title, notes for 40 musicians, that's 80 pages per number, 12 numbers per LP, so overall that's almost a thousand pages per album! And we recorded around 150 albums that way – that's a lot of little black notes!

There were even times when I was recording at several different places at the same time. While the string instruments were in the hall preparing for a *Classics* LP, the choir was practising for a *Beachparty* album in another studio, and just a hop and a skip away the latest *Non Stop Dancing* was being mixed. I was so inundated with work I barely had time to really register my growing popularity.

Two Boys from the Waterside

In the studio I made a conscious effort to create a particular ambience. I was convinced that a good atmosphere was discernible, so it was important to me that everyone was feeling good – and in fact there was a great atmosphere at most of our recordings. I had a small kitchen built into the studio and hired a woman to cook for us, so our creature comforts were always seen to. This positive working environment was certainly an important factor in our success: I'm convinced our good mood can be heard in our music.

Arranging and recording were not the end of my work. There were plenty of things outside of my musical world that I had to deal with. There were the regular Polydor in-house marketing sessions, for instance, which were mainly designed to motivate the sales representatives to sell their different products. I would grab the band and play at these meetings, exclusively for the marketing people. I went from table to table and chatted with all the staff, told them about our new projects and assured them how great they were in their work. I wanted to give each and every one of them the feeling that they were just as important as I was, as everyone who worked on our common success. That was incredibly motivating for these people. I was 'their' Hansi!

Another important link in the chain of success was undoubtedly the design of the record covers. That was very much Werner Klose's playground. At first I had very little to do with it, since I was not shown on any of them. The preferred motifs were lovely ladies, like the half-naked beauty on *Beat in Sweet* or the swinging girl on *Ännchen von Tharau*, who impressed one fan from Vancouver so much that he wrote to Polydor to request her address: the ardent suitor harboured serious intentions of marriage.

But my increasing popularity soon led to me having to appear on the covers in person. My first time was for the album *Rock Around with Me*, which shows me styled like a rocker in a denim jacket and sitting on a motorbike. I was supposed to convey a more mature version of James Dean!

From that point I also had to squeeze endlessly long sittings in the photo studio into my schedule. In chunky clogs or as Käpt'n James or as a torero – the formula was 'Hansi plus costume'. This was supposed to indicate to the public at a glance what type of music to expect from the new record. Klose was constantly coming up with crazy new ideas and I had to pose in the most unbelievable costumes. What's more, there were the national differences, since not every cover was equally suitable in every country.

The album *Voodoo Party* is a good example. On the German version the entire band was depicted wearing rather ludicrous carnival jungle costumes, but the people from Polydor in Britain wrinkled their noses at this. 'You won't sell a single record here with that cover. We have to do it differently.' So in England the album was released with a voodoo mask against a black background. In Japan they usually used different layouts, mostly romantic landscape photographs taken with a soft lens. A regular market for collectors has now evolved out of the many different cover designs worldwide. There are fans who have collected several thousand (!) of these covers and still always manage to find something new.

On top of that there was the inimitable 'James Last' signature. The characteristic shadow was initially designed to improve its legibility on the cover, but it soon became my trademark in every conceivable colour combination. Later, towards the end of the 1980s, a new Polydor crew wanted to restyle my image from that of the 'happy party king' to one of an 'elder statesman of music'. They did away with the distinctive logo and replaced it with rather arbitrary, constantly changing type fonts – a marketing misjudgement that wasn't corrected until 1999.

Another important marketing instrument was our cooperation with the print media, like the radio programme guide *Hör Zu* or the illustrated magazine *Stern*. Henri Nannen, publisher and editor in chief of *Stern*, was particularly in favour of linking his magazine to popular music. Some of my productions appeared as *Stern* records, including advertising supplements. Today this would be called cross-promotion. Nannen landed some particularly big events with publicity potential, such as a gala celebration for the award of a gold record by the German Federal Minister for Finance – coverage in all the media was guaranteed.

Every two weeks I would meet privately with Werner Klose and Ossi Drechsler for a brainstorming session to discuss new plans and current projects. It was always important to us never to put an idea, no matter how good, into practice according to conventional patterns – there always had to be something unusual and creative. The title of the album, individual songs, the cover – something had to be there to trigger discussion in the press or among fans, otherwise the album would never make the top.

Sometimes the ideas for a new production came from Werner

or Ossi and sometimes from me. A regular bazaar of ideas would develop, something like this: Werner wanted an LP with marching music, but that wasn't quite my taste, so we'd trade. I'd say, 'OK, you'll get your marching music if I get a modern choir LP.' Whenever I had finished a new production that was particularly close to my heart, we'd meet at midday at my place, I'd pull the curtains, light a couple of candles, put a bottle of wine on the table and just say, 'Relax and listen.'

Naturally, television also played an essential role. From 1968 onwards, I found a constant forum in the *Starparade* on the station ZDF (Germany's Channel Two) but more on that later. At this point, however, a critical piece in the jigsaw puzzle for success was still missing – the tours, immediate contact with my audience.

What would become an essential link between me and my fans – and ultimately distinguish us from all other orchestras – was still unthinkable in 1968. No promoter wanted to take on the risk of sending a purely instrumental group on tour. The idea had never been tested. Of course, we had appeared live, just like Max Greger or Hugo Strasser, but that happened either on television, at dance events and balls, or as the orchestral accompaniment to a singing star. So it was only logical that initially I should be teamed with a singer who could pull the crowds – Freddy Quinn, for whom I had written the arrangement of his million-selling hit 'Junge, komm bald wieder' (Come Home Soon, My Son) six years previously.

We had met for the first time in 1954. After many turbulent years of wandering, Freddy was finally quite eager to land his dream job of singer, actor and entertainer. He got the chance at NDR, where he was to record two songs – 'Hallo Joe' and 'Karte genügt' (A Card Will Do) with the popular radio orchestra under the direction of Alfred Hause. At that time I played double bass in the orchestra. There were no playbacks, no text monitors or suchlike: everything was live. So the young lad was naturally nervous in the studio and his stage fright was more than obvious.

I decided to look after him. 'Listen, it'll be all right. Just look over at me, and I'll give you the sign when to start,' I told him.

During the recording he was looking over at me with one eye and at Alfred with the other, and, thanks to his talent, but perhaps also to a little help from me, he met the challenge of his debut without a hitch. Two years after this episode he had his great breakthrough with 'Heimweh nach St. Pauli' (Longing for St Pauli), which sold over a million copies and broke all records at the time.

By 1968 Freddy Quinn had long been one of the biggest stars on the German pop scene. Although he was actually born in Vienna, Freddy was seen as a 'boy from the waterside' and that seemed to fit with Bremen boy James Last. So they put us together and together we set off on our journey through the concert halls. In contrast to today, where I always travel with my musicians in the same bus, back then I had to travel with him in his private, chauffeur-driven car. He spent a lot of time philosophising and was often dissatisfied. But Freddy is, after all, not your run-of-the-mill person.

'I am a sailor' was his standard phrase. He always had his kitbag packed, with his passport and 15 different currencies – 'I can clear out at any time.'

Apart from Freddy's songs, we also played the 'Anvil Polka' on this tour, and that expanded my musical palette by yet another colour. It was the foundation stone for the *Polka Party* series, a musical concept that still makes ripples today. There is barely a folk-music programme without a *Polka Party* sound imitator. Legions of folk-music bands were formed, all wanting to sound like my orchestra on the *Polka* LPs.

Yet a lot of hard work went into these arrangements. For almost two years I racked my brains about how such a polka record should sound. Which instruments should be in the foreground? What should the phrasing be like? How could we alter the rhythm? Take the 'Wiener Praterleben' waltz: during the 1920s it had often been played during the popular six-day races at the Berlin Sports Palace. We turned it into a polka, the 'Sports Palace Polka'. At that time there was a guy in Berlin who was known throughout the city as Crutches, because he could only get around on crutches after an accident. Crutches became known because he would constantly 'improve' the 'Sports Palace Waltz' with loud whistles, and we built that into our polka. Today this piece is played by every police band, but no one knows this polka was once a waltz.

The tour with Freddy also had an important effect on my orchestra. Most of the musicians I had engaged for the studio recordings had come from NDR. Since they were salaried employees there, they couldn't or wouldn't come on tour with me for weeks on end, so I was forced to choose new members for many parts of the band. This is how Bernd Steffanowski and Helmut Franke (guitar), Wolfgang Ahlers and Conny Bogdan (trombone), Harald Ende (saxophone) and Manfred Moch (trumpet) came to join the band.

Manni Moch had previously been a soloist for Bert Kaempfert, but had parted from him. Manni's very relaxed trumpet style – very airy and most noticeably behind the beat – delivered exactly the right sound for titles like 'Touch of Your Lips' or 'Memories of Rubinstein'. He called it 'playing the slather rag'.

With this new team, slowly but surely an orchestra of freelance musicians evolved for whom I felt responsible, and whose livelihood I had to ensure if I wanted them to remain committed to me.

part three:
Jet Set

Beach Parties

In autumn 1969 a special adventure awaited my wife and me. We travelled to Brazil, where I had been invited to be a member of the jury for the Festival Internacional da Canção Popular, the Rio Song Festival. The invitation came as a great surprise, and I saw it as a great honour. Before me, and since, there have been such illustrious members of the jury as Henry Mancini, Francis Lai, Ray Conniff and Paul Simon. I had had no idea that my records were even known to people in Rio de Janeiro.

This was the fourth time the great Brazilian music festival had been held. More than 2,000 entries from 40 nations had been submitted and the sold-out final took place in front of 100,000 spectators in the Maracana stadium – an unforgettable experience. Henry Mancini, at first sitting alone on stage in the middle of this enormous stadium, began to play his world hit

'Moon River' on the piano with just one finger – and 100,000 people hummed to it. Then the strings joined in, and that created an indescribable atmosphere. Even today just thinking about it gives me a tingling feeling.

The winning title at that year's festival was deeply controversial. The public favourite was the American Bill Medley, the distinctive voice of the Righteous Brothers who had landed worldwide hits with 'You've Lost that Lovin' Feelin'' and 'Unchained Melody'. Bill Medley's entry was 'Evie', a wonderful composition by Jimmy Webb, but the winning song was 'Cantiga por Luciana'. The public was not at all pleased with this decision and raised all hell.

I was so impressed by my excursion to Rio that soon after my return I produced a record that attempted to capture my memories of Brazil. It was a rich sound of strings with cellos and double basses, supported by the choir and mandolins, with strong accents set by the guitars and flutes, and with trumpets, flugelhorns and trombones – a full orchestra. The album appeared under the title *With Compliments* and apart from the festival songs 'Evie' and 'Cantiga por Luciana' also featured a previous winning title 'Andanca' and some of my own compositions. A visit to one of the famed samba schools of Rio had also left a lasting impression on me. The vitality and zest for life that this dance expressed – and perhaps also the beautiful dancers – inspired me to write the exuberant 'Happy Brasilia'.

But all that composing, arranging and producing left me less and less time for my family. My life accelerated more every year, becoming more demanding and nerve-racking. When I left the studio late at night, all revved up and restless because, for example, we had just finished recording a new *Non Stop Dancing* LP and the party had gone on longer than expected, I couldn't just drive straight home. My mood motor was running at top speed, so I'd go on the town with my musicians, sometimes ending up in clubs with a certain reputation, painting the town red. I might not have ended up in bed with some of the girls on these excursions, unlike many of my musicians, but the sun was often high in the sky before I made my way back home.

If the children were up and about, I would collect them all, mine and the neighbours', and we'd go sledding or descend upon a clothes shop for kids and I'd deck them all out in chic gear. When their parents woke up, the children would be standing at the door in new clothes.

Every mother and every father knows how amazingly fast time flies when you measure it by how your children grow up. In my case I think the clockwork went into overdrive. Were Rina and Ronnie teenagers already? Had the children really cast aside their cute little primary-school bags so soon? I could hardly believe it: in no time at all they were both going to secondary school. After school they would look in on me in my study and I had to play what I was working on for them. Or they'd come with me to the studio and join in on the *Non Stop Dancing* recordings.

I must admit that the lion's share of their upbringing was left to Waltraud, and she did this with great dedication and sensitivity. My wife always strove to give our children a more or less normal childhood despite the increasingly intrusive fuss about my fame. It is thanks to her that our children made something of themselves. Her quiet composure offered the necessary balance to her crazy husband. She looked after everything at home, clearing the way for me and providing me with a completely carefree life. This was all a sign of her great strength and generosity.

I, on the other hand, was far from generous, and I could get jealous very easily. If I saw her standing with another man for too long, I immediately demanded to know what was going on.

We continued living in Hamburg-Langenhorn, but in 1969 we moved from 71 Holitzbergstrasse to number 61. This house lay a little way back from the street so we weren't quite as exposed to the groups of fans, who by now were coming in hordes on buses to look over our garden fence. My brother Werner and his Norwegian wife Hjördis took over our old house.

Despite all the work, there was one period in the year that Waltraud, the children and I always spent together – the school holidays. In winter we would go skiing to Obergurgl in Austria. Waltraud was not a particularly good skier, but we always had a party going. No sooner had we arrived than we would invite other skiers and instructors to join us for a party – the success of our holiday was always pre-programmed.

For many years we spent the summer at a camping place on an island called Sylt, at first in a tent and later in a caravan. That was before the in-crowd took over this lovely place. The North Sea has always held a great attraction for me. My first real trip, fairly soon after the war, took me to a beach near Cuxhaven. I set up my tent and after a while two girls trotted up on their Friesian horses and the three of us sat looking out over the mudflats. It was low tide, no sign of water. That was the first time I had been to the seaside and there was no sea to be seen!

On Sylt we met up with the same group of friends every year. They weren't musicians, but a colourful mix of people who were thrilled every time the fun started up again. In the morning we would pack lots of bread rolls and head out to the beach for the rest of the day. We'd play volleyball for hours on end or trek for miles through the dunes – that was back in the days when you still could; nowadays it is forbidden in order to protect them. The kids would have their surfboards with them and we couldn't drag them out of the water. Werner, Hjördis and their two children, Werner and Steven, were always amongst the crew.

jet set

Our beach parties were legendary. We bought mussels by the kilo, giant buckets of them. At the camping ground we scrubbed them thoroughly and, when the other swimmers had left for the evening, we put them on to cook with wine, onions and water in the lifeguard huts. Then the party could begin. We set up beach baskets and torches and we ate, drank and got up to nonsense until the early hours of the morning. A few years later, the covers of my *Beachparty* albums were created in memory of these times.

The weather didn't matter to us at all. If it was cool, the adults drank tea and kümmelschnapps while the children all ran around wearing similar pullovers knitted by Grandma. When the five or six weeks were over, everyone trotted up with their towels and bed sheets, and there was endless waving and goodbyes with copious tears at the car train. The children would spend the rest of their holidays with their grandparents in Bremen, Opa Louis and Oma Martha. They loved being there: they were allowed to stay up late watching television and only had to have a quick wash before bed. Waltraud's mother, Oma Meta, was much stricter, and every day the kids would be thoroughly soaped from head to toe.

Once we even spent our winter holiday on Sylt. Initially, we'd driven our caravan to the Harz mountains to go skiing. It could be quite cosy in the heated caravan, but after a week we'd had enough. All through that night it had snowed, so in the morning we had to dig the caravan free and pull it out of the snow with a tractor. Then, in the middle of winter, we drove straight up to Sylt and had the whole camping ground to ourselves. It was wonderful: walking along the North Sea beaches, gathering flotsam and jetsam, making sculptures out of old wooden slats and tar pots – better than any mountain.

However, the more I grew from Hans into James Last, the more difficult it became on Sylt. Soon we were hounded from morning till night by autograph hunters, and then came the reporters and photographers. Rina hid for hours under the table in the caravan – even then she was quite camera shy. Ron was better equipped to get by, but our idyll had been broken.

Our holiday in the summer of 1970 was to be our last on Sylt, but it wasn't due to the fans. For my part, I enjoyed the popularity. I liked the actual contact and thought it was great when people recognised me on the street because they shared my sense of music – even if I had to run through the city because so many people were following me. Since then things have become more sedate, as the fans have grown older with me and they don't run quite so quickly any more. Our times for the 100-metre sprint have definitely settled well outside the 15-second mark...

No, the reason why we stopped going to Sylt was much more dramatic.

Speed Rage

We were on our way from Sylt to Hamburg, full of sand and dirt, when I noticed that the exhaust of our blue Opel Diplomat was getting deeper and deeper. Money didn't mean much to me back in the early days of my success – after the modest circumstances of my childhood, this was something I couldn't quite come to grips with. So I said cheerfully, 'Let's just drive on to Düsseldorf to Auto Becker, the car dealer, and see if we can get a new car...'

Auto Becker had the greatest cars in the world in stock – Ferrari, Lamborghini, Jaguar, anything your heart desired – and back then I was quite a car freak. Even when I was Hans Nobody, I was fascinated by powerful engines and well-designed bodywork. After all, I come from Sebaldsbrück, home of the car factory of the brilliant design engineer Carl Borgward. One of Germany's most legendary vehicles was constructed in this factory, the famous Borgward Isabella. Naturally, my first car was also a Borgward, a little Goliath model, but even back then I would stand longingly in front of the showrooms of BMW and dream of owning a snazzy little sports car myself one day – and somehow I knew that that day would come.

Now the moment had arrived. We drove straight on past Hamburg and directly to the Ruhr area. It turned out to be a bit further than we had thought, so it was already 6pm when we arrived in Düsseldorf. Becker was just about to close shop but immediately recognised that he could land some good business with me. So he let me look at a few cars and then said, 'Ah, Mr Last, we have a really lovely one here – the fastest four-seater in the world, an Iso Rivolta Fidia.'

Superb! A quality saloon car from a small, classy Italian sports-car manufacturer, V8, 5.8-litre engine, sensational design and a top speed of 220km/hr – and all that in 1970! It didn't take me long to decide. 'That looks good, silver and brown is fine. We'll buy it!'

I signed the contract and Becker congratulated me, 'Well done, Mr Last, an excellent decision. I'll bring you the car next week.'

We hadn't reckoned with that. 'No, since we've bought it, we want to take it now!'

'I'm sorry, Mr Last, you can't. The car has to be registered first!'

We conferred with Mr Becker senior, who had a brilliant idea: I would become their employee! For the first time in years I was a salaried employee again – even if only for three days. As a staff member of Auto Becker, I was permitted to transfer the car to Hamburg, thus allowing me to take my dream car home straight away. I was overjoyed with my speedy toy. How could I have known it would change the life of my family so fundamentally and in a way I would never have guessed?

Some weeks later Waltraud and I were sitting together one evening enjoying a glass of wine. I had a long day in the studio behind me and another one ahead. 'You know, if you don't have anything planned for tomorrow, maybe you could drive the Iso to Düsseldorf for its first service check,' I suggested.

'No problem,' she said, 'I can do that.'

The next morning we said goodbye to each other, just as we did every day, and I set off for Studio Hamburg, just as I did every day. I had to record the playback tapes for a production with Frida Boccara, the French Eurovision Song Contest winner of 1969. In the middle of this work, towards the evening, I got a phone call.

'Mr Last, this is the police from Bad Bramsche. I am sorry to have to tell you this but your wife has had a serious accident and is in a critical condition...'

My heart stood still. It was a bolt out of the blue. One minute I was creating a cheerful Happy Sound, the next my world was collapsing.

I immediately broke off the recording, grabbed a colleague's car and rushed off. Waltraud was in the hospital in Bad Bramsche, near Osnabrück, in the intensive care ward. When I arrived there that night, she was conscious, but barely responsive.

The doctors and police described what had happened. Waltraud had been overtaking a lorry on the autobahn when it had suddenly pulled out and cut her off, causing her to skid out of control. The Iso had broken through the crash barrier at high speed and spun up the side of a small hill. She had been flung out as the car overturned, but the heavy vehicle had slowly rolled back down the hill, before finally coming to rest directly on top of her. The smouldering hot exhaust pipe had caused dreadful burns, affecting the whole of her left side. In addition, she was suffering from multiple fractures.

It became a life-or-death fight. Waltraud lay in hospital for many weeks. She wasn't fit enough to be moved until a month later, when she was transferred to a Hamburg clinic. All told, she spent six months in hospital. But she survived.

During this time, Waltraud's mother looked after our two children and the neighbours lent her a hand. Our friend Lilo visited Waltraud in hospital almost every day, taking her soup and juice to build her up. It was at this time that my life was taking on a faster pace. Among other things, my first German tour was about to begin, the contracts having long since been signed... Waltraud certainly didn't get the attention from me she deserved.

Once she finally got home after being away for so long, her reaction was typical of her. She just said a quick hello, took the car keys and drove off. She was convinced that, if she didn't get behind the wheel of a car straight away, she would always live in fear of driving and never do it again. This courageous yet clear-headed attitude was characteristic of her.

After the accident I bought a second Iso Rivolta, but someone drove into me as I was on my way home from the studio. 'That's it,' I said to myself. 'This car only brings us bad luck.' The next morning, someone from Mercedes was standing at the door – he had probably been listening to the police frequency on the radio and heard of my mishap. In any case, he left a Mercedes at our disposal. Very smart.

Canadian Last Fever

One question that became more and more insistent towards the end of the 1960s was whether it was feasible and affordable to send us on tour as an orchestra alone – without a crowd-pulling singer. Could we sound as good live as we did on a record? Would our audiences want to listen to two hours of orchestra music without a singing star? The answer was a clear maybe.

The tour with Freddy Quinn had been very successful, the credit being mostly due to Freddy. Our appearances at several balls had also been well received, but people went there to dance, drink and chat, so we couldn't really draw any conclusions from that. Then came our live appearances in Canada – now they were a real yardstick.

One fine day, Werner Triepke, who worked for Polydor International, received a telegram from our Canadian branch saying, 'Send by return 5,000 copies *Trumpet à gogo* – stop – plus 5,000 copies *Ännchen von Tharau* – stop – ASAP.'

Whatever could that mean?! Ten thousand LPs to Canada? Not a soul there knew who we were. We'd never done any advertising there, so what made them think of James Last? Triepke telegraphed back in disbelief: '5,000? – stop – please confirm quantity – stop.'

The answer was prompt: 'In words – stop – five thousand – stop.'

That was the beginning of a long love story between our music and the Canadian public. I was told that in 1969 a Last number could be heard on any of the Canadian radio stations at any time – Last fever had broken out in that great land and was threatening to become a veritable epidemic. Five per cent of the entire Canadian record sales were my music! The record company wanted to profit from this and asked if we could play a couple of concerts in Canada. That would be a completely new, extremely exciting venture! I thought about it briefly and finally accepted. Just to be on the safe side, we also took two stars with us as an additional attraction, Renate Kern and Bata Illic.

All the same, one thing was clear: the concerts couldn't take place without my tried and tested sound engineer, Peter Klemt, so

I asked him if he wanted to come to Canada with us. Initially, Peter was anything but excited. Doing sound at a concert? Now that was something that lay far beneath the dignity of a successful sound engineer. That was something for trainee technicians!

But it was extremely important to me that we produced the same sound on stage as we did in the studio – the audience had to get the same quality live as they were used to from our records. Finally, Peter allowed himself to be persuaded – and I believe he has never regretted it. Bit by bit he came to enjoy life on tour as a welcome change to the studio routine.

However, at the end of the 1960s there was next to no suitable equipment for the stage – no proper mixing consoles, no special loudspeakers and least of all stage monitors. So I bought an amplifier with six control knobs for six microphones and it was installed on stage – that became Peter's new workplace. He was given stage clothes like the musicians, and now had to conjure up our studio sound with the most primitive technical devices. But he wouldn't be Peter Klemt if he didn't achieve that in the shortest time!

The first three concerts were to take place in the open air on the grounds of the World Expo in Montreal, on the gigantic Place of Nations. When we arrived in Montreal, we discovered that the 5th Dimension, who at that time had 'Let the Sunshine In' and 'Aquarius' from *Hair* in the charts, would be performing at the same venue the evening before us. We drove straight there to hear them, but, when I saw this incredible mass of people who had come to see the 5th Dimension, I was dismayed. For the first time we would have our own real concert, but it was against this backdrop! That evening at the hotel I fell to my knees begging and praying, 'Dear God, please let it rain tomorrow! Then we won't have to play. Or at least let there be a good excuse why so few people could come.'

It didn't rain. We arrived at the grounds for the sound check and I couldn't believe my eyes: the grounds were already half full, with about 20,000 to 25,000 people – and the stream of people wasn't letting up. In the end there were 50,000 spectators. During the concert a wind got up, distorting the sound and making the evening a game of chance, especially for our bassist Benny Bendorff. Benny was new to the band and only knew the numbers from our recording of *Hair*, for which I had engaged his services just before the tour.

But the audience was amazingly enthusiastic. They could sing along to our records from the first to the last note, and kept calling out titles they wanted to hear: 'Hansi, play this! Hansi, play that!' The concert ended in a gigantic party, and it was just the same at the other evenings. We had performances in Toronto and Kitchener, playing to a total of 210,000 people. One thing was clear: my music didn't just work on record: it could captivate people in concerts too.

Nothing more stood in the way of a tour through Germany. Or so I thought.

Polydor's marketing chief Werner Klose had presented several concepts for a James Last tour to the concert promoter Hans-Werner Funke, but he was still a little reluctant and hadn't quite swallowed the hook. So, in collaboration with *Jasmin*, a very trendy glossy magazine, Klose organised several test concerts for invited audiences. The gratifying result of those experiments finally wiped away the last of Funke's scepticism and we set about planning our tour.

Despite our experience in Canada, we were still of the opinion that our show wouldn't work in Germany without the support of a crowd-pulling singer. During the 1966 German pop festival in Baden-Baden, I had met a young amateur singer who'd made an impact with some very well-performed blues songs. Her name was Katja Ebstein. Now, four years later, her song 'Wunder gibt es immer wieder' (Miracles Are Always Happening) was a big hit after coming third at the Eurovision Song Contest in Amsterdam. I asked if she wanted to join us on tour and she immediately said yes.

The first James Last concert in Germany took place on 10 October 1970 and it was a fantastic success. Our tour of Germany and Denmark was supposed to take four weeks, using a reduced-size band with no strings and only a single spotlight for the stage. All the concerts were completely sold out, even the huge Westfalen Hall in Dortmund, which held 12,000 people, for three nights in a row. Halfway through the tour, Funke asked if we would agree to extend it by 14 days. In our great euphoria, we didn't need to discuss it long: Katja, the band and I all immediately agreed.

The one person I did not think of was my wife lying in hospital seriously injured after the car accident. Naturally, Waltraud was disappointed that I would be on the road for another two weeks without having discussed it with her, but at least I took every opportunity to come and visit her in hospital between the performances. It was a situation that would repeat itself – under much more tragic circumstances – many years later.

Since our debut we have been on tour almost every year in Germany, Austria and Switzerland, in Scandinavia and the Benelux states, in France, Great Britain and Ireland, in Russia, Africa, Asia and Canada, in Australia and New Zealand. My musicians and I have travelled almost the whole world together and experienced all sorts of things. During our tour with Katja, I said to the band, 'As great as our success is, it certainly can't go on like this. At 60 I will probably be playing a barrel organ for the bathers on Sylt.' Katja and her then boyfriend Christian Bruhn – now chairman of the board of supervisors of GEMA (the

German society for music performance rights) – ended up giving me a barrel organ. It is still standing in my house in Hamburg, but I have yet to use it!

Pier 66

Waltraud's accident was to change a great deal in our lives – both directly and indirectly. One aspect was that she didn't want to be seen in public with a large burn scar on her body. Until then we had been great fans of naturism, but now that freedom was over. 'I can never go to the beach again with these burns,' she said. That meant the topic of holidays on Sylt never came up again, but I had a suggestion.

'Let's buy a boat! You can walk around however you like on board.'

So we went to a large boat fair in Hamburg to look for something suitable. Gigantic yachts were standing on display, looking twice as big on land as in the water, when suddenly a school class spotted us: 'That's James Last over there!' Once again we had to flee so we climbed on to a large cruising yacht to hide. As we looked around, we thought, Hey, it's quite comfortable in a cabin like this!

Eventually, the representative of the boat's manufacturer, a very pleasant man called Hans Otto Noll, came to sit down with us and poured us a drink... By the time we left the boat, we had signed a sales agreement for a 48ft yacht.

To collect our new boat we had to travel to Fort Lauderdale in Florida and a marina called Pier 66. We went on board and were bowled over. Waltraud had chosen the colours for the materials, blue and green, and they matched the pale turquoise of the sea perfectly. We had had an autopilot installed; back then that consisted of attaching two compasses, one at the front on the bow and one at the stern. To adjust this device, we had to sail through different canals aligned exactly according to the points of the compass. In doing so, we sailed by the fantastic villas of Fort Lauderdale and instantly my imagination was on fire – it would be great to retire here, that would be so lovely! In front of some of these magnificent houses were signs with FOR SALE and a telephone number on them. On the spur of the moment I rang up one of the estate agents.

'Hi, folks,' he said as he answered the phone, 'you want to buy a house?'

'I'd be interested to know just how much a house like that would cost.'

'Never mind, just have a look!'

We let ourselves be talked into it and went to look at several houses the next day. One of them was particularly impressive. Ronnie and Rina knew straight away which rooms they'd choose and were bubbling over with excitement. 'We can go for a swim in the pool every morning, we can grill over there, and back there we can play volleyball!'

We returned to our boat and that evening, fanned by the gentle ocean breeze, thoughts of the house danced in our heads. But, when we passed by the next day, SOLD had been written across the sign in front of the door. Great cries of disappointment. But we had also seen other houses for sale. One was a little expensive and actually too big – we just wanted a bungalow for our holidays, if anything – and the owners still lived in it.

But things happened as they did on our visit to Auto Becker. We came in from the beach, all full of sand. I said to the owners, 'Our plane back to Germany is leaving soon, but I think we should buy a house before we go. You can hear how upset the kids are.'

The owner, Chauncey Huber, looked at us in confusion. 'How do you want to pay, then?'

'Well, cash!'

He was flabbergasted. Back then, that was very unusual, even in America. 'My beautiful bedroom, my kitchen, all gone!' sighed his wife. She didn't really want to give up her home so soon, but in the end it wasn't so bad. The Hubers built a new house in the neighbourhood and became good friends of ours.

Two years later, in 1973, we moved into another house – huge, with 15 rooms, almost all with their own bathroom, and a tennis court in the garden. It lay directly on the Intracoastal Waterway, which runs along the leeward bay side of Florida right up to Chicago. We also took over the caretakers, Dan and Rose.

Also in our new neighbourhood was a dog, which would wander into our garden every now and then. When Ronnie's new friend, an American girl, was visiting us for the first time, she came running into the house, all agitated. 'Der Hund des Nachbarn scheißt bei uns in den Garten!' (The neighbour's dog is shitting in our garden!) It was her first German sentence. Well, the dog turned out to be pretty lucky, because our neighbour was Raymond Albert Kroc, founder and owner of McDonald's. By strange coincidence, the boss of Burger King lived just a few doors down, although happily he didn't have a dog.

For over 30 years now, I have stayed in Florida. I now live in Palm Beach, at my fourth address (after Fort Lauderdale and Coral Springs) in this wonderful, sunny land.

We ended up having our new boat brought back to Germany. (Incidentally, the German Olympic Committee rented it as an adjudicator's boat for the 1972 Olympics sailing competitions in Kiel.) Now we had a boat in Hamburg, but a house in Fort Lauderdale. The result was that I was only on board two times, once during a short holiday in Denmark. Even then we had to cut that short and charge back to Hamburg because my father had been taken to hospital after a stroke.

He never really recovered from it and Louis Last, who had bestowed on his sons his great heart, his humour and his musicality, passed away in 1972, almost 84 years old.

My mother, Martha, followed her husband five years later. I was in Florida, when she was admitted to hospital with internal bleeding. I leaped on board the next plane to hold her hand one last time but arrived in Bremen seven hours too late. She died shortly after her 80th birthday, which we had celebrated together just 14 days previously.

I had already developed a way – probably at the death of my half-brother, Bernhard – of coping with such experiences. It is a well-trained repression mechanism that helps me through these situations, at least on the surface. It wasn't until many years later that I had to learn, quite painfully, that this trick doesn't always work. But, at the time of my parents' deaths, I didn't have much time for mourning or deep reflection. The cruise control for my life was set on high speed – and not only on a professional level.

King Hussein's 'Cigarette'

At the end of the 1970s, when saving fuel was high on the agenda even in the USA, people waved goodbye to big boats. We sold our yacht, too, and decided on a so-called Cigarette. These are slim-lined, very stylish racing boats that can flit across the waves at a breathtaking pace. Although I hadn't the faintest idea about them, I was fascinated. The owner of the best-known Cigarette boatyard in Florida was Don Aronow. First he showed us his latest model, a small 28ft boat, but he said he had another larger boat in the shed. Did we want to see it?

Of course we did. This Cigarette looked gigantic, really wicked, with two 500hp motors at the back. It had been built to order for King Hussein of Jordan.

We spent a long time chatting with Don, one of the most colourful characters you could meet. He had invented the powerboat, super-fast offshore racers that could speed across the waves at far in excess of 100km/hr even back then. He was also a well-known champion, having won many a high-speed race in his Maltese Magnum.

Several years later, in February 1987, a black Lincoln drove past his office in Thunder Row at walking pace. Someone fired off a few volleys from a machine gun and Don was dead. Even today, wild rumours still circulate about his death. No one ever found out who had set the killers on to him or what the motive was. Was it to do with drugs? Politics? The fact was Don Aronow, a friend of the then president George Bush, was due to stand witness in a drugs trial the day after his murder.

Whatever the truth of the matter, when Don showed us his boats that day, he was on top of the world. 'Actually, I like you guys a lot better than King Hussein. If you want the boat, let's put it to water.'

A little while later, we were off. The man could drive like an ace – we had never experienced anything like it. In the end we bought King Hussein's Cigarette and took it with us. As we were leaving, Don Aronow said, 'Do me a favour and don't drive straight out on the open sea. Get to know the boat first.'

But of course we didn't have the patience and did exactly what he'd warned us not to do. On our first excursion Ronnie, our road technician Jürgen Mayer and I jetted along from Miami to Fort Lauderdale, and, before we returned into the marina, Jürgen suggested, 'Come on, let's head out to sea.'

Fine! Brashly, we tried out a little of what the Cigarette could do. All of a sudden a giant freighter appeared, throwing up enormous waves. We made the typical beginner's mistake: we dropped speed instead of stepping on it – and the Cigarette speared into one of the waves like a submarine. The water stood half a metre high in the boat and we were soaked to the bone. We panicked for a moment but the pumps started up immediately, and in the end the shock was greater than the damage done. A long swig of vodka helped calm our nerves.

New Faces in the Family

At the beginning of the 1970s some of my musicians had got salaried jobs at NDR and, since we were often on tour now, I couldn't use them to the same extent. I took the opportunity to make an international orchestra out of what had been until now a purely German band. New faces were supposed to provide new swing and a modern sound.

The first 'foreigner' was Barry Reeves (percussion), from England. Then came the trumpeters Rick Kiefer from the USA, Leif Uvemark and (a little later) Lennart Axelsson from Sweden, and the trombonist Georges Delagaye from Belgium. Finally, Bob Lanese, also from the USA, joined us. He was to become my lead trumpeter for many years.

It was pure chance that brought Bob to the band. For my work in the studio I sometimes engaged Ernie England, an American living in Hamburg, who would leap into the breach whenever a trumpeter in my regular team couldn't play. In October 1971 it happened again when we were due to record *Beachparty 2*, so I called on the 'American trumpet'. We were about to start the first number and Ernie still hadn't appeared. Instead, a rather big, beefy bloke planted himself in front of me, armed with a trumpet, flugelhorn and piccolo trumpet.

'Who are you, then?' I asked.

'I'm the American trumpet – you hired me.'

'Where's Ernie?'

'In Sweden.'

'All right, then you can play!'

Bob didn't have the faintest idea what sort of music we played, but he was prepared for anything and delivered a faultless performance. Over the years he has become one of the most distinctive and best-loved faces in my band. When Leif Uvemark left us, Bob took over as first trumpeter, a very important job. The lead trumpeter doesn't act as a soloist, but – along with the drums – has to hold the troupe together.

In this respect the musicians generally had a lot of leeway. They could play a piece as far as possible according to their own personal feeling. Through his classical training, Bob was predestined for many difficult recordings in the *Classics* series – our version of Haydn's *Trumpet Concerto*, for instance. Leif Uvemark played the first part, Bob the second – and the whole thing twice so that it became a four-part phrase.

We once played this concerto live in ZDF television's *Starparade*, with Manni Moch, Rick Kiefer, Dieter Kock and Bob the four wind players. The broadcast began and I opened the score to give the trumpeters their cue, but instead of the musical notation a pair of voluptuous breasts smiled up at me. The devils had smuggled a *Playboy* centrefold into my score and written 'Have fun!' – and all of them had signed it. It was a real feat of self-control to stop myself bursting with laughter in front of the camera – no doubt my features were contorted quite comically.

With our new band members, our music also became more international. Now I wanted to have a choir to match this style and who could perform the hits convincingly in English. So I flew to London and engaged ten singers from the cream of British session singers. The best known were the sisters Sue and Sunny Glover, both stars on the scene. They had worked with Tom Jones, Cat Stevens and Shirley Bassey and became famous as the two female vocalists on Joe Cocker's brilliant version of 'With a Little Help from My Friends'.

Madeline Bell, who I had met at the Song Festival in Rio, was also the stuff of stars. She was the lead singer in the pop group Blue Mink and had recorded background vocals for Dusty Springfield and Elton John.

When I arrived in Hamburg with our new choir to record our first album together – *Beachparty* – the boys and girls naturally wanted to see something of Hamburg, so I dragged them off to the Reeperbahn, our great amusement mile. You don't find just theatres, restaurants and bars there, but above all a variety of red-light places and it was obvious that sooner or later we would end up in one.

Of course, there was the usual striptease, and the climax of the show was supposed to be when one of the scantily clad ladies appeared on the darkened stage with a tray full of burning candles to illuminate her perfect body with flickering flames. The girls from my choir promptly stood up as one and spontaneously belted out 'Happy Birthday to You' to loud guffaws in the darkened room.

My English singers were significantly better suited for the international market than our German *Non Stop Dancing* choir. Under the new trademark James Last and Company, we recorded a series of choir LPs reflecting the then current flower-power sound. With hits by Simon & Garfunkel, Neil Diamond, George Harrison, John Lennon and Santana, the *Voodoo-Party*, *Happyning*, *Love Must Be the Reason* and the *Beachparty* series are among my very favourite productions.

It was new and exciting working with the choir in the studio, especially as far as the phrasing of the voices was concerned. I arranged the four-part choral movements in just the same way as a string movement and the choir's performances live on stage were particularly successful. Numbers like 'MacArthur Park', 'Bridge over Troubled Water' and above all 'Don't Cry For Me, Argentina' regularly brought audiences to their feet.

The choirs always had an unfair advantage at our concerts. While the band and the string section were on stage constantly, the singers only had to appear for a few songs. They were the first to get a cool drink while we had to still sweat it out on stage.

In the early years the voices of the choir were a little more solemn, but later I wanted a more dynamic sound that had a more soulful feeling but was still based on polyphonic harmonies. That happened around 1978 when Simon Bell joined us. Simon is the only singer from those days who is still with us, because a more aggressive style has asserted itself in the choir as it has in the instrumental area.

Today the choir is no longer a multi-vocal ensemble, but rather a combination of strong personalities from England, the USA and Trinidad. Witness, for instance, the unbelievable energy bundle Tracey Duncan, or Mac Kissoon who had great success in a duo with his sister Katie in the Netherlands, or Ingrid Arthur, a gospel singer with a powerful voice that reaches from Hamburg to Los Angeles. Each of them has much more musical leeway than previously, and each can deliver a brilliant individual performance on stage. It is unique that they work as a choir and yet each of them is a soloist.

In 1994, after a very long break, we recorded another choir album, *My Soul*, using old Motown songs by the Supremes, Marvin Gaye, Diana Ross, the Jackson 5 and others. At that time Motown Records had just been taken over by Polydor and, to celebrate this deal, they asked me, of all people, to make a record to suit the occasion. We recorded the choir in London, superimposing several parts and phrases one above the other – just as we did with the strings. The resulting sound was fantastic. Everyone was completely behind the project – until someone found out that Polydor didn't hold the publishing rights for the songs. Putting it in business terms, there just wasn't a lot in it for Polydor. The company's enthusiasm for the project plummeted and there was no advertising for the CD at all – it simply trotted along as a sideline in the sales. It was such a shame, since *My Soul* was for us a very modern album full of effects.

Shortly after that, we recorded *Beachparty '95* with my choir and black gospel singers from Florida. We recorded the gospel choir at New River Studios in Fort Lauderdale, with Mac and Katie Kissoon there as support. Their job was to familiarise the gospel singers with my arrangements, since choirs like this often sing by ear as many of the singers can't read music. For this CD I arranged songs by Madonna, George Michael, Billy Joel and a completely unknown group called World United. Where did this mysterious group come from? The Caribbean? Africa maybe? In any case, the refrain was sung in Swahili.

We released one of the three songs by this group as a single and sampled it to several German radio stations. It started well and was played quite often – until our record company announced far too soon that World United were none other than James Last and his musicians. That was the end of the air play. The old mechanisms kicked in straight away. Just as narrow-mindedly as Deutsche Grammophon had refused to bring out my *Threepenny Opera* on its classical yellow label, the pop radio stations didn't want to play a song by James Last. Under the pseudonym World United, we had wanted to try out a new direction and open doors that wouldn't have opened for James Last. The radios could have played us without the prejudice that has built up over the years against the brand James Last. 'Leave my name out of it, let's just make music,' I said over and over again. But there is no cure for the pigeonholes in our heads.

We still have the choir with us on our tours, and every time I arrange one or two new songs for them. But it would be very appealing to work with the choir again in the studio. I think a gospel album would find a good place in my gallery.

But I have hurried too far ahead in our story. Let's go back to those colourful 1970s...

Cowboy Betty and the Holy Spirit

Our first performances in Canada in 1969 had triggered such enthusiasm that Polydor Canada set its heart on getting us back to that magnificent land. In 1973 that time had come. The company hoped our tour would be 'the most successful event in the history of Polydor Canada'. To achieve this goal, enormous sums were invested in radio and TV commercials, press conferences were held at all the tour locations, a James Last month was announced, and in a Polydor letter they wrote, 'The advertising budget for this tour beats it all. It will be the greatest tour since the Rolling Stones.'

That much enthusiasm entails some obligation. The concert tour was set for four weeks in May and June and was to be our most strenuous ever. We were appearing not only in large cities like Vancouver, Montreal and Toronto, but also in small remote places like Saskatoon, Edmonton, Winnipeg – spread over the immense expanse of the Canadian forests. In total there were 17 concerts on our itinerary. The most bizarre concert took place in the Winnipeg arena with an audience of 5,000. We were just playing 'Moscow Nights' when I became aware of increasing laughter, first from the audience and then from my musicians. Unobtrusively I checked my suit. Had a seam split? Was there something wrong with my 'grooming'? Finally I spotted the reason for the boisterous mirth – unnoticed by me, an older lady had clambered on stage and shed her clothes. Now she was gyrating and jiggling her more than ample curves, wearing nothing but a bullet belt and two Colt pistols. Two more fans followed her example. Although Cowboy Betty only wanted to demonstrate her enthusiasm for our music, I must admit I capitulated in the face of her voluminous nakedness and temporarily left the stage.

The longest stretch we had to cover was from Montreal to Vancouver on the west coast. It was at this point that misfortune caught up with our bass trombonist, Conny Bogdan, which he managed to overcome at the last second with the help of the Holy Spirit. The evening before we were due to fly out, Conny received a visit from a family he knew, or perhaps was even related to – we could never get the details out of him. The degree of relationship must have been so intense that good old Conny spent the evening and then the night with this family. Normally, Conny was a reliable and punctual chap, even if he did sometimes drink so much that he didn't notice we had filled his bottle of Underberg with Maggi spice instead of schnapps. But that's another story.

In the morning we were told everyone was there, so we could set off to the airport. Since Conny Bogdan was always there on time, it didn't occur to the otherwise preoccupied tour manager, Conny Güntensperger, that our bass trombone was missing. We drove to the airport, where the tickets were distributed – we each got any old ticket, as nobody paid attention to the names. But one boarding card was left over. Conny Güntensperger was perplexed. 'Who could it be? It says Detlef Surmann on the ticket but he's here, so that's not the problem.'

On the plane he started counting again. 'I can't work it out. Who is missing?'

Finally, the individual instruments were called out: 'Four trumpets? They're there, good. Three trombones? No, only two. Who's missing? Conny Bogdan! Where is he?'

Missing! No one had seen him. That meant we'd have to get through the evening without him. But when we finally reached our destination after an infinitely long flight and went to rehearse, to everyone's surprise, Conny Bogdan was already sitting in his place with a broad grin on his face and a Bible in his hand. 'What's kept you then, what's kept you then?' he said cheekily. 'I've been here for ages, for ages! What's kept you then!?' Conny *always* said everything twice.

What had happened? Conny had arrived back at the hotel in Montreal far too late. Now Conny was a lovely chap, but he didn't speak a word of English, he didn't have a cent in his pocket and he had no plane ticket. He stood alone in the hotel and pondered: 'Where on earth did they go today, where did they go? I don't know what our next stop is, I don't know.' In his suitcase he found his tour contract, which had an itinerary attached... 'Today is Thursday, I should really be on my way to Vancouver, Vancouver! Where is Vancouver? Four thousand kilometres away! How do I get to the airport with my suitcase, how do I get there with my suitcase, without money, with no money? Walk!'

So he dragged his suitcase across the highway to the airport, and there the drama continued. 'Who can understand me here? Lufthansa! They should be able to speak German, yes they should! I am from the James Last Band and I must get to Vancouver, yes I must!' Now it just so happened that at that moment a minister of the church was standing next to him. Not only did he speak a little German, but he invited him to come with him in a private plane. While our plane was stopping in every town, Conny was flying non-stop to Vancouver and so arrived much earlier than we did.

His pious new friend also gave him a Bible as a parting gift, and from that day on it lay on Conny's music stand at every one of our Canadian concerts. During this tour we were also booked to do four concerts in the USA, but, for reasons which I'll explain later, these performances were cancelled. As a result we had a few days off and, instead of sitting around idly, on the spur of the moment I invited the whole band on a short holiday to Las Vegas.

Seven Lincolns in Las Vegas

I had been introduced to the notorious gambling city in Nevada when Polydor boss Heinz Voigt and I had gone there a few years previously to watch a few shows. I'd heard a lot of interesting stories from Heinz when I was doing a few productions with Brenda Lee and Connie Francis, and it had never been really clear who or what had been behind them. For instance, Heinz was offered a particular hotel and, when he didn't use it, he immediately got a phone call: 'Why didn't you do what we told you to!?' Another time a rental car was waiting for him in front of the hotel and no one knew where it had come from. I wondered to myself why these things had happened. And how was it that we got into every show, even when they were sold out?

Ronnie had always said, 'Paps, if you ever get an offer to play in Las Vegas, don't do it!' But, despite knowing of Las Vegas' shady aspects, and a little annoyed about the cancelled US concerts, I had itchy feet. I had the promoter order seven white Cadillac convertibles. The poor man was in despair: 'Where on earth will I get them!?'

'Well, from Hertz, of course!'

'They won't have seven white Cadillac convertibles there!'

'Just ring up and find out,' I replied.

He did so and came back: 'See, I told you! They don't have them.'

'Then ring up Avis!'

It went on like that a couple more times and finally we had an offer of seven white Lincolns. Great! So we flew to Nevada, arrived at the Sands Hotel, left our luggage in the lobby and marched straight off into the casino. Everyone was thrilled, the slot machines rang and spat out their cent pieces. Suddenly there was an announcement on the intercom: 'Telephone for Mr Last!' I went to the phone – there was one on every pillar – and it was the bell captain. 'Mr Last, your seven white Cadillacs are here.'

'Oh, what a shame! We don't need them any more. Send them back. We have seven white Lincolns now!'

During our stay Diana Ross was performing her opening-night show at the famous Caesar's Palace. I didn't want to miss her, so I asked for tickets at Sands. 'We'd like 32 tickets for the Diana Ross show.'

He laughed out loud. 'You're joking! The show has been sold out for weeks.' And then the power of certain magic words in this city was proven to me again: I just mentioned the name of a man Heinz Voigt had told me about. The man at the desk nodded discreetly and in next to no time we had our tickets. That evening the audience were standing in queues but we, the James Last party, were waved in and first to enter the hall. We saw a wonderful show and a fantastic performance by Diana Ross.

A few months later we were in Dortmund for another *Starparade* appearance. After the show we were sitting with a few of the other artists, telling them about this fantastic show in Las Vegas. One of them, a well-known German pop singer, stood up and said, 'What's the big deal? That's small fry! Have you ever seen one of my shows in Bielefeld?!'

Rockers on the Lüneburg Heath

As a result of the many album recordings, tours and other performances, I was finally able to afford my own orchestra. The musicians were practically always there for me when I needed them, but that entailed a high degree of responsibility on my part. I had to make sure they were all sufficiently busy and earned well. There would be times in my working cycle when the orchestra had nothing to do – when I was brooding over new arrangements, for example – so the orchestra was free to take on other engagements.

As bandleader and employer of so many highly qualified specialists, it was important to me that I ensured the right creative atmosphere. No one can perform at a high artistic standard if he is weighed down by personal problems or doesn't feel comfortable. You can usually only make good music if you enjoy it, so you make it with friends and not boring strangers.

My musicians and I spent a lot of our spare time with each other – sharing holidays, weekends, sporting events and excursions. A sense of community and team spirit were an essential part of our success. But a real family means a wife and children, and they were the ones we always had to leave at home when we were in the studio or on tour. So the idea evolved of creating a shared home for this big James Last family. By chance we got an opportunity to buy a suitable piece of land in Fintel, a small village south-west of Hamburg, so I decided to build a cottage with a few guest rooms on the Lüneburg Heath. When we wanted to relax with our wives and families, we would have something like a common home.

No sooner said than done. When we laid the foundation stone, I had a gold record bricked into the fireplace, and in September

1973 the house was inaugurated. Every musician had a key and could use our recreation centre whenever he wanted.

There was a huge living room with a quadraphonic sound system and a bar generously fitted out in every respect. There were eight double rooms arranged around this room, each with a bath and toilet and each in a different colour, so you could leave the bar and fall straight into bed. The freezers were always full of steaks, seafood and sausages, and the wine cellar was well stocked. We had a mini-golf range, a tennis court and a football pitch, where we played some great games. Sometimes we staged charity matches, for instance against the *Hamburger Abendblatt* newspaper or the German national women's team. All of my musicians wanted to cover their left winger, who incidentally was really quite good looking.

Behind the house were a field and a small brook, over which cows would gaze at us through the morning mist. In the evening we would cook and grill, light gas lanterns and party till the early morning – and I was usually one of the last to find his way to bed.

Once we had a wonderful Christmas party there with the Bergedorf Chamber Choir. Outside lay snow, but in the middle of the living room stood a giant Christmas tree and the choir sang – that was a picture-book Christmas.

We all took our children to Fintel – after all, we were no longer young pop idols and so we all kept an eye on each other's offspring. It was a special community with a very special atmosphere. Often friends came to visit – rock stars like Peter Maffay and Udo Lindenberg, or the comedian and actor Otto Waalkes. Otto was always a nutter, dashing about with his hair billowing behind him. He'd already appeared on stage as a very young lad in the early 1970s in the auditorium at Hamburg University, where he'd been studying art. I'd known him since those days, and I would describe Otto as a friend. Udo Lindenberg, too. At the beginning of his career I once rang him at home late in the evening to tell him I really liked a particular song of his.

'Hallo, this is Hansi Last.' There must have been a party going on at Udo's, but in any case the voice that had answered sounded fairly drunk, and bang, the phone was back on the hook. Udo must have thought it was a joke. It wasn't until I rang back that he finally realised it was true. He still comes to our concerts today, and we share a mutual respect for each other's work.

Otto, Udo and even Peter Maffay have all remained perfectly ordinary blokes, old rockers like me, mates who fitted in wonderfully with us. And Fintel was the ideal place for a party without all the press people getting wind of it. We got on extremely well with each other, and that remains so today. God knows you can't say that about all your peers!

In Fintel, we listened to a lot of music and discussed new ideas coming from the USA. We all liked Blood, Sweat & Tears a lot. Their jazzy phrasing of wind instruments certainly inspired me. If you listen to their early records from the late 1960s – the song 'Sometimes in Winter' for example – and then to my arrangement of *Hair*, you can recognise distinct echoes of them. Or the soul-funk band Tower Of Power with their dense, precise horn section. Or the group Chicago – they had their first big hit in Germany as a soft rock band with 'If You Leave Me Now', but in the first ten years of their career, from 1968, they were a hard-as-nails jazz-rock-fusion band who could show us all a thing or two. It wasn't until the death of their truly excellent guitarist, Terry Kath, that their music became softer. We listened to these records for days on end and talked about them – that gave me a crucial impetus for my work.

For a while the Brazilian Deodato and his form of Latin jazz was my band's favourite. They often played his music on the bus when we were on tour and sometimes the driver had to do a lap or two around the block because a certain song wasn't finished and we didn't want to get out. When we met Deodato in person during a festival in Venice, it turned out to be a rather bitter disappointment. Ennio Morricone was there, my band and Deodato. I was looking forward to his show, but what he delivered was pretty meagre. A pity. Unfortunately, Deodato has now silently disappeared from the international scene.

By the mid-1970s my band had grown as thick as thieves, not least because of the recreation centre in Fintel. Even outside of professional commitments we had a lot of fun together. Tour leader Conny Güntensperger, road technician Jürgen Mayer, our tailor Karl-Heinz Cisek and bus driver Rudi Gies were also part of this family, as were Elke Albrecht – who was responsible for my personal office – and Inge Schierholz, my link to the Polydor company. I saw my role not so much as a boss more as some kind of head of the family who had to look after of the well-being of his fosterlings.

That was also the way I did my arranging. Since I knew the strengths and weaknesses of every single musician, I could always write his part within the limits of his abilities. In the 40 years of my career there were only three occasions when I had to fire a member of the band. In two cases they were people who hadn't been with us for long and had committed crass breaches of discipline. The third occasion was much more dramatic, and the memory of it still hurts me today – I had to fire my own brother.

Robert and Werner

There must be some kind of mysterious connection between the Last family and the USA. My father used to proudly show our visitors a photo in which he was sitting in a canoe with a Native American. The American was rowing and my father was playing the accordion! The photo was taken in Louisiana. Before my father became a civil servant in Bremen, he had travelled around parts of the USA as a stoker on a ship. Now I had bought a house in Florida, and my two brothers, Robert and Werner, had earlier emigrated to the USA for a while. Both soon returned to Germany – America was a difficult place for musicians because of the strong unions, which didn't tolerate competition from outside.

Robert, the eldest of us three, tended to be the quieter, more serious type, with a dry sense of humour. In that respect he was like our mother. In 1944 he married Marianne, and, since we were all glad to have a roof over our heads at all after the war, we all lived together in our parents' house in Bremen for a time. And, as I mentioned, one of my mother's greatest talents was to create a family atmosphere in such a confined space without any of us getting on each other's nerves.

Robert had trained as a timpanist at the Hamburg State Opera House and in 1956 he decided to try his luck in New York. Once there, he had to work hard as a waiter just to keep his head above water. Finally he acquired his coveted musician's licence and started training under Sonny Igoe, the drummer in the Woody Herman Band. He managed to last a whole six years in the USA and his younger son, Roy, was born there.

The day before he was due to return from New York, someone in Hamburg was looking for a percussionist for a recording who could play Ravel's 'Bolero' properly.

'You should use my brother!' I suggested.

Now 'Bolero' is about the worst thing you could do to a drummer: it's a very tricky piece of work. Well, Robert arrived home, tired from the trip and the time difference between the two continents, and now stylistically honed to US swing. The first thing he had to do the next day was head to the concert hall, stand alone in front of his small drum with hundreds of musicians around him and produce the complicated 'Bolero' rhythm. His palms were sweating – it was a tough job, but he mastered it.

Robert has drummed in many orchestras. He and Werner had even been in my first orchestra at Radio Bremen, so, when James Last finally came into being, it made sense that I should get him in my band. He was hard working and technically brilliant, with a very idiosyncratic style, excellent timing and his own special ways of playing drum-fills. There are even people today who copy his style or sample his drum beats.

Robert played for us for many years but in the early 1970s he ended up with the record company Teldec, because they wanted to have the name Last in their roster. He recorded his own albums and Les Humphries wrote the arrangements for him. When I heard about his record contract, I warned him, 'If you think there might be loopholes in your contract, talk to me.' I had already gained some experience on that score, but Robert wanted to sort things out himself and ended up keeping fewer rights to his music than he might if I'd negotiated for him.

Finally, it came to a situation that hurts me even today, although it happened over 30 years ago. We were on tour in South Africa, about which I'll say more in the next chapter, at a time when Robert was making records himself but still played in my band. Robert must have felt like a king that evening. He had drunk a little too much at dinner and eventually started ranting and raving and insulting me and my musicians. That was bad enough, but things like that can happen if you drink a bit more than you should.

But then Robert took off with a black girl – forbidden in South Africa at that time due to apartheid – and locked himself in his hotel room with her. The worst problem was, though, that he simply didn't come out again, not for breakfast and not for lunch.

jet set

We were in Johannesburg, the venue was sold out, and we had to play 13 concerts in seven days. Robert didn't turn up at the bus, and he didn't come to the afternoon performance. Our percussionist Barry Reeves took over the drums – a monumental achievement for him, since it was the first time for him – and he carried it off perfectly.

After the concert I rang Waltraud in Hamburg. Robert had often gone a bit off the rails in the past, but this time it seemed a lot more serious. I asked my wife for her advice. 'If something like that happens once,' she said, 'it will happen again, and that could cause you a lot of problems.' It was a very difficult decision.

That evening Robert turned up as if nothing had happened and wanted to play. But I had to stay hard: 'It doesn't work like that. From now on Barry is playing drums.'

I think this episode left more of a mark on me than on him, and our relationship was affected by it till the end. I have always got on with his family – his wife and the children – and, when we were in need of help or he needed to earn some extra money, he would sometimes play on our recordings. But our relationship was never again as easygoing as it used to be.

When Robert was in hospital with heart trouble in the mid-1980s, he desperately wanted to talk to me, and then it all came out. He spoke of how so much of what he'd done had been wrong and how sorry he was. His wife told me that sometimes he used to secretly hang around the studio when we were recording, just to get that feeling of what it had been like when we had made music together in harmony. But he never once said, 'Hansi, let's forget all that crap! I want to play drums with you again.' He couldn't bring himself to do it, not until the end. I sat by his bed for many hours, and he talked and talked. He had to get it all off his chest and make his peace. The next day Robert died.

Werner was the most temperamental of us, apparently having inherited a lot of our father's character. But, just like father Louis, he was also a great storyteller and comic. When he really let go, we would all end up doubled up with laughter. He had started studying music theory and theory of composition, and he too went to America – with his wife Hjördis – and worked as a trombonist in a big band. Some years after his return, Werner took over our house in Holitzbergstrasse. He had already sold his place in Bremen, but our new place wasn't ready yet, so the eight of us lived together for a while in one household – not just with his wife and their two sons, Steven and Werner Jr, but also their dog, a boxer called Citro.

Werner was a very bustling person, who always had an incredible amount to do, who often experienced little mishaps, and who liked to play the clown. Shortly after I did – in 1966 – he also got a recording contract with Polydor, and he, like me, also got a new name from the advertising strategists. As Kai Warner, he eventually became a well-known bandleader, hit songwriter and record producer.

Yet Werner also had his serious, introverted side and that, in my opinion, cost him his life. Werner chewed himself up because he never achieved in life what he had really set out to do. His dream had always been to write a symphony. Since I was the first of the three of us to earn good money, I said to him, 'Go spend a year up in the mountains and write your symphony. I'll finance it for you.' But Werner never took up the offer. Later there were marriage problems on top of that: he constantly had affairs and drank a schnapps or two too much every now and then. Finally, his liver gave up. He, too, died far too early, in July 1982, at the age of only 59. The pop singer Renate Kern, whose records he had produced for many years, held the eulogy at his graveside.

His son Werner, who incidentally took trumpet lessons with Bob Lanese for a while, is enjoying his own success with the Ballroom Orchestra, which is swimming on the tide of the new popularity of ballroom dancing. Another musician also emerged from this generation of Lasts: Robert's son Roy was a guitarist in his own metal band, the Roy Last Group. Tragically, he too died young, at 48, from a stroke in July 2004.

My relationship with my brothers was always something exciting, because we had fun with the audiences and had our own special way of communicating with people. It had been like that since we'd played music together in the American clubs after the war, and their early deaths left a void in my life that has never been filled. Perhaps that is why it has always been so important to me to have a family relationship with my musicians.

part four:
Around the World

South of the Equator

The fun my musicians and I have on stage always carries over to the audience, and that is exactly what I want to achieve with our performances – to convey pure joy for life. Every musician in my orchestra lives for every minute of the concert, even if he has a short break from playing. Some time ago I was watching a show from Las Vegas on television where everything was perfect: the star, the dancers, the light effects, the sound – everything. But the performance nevertheless seemed lifeless and sterile. I used to think it was impossible to be better than Vegas. Now I know you certainly can be, because our band lives: the show isn't a *show* – we *live* on the stage. That is what makes us different from everyone else.

My friend Max Greger once said, 'I had the best jazz musicians in the world in my band. They take their saxophone, play, put the saxophone down – rest. Then the next: trombone – solo – rest. In your band you can look from left to right, from top to bottom, and there is always something happening. The people have always got something to look at.' That sort of thing can't be rehearsed, you have to feel it. People like this vitality, and I see my task as giving it to them – even if it isn't always the hip-hop polka. Whenever two or more of the musicians in my band meet, not ten minutes will go by before they start recounting endless stories of their experiences on our big world tours.

The first of these trips around the world took place in 1972. We flew to Johannesburg in South Africa, where we gave 13 concerts in a row in a theatre called the Colosseum (it was this part of the tour that led to the rift with my brother Robert). All of the performances were sold out and 2,500 people welcomed us each time. Although we had never appeared in Africa before, the audience gave us the feeling that we were long-awaited old friends. Of course, the folk songs and sea shanties went down well with the many South Africans of German background.

Our Belgian trombonist, Georges Delagaye, experienced one very unusual evening in Johannesburg. A golden boy with a broad, beaming smile, Georges was a bachelor in his mid-thirties and certainly one for enjoying life. Wherever we performed, he managed to get the phone number of a good-looking girl from one of his local musician friends. In Johannesburg Georges was, as usual, looking forward to meeting a lovely unknown lady with whom he planned to sweeten his stay. He was waiting with us at the bar in cheerful expectation when the door opened and in walked Georges's companion for the evening. And what an entrance! A woman of about 60, her best days long behind her, entered the room, dressed up to the nines. 'Hi, folks!' she announced in a loud voice. 'I'm looking for Mr Delagaye!'

This rendezvous was of course the result of a practical joke that the band had thought up. But Georges, the perfect gentleman, stood up, offered her a chair and spent the entire evening chatting with her.

From South Africa we flew on to Perth, Australia. We arrived in the morning in good time, and a bus picked us up at the airport and took us to the hotel. We were all tired, hungry and thirsty from the night flight, and everybody was looking forward to breakfast and getting to bed. But it was a small hotel and there was trouble assigning the rooms. The desk clerk kept looking in his book and at every name he shook his head. Mr Platzek? No, no booking. Mr Lanese? Sorry, nothing for him either... While this procedure continued for what seemed like an eternity, our hungry gang tired of waiting patiently in the lobby and descended on the breakfast buffet. When all the platters and plates had been eaten clean, the penny dropped with the slightly desperate hotel manager: we had landed in the wrong hotel.

Our music was particularly well received in Australia and during our stay we received an incredible 43 gold records. The concerts in Sydney, Melbourne, Brisbane and Adelaide count among the very special memories of my touring life: there was no one who hadn't heard of our records. Our performances regularly turned into one grand, enthusiastic happening. The audiences could hardly restrain themselves and we didn't hold back either. We ate in the best restaurants and after every concert a party atmosphere reigned into the early hours as we consumed vast amounts of alcohol.

Günter Platzek once kept count of what we guzzled on one of these tours. The result was, I'm afraid to say, quite sobering – or, more accurately, shocking. There were copious bottles of scotch, bourbon, vodka and gin – it seemed we were all well on the way to becoming alcoholics. One hotel manager even went so far as to put gin and tonic into babies' bottles because he knew that the airline we were using didn't serve alcohol. There's a saying in Germany: once your reputation is in tatters, there's nothing more to be embarrassed about.

A few years back I ran into a man in Hamburg who greeted me effusively. 'Hello, Hansi! Remember me? I'm the one who first imported Beefeater Gin and Myer's Rum into Germany 30 years ago – just because of you lot!' It was no joke. Apparently, their import trade had boomed from the time my orchestra started touring.

All the same, I never had the feeling that I would become dependent on alcohol. Some people get quite testy when they've drunk too much. Alcohol makes you unjust and self-righteous: I notice that even now when I drink one too many. Then I know that I'd better hold my tongue! But I have never drunk out of frustration, always out of enjoyment – I believe that makes a big difference.

Today the booze sessions are long gone. These days you'll find us all at the golf course first thing in the morning, and the most popular drink is mineral water.

We returned to Australia in 1975, and this time we had the singers with us. This gave rise to one of the band's most legendary stories. We arrived in Melbourne in the afternoon and were taken to a luxury hotel – unshaven, bleary-eyed and all wearing Bermuda shorts. When we checked in, I wanted to book a table for the band for dinner at 8pm. The manager looked us up and down and said arrogantly, 'You can come at 6pm.' Presumably, he wanted to keep us away from his evening guests. I insisted on 8pm, so he had little choice. 'All right then, but please come in appropriate clothing.'

Well, was he going to get a surprise! I sent word to everybody: 'Dress to the nines. If necessary, put on your stage suits.' I wanted my band to surpass all the other guests where dress was concerned.

At 7.30pm we met at the bar, far more elegantly dressed than the rest of the guests. We marched together into the large dining room, where pleasant waiters in tuxedos led us to our table. We all sat down but two people were missing: Sunny from the choir and Ryno Ericsson, a trombonist who had stepped in for Conny Bogdan on this trip. At 8.15pm they made their entrance. A double door flew open and Sunny and Ryno appeared arm in arm. Sunny was in full regalia, wearing an evening gown, a silver hair circlet, a fur stole and a ring on every finger (she'd borrowed them from the other choir members). Ryno, who was very tall, slim and elegant with a grey Dick-van-Dyke beard, was wearing hired tails and a top hat. Infinitely stately, they proceeded through the door into the dining room. Ryno took his hat, gloves and cane and passed them to the waiting maitre d' without even deigning to look at him. Very slowly, like a duke and duchess, the two of them made their way to the table. It was brilliant – the whole band stood up and applauded. At that the other restaurant guests rose and joined the applause: they were convinced the two of them had to be very important people!

In Adelaide Jürgen Mayer allowed himself a far more high-spirited joke. The band was standing in the hotel lobby, waiting for the bus, when the phone at reception rang. No one was answering it – the desk clerk must have disappeared for a moment – so, on the spur of the moment, Jürgen picked up the phone. 'Good morning, sir, how can I help you?'

'Could you please have someone collect the luggage from room 215?'

'Everything?'

'Yes, everything.'

'No problem, sir. I'll see to it.'

Without Jürgen even saying a word, six others ran upstairs with him to room 215. Five minutes later Jürgen returned with a suitcase, then Harald Ende and Günter Platzek with the television, Conny Güntensperger with two chairs. Bob Lanese and Dieter Kock were dragging the mattress, and Georges Delagaye brought up the rear with the bedding. They had cleaned out the room. As the guest stood astounded in the lobby, Jürgen asked him with an air of utmost innocence, 'Shall we put it all in the taxi, sir?'

In wonderful Sydney we appeared in the brand-new opera house: the first orchestra to give a pop concert there. The string section from the Sydney Symphony Orchestra played with us, one of whom was Anne-Louise, a stunning-looking viola player, only 18 or 19, who certainly showed off what she had to offer – and that was quite a lot. Rick Kiefer had a solo in 'I Left My Heart in San Francisco' and played only to her. The audience was sitting below him, but Rick played up to Anne-Louise.

Many years later we were on tour in Germany and one of our young string players told us about a colleague, an Australian viola player who had studied with her at university and said she'd played with us at one time. That had to be Anne-Louise!

I asked for her number straight away and called her at midnight. 'Anne, how are you? Would you like to go on tour with us?'

'Yes, but when?'

'Whenever you want – tomorrow even.'

So, instead of four viola players, we now had five. Our tour then led us to London, where we heard Buddy Rich was in town to appear at Ronnie Scott's jazz club. We all wanted to go, but how were all these people going to get into a sold-out concert in a small venue? Our British tour manager, Liz Pretty, convinced the club manager: 'Listen, every one of us will buy a bottle of champagne, and we'll stand.'

So, more than 40 of us stood in the club, each with a bottle of Moët & Chandon in hand, and enjoyed the concert.

All the while, Anne-Louise was flirting outrageously with

Buddy Rich's first trumpeter, a good-looking, dark-haired American called Bob. After the concert, Bob accompanied our new viola player back to our hotel, and, four or five days later, somewhere in the Midlands, Anne-Louise came to me and said, a little embarrassed, 'Hansiiiiiiiii, Bob would like to see me again.'

'Well, what's the problem?'

'He's still playing in Ronnie Scott's and we're moving on.'

'OK, when does he have his day off?'

'Monday.'

'We'll send someone to pick him up.'

On Sunday evening a Rolls-Royce was waiting outside the club. Buddy Rich wanted to make a joke and called out to his musicians, 'See, guys, that's my new car.' But Bob set him right: 'Sorry, boss, but that's *my* car.' And with that he got into the Rolls, right in front of his boss, and drove off to his Anne-Louise. After that he was fired.

Well, Anne-Louise Comerford and Bob Coassin ended up getting married. They now have two grown-up children in Australia, yet they both still play in my orchestra. Anne-Louise is the first violist at the Sydney Opera, while Bob is lead trumpet with the Australian Art Orchestra and considered one of the country's most prominent trumpeters. He has worked with Ray Charles, Dizzy Gillespie and Frank Sinatra, and been a member of the famous Tower of Power horn section. Despite all that, they still come all the way from Down Under whenever we go on tour – it's hard to imagine a greater compliment.

Our Australian fans haven't forgotten us either. Once, after a long stretch in the bus on the way to a concert in Innsbruck, we took a short break at a rest stop in Inntal. The band went into the restaurant but I preferred to stay in the bus, since there are usually too many back-slapping Hello Hansis to be able to eat in peace. After a couple of minutes a red English double-decker bus pulled up next to us, full of young people who peered inquisitively through the windows. 'Where are you from?' I asked.

'We're from Australia. We hired the bus in London and now we're touring through Europe with tents, but we've only had bad weather so far! And who are you?'

'I'm James Last. I'm touring with my band.'

'What!!? James Last!??' they cried in disbelief.

'We're playing a concert this evening in Innsbruck. Would you like to come?'

That sparked a lot of excitement. I rang our hotel in Innsbruck to see if another 20 double rooms were available. No problem – that would be OK. 'All right – if you head on to Munich, you'll have to sleep in your tents tonight. If you come with us to Innsbruck, you will all have a hotel room.'

I invited them all to dinner, and in the evening they came to the concert, sat to the left and right of the stage, and had a lot of fun. Weeks later I received a letter from them saying it was the loveliest evening of their entire trip through Europe.

Exotic Charm

Our world tours even took us as far as New Zealand, where we gave concerts in Auckland, Christchurch and Wellington. One really fascinating experience was our visit to the Maori. When we got off the bus in one of their villages, they rushed towards us – their faces painted in a frightening pattern and holding spears – and carried out a wild tribal dance. There was fierce drumming and suddenly we were surrounded. Children and old people stood around the group of dancers, humming loudly. Suddenly, the chief raised his spear and a deep silence immediately descended.

My study in our house in Holitzberg – this is where I developed most of my arrangements and compositions.

Above: A rehearsal for the first German tour. I am pictured duetting with Katja Ebstein
Below: If the hotel kitchen is closed …with K.H. Lüer, Bob Lanese and Harald Ende.

Above: With my band in front of St Basil's Cathedral in Moscow.

Below: Confrontation in Moscow: it was 'power to the people' when the Soviets turned off the power.

Above: Warming up for the first *Sing Along* fête.

Below: Well-protected for a television broadcast in Allgäu.

Souvenir hunting in New Zealand.

Above: An actor who always hits the right note: my good friend Hein Reincke.

Right: Ron slowly grows into his job as my new sound engineer.

A gold record in the future chimney of our recreation centre in Fintel.

The Last family together.

A moment later he broke the spear with a dramatic gesture and we were heartily welcome.

We were so taken by this performance that I invited the whole group to our concert. That took place in an old cinema, where the stage was very high. The white audience sat down below while up in the gallery – at eye-level with us – were the Maori.

'Yesterday evening the Maori gave us a fantastic reception,' I announced. 'The entire band really enjoyed it.' But that didn't go down at all well with the white New Zealanders. Icy silence reigned in the stalls, but up in the gallery an enthusiastic cheer came from the Maori. The white audience evidently found the presence of the natives inappropriate and objectionable. It was only then I realised how extreme the tension was between the former white intruders and the Maori. It would take another 20 years before the New Zealand government made the first gestures of reconciliation towards the natives of this magnificent land, defusing the conflict step by step.

Then we experienced some dramatic moments on the flight from Auckland to Christchurch on South Island. We had already taken off, but the aircraft had to turn back because there was such a heavy storm the plane couldn't land. We waited three boring hours at the airport, knocking back a gin and tonic or two. Finally, the pilot came over to us: 'I'm going to take another shot at it. Ask your boys if they want to come along.' No problem – the gin had given us courage and we all agreed.

We took off and at first everything seemed quite harmless. But then we got caught in the most violent turbulence I have ever experienced. Glasses flew through the cabin and the stewardesses were sitting trembling on the floor, but we made it through to Christchurch unscathed. At the airport a mob of reporters was waiting for us. They'd heard of our odyssey and were ready to cancel our concert for us, since not only were we late but the equipment, which was coming by ship, still hadn't arrived.

But under no circumstances did I want to cancel. 'We're driving straight over to the radio station to announce that the concert will take place, no matter how late it is, even if it's two o'clock in the morning. If the people want us to, we'll play.'

The concert was due to start at 8pm and 3,500 people were expected. We arrived on time at the hall, which was already chock-a-block. The stage, on the other hand, was gaping bare. Literally nothing was ready. Finally, the truck with our equipment rolled up, and then something truly unique happened: the entire band, including myself, set up the stage equipment together, including the sound and the lights. Every time one of us came on stage with a spotlight or a cable, 3,500 people applauded. Eventually, at midnight, we were ready to start. It was one of the most memorable – and certainly the most southerly – concerts we have ever played.

From New Zealand we flew on to Hong Kong. On our second Asian tour in 1975 we also played in Kuala Lumpur, Malaysia and Singapore. For some strange reason long hair was forbidden in such a highly modern city, so our guitarist, Peter Hesslein, had to constantly hide his well-over-shoulder-length adornment under an enormous cap. What's more, in the middle of the first part of our concert our mixing console failed, and I – of all people, who hates making long speeches – had to entertain the audience with anecdotes for 40 minutes until Peter Klemt had set up the back-up console.

All told, we were travelling for about six or seven weeks and, after the exertions and stress of such a long concert tour, all of those involved had earned a break. So I invited the whole band to a luxury hotel in Penang for fours days – four days of relaxation, a wonderful warm ocean, palm trees and cool drinks, before we had to launch into studio appointments and a tour of Germany straight after our return home.

In 1972, the travel costs for the entire six weeks in Africa and Asia amounted to about DM 160,000 roughly what we have to spend per day for a European tour today.

We began our third big trip through Asia in 1980, when Bangkok, Singapore, Hong Kong, Malaysia and the Philippines were added to the itinerary.

It was on this tour that I first became aware there were fans who followed us halfway round the world. The following article appeared in the *South China Morning Post* from Hong Kong: 'Their hobby – the music of James Last – has already cost the Crow family from London the equivalent of a new bathroom and a new car. But the family says they are glad to bear these expenses. They are avid fans of the bandleader and for three years they have been following him everywhere – even to his concerts in Asia. Mr Crow invests £2,000 to £3,000 in his hobby every year. He only regrets that he didn't already have the financial means earlier.'

In the Philippines we played to audiences of 20,000 in large stadiums, including the one in which Muhammad Ali had defended his world heavyweight title against Joe Frazier in the 'Thrilla from Manila'. It was incredibly hot, cockroaches the size of sparrows scurried around the dressing rooms, and the amplifier of our sound system had to be cooled with ice and fans. We were also invited to dinner at the home of Imelda Marcos, the wife of the dictator. However, she wasn't there in person – presumably she was too busy counting her shoes.

Meanwhile, dozens of extremely young girls were constantly hanging around our hotel, fluttering around my musicians like colourful butterflies. They would arrive carrying evening gowns on hangers, in the hope they would be asked to dine with the band in the evening. I had no idea where they came from, but they were beautiful and their soft voices sounded so sweet, like the upper register of an organ. To these girls, my musicians were real superstars, and they probably wanted to meet someone who could take them away from their poor living conditions.

For a change, my wife accompanied me on this tour, on something like a honeymoon to celebrate our 25th wedding anniversary. During the day, all these girls would sit around Waltraud at the side of the pool as if she were their mother hen. Our concert master, Eugen, who was in his mid-seventies, casually leaned back at the edge of the pool, cigarette in mouth, a girl to his left and right, a blissful smile on his face and gushed, 'Hansi, what a life!'

In contrast, Stefan Pintev, our concert master today but then the band's youngest member, encountered a rather delicate problem. He had engaged in a rather too intense exchange of thoughts with one of these beautiful girls, causing her parents to turn up and interrogate him as to what he did, what religion he was – and finally invite him to dinner. After that it was understood that Stefan had to marry the young Filipino girl. As was so often the case, it was left to me to sort it all out. But I managed to put things right, since I had already gained some experience on this score. After all, one of my musicians had already brought home a wife from a country which in those times was still quite 'exotic' – the Soviet Union.

Comrade Nyet

In May 1972 we started on a tour that had been long in the planning – through the deeply communist Soviet Union. It took place as part of a cultural exchange between West Germany and the USSR: the Russians sent us the Leningrad Philharmonic Orchestra and I had the honour of representing my homeland in Brezhnev's country. We weren't, however, the first band to have toured the Soviet Union. Max Greger had played there in 1956, with a very interesting young man at the piano – Udo Bockelmann, later famous as Udo Jürgens. It wasn't possible to buy James Last records in 1970s Russia, so the people only knew our music from smuggled tape copies and BBC radio. The communist bigwigs clearly had no idea of what happened at our concerts. Apparently, they believed we were something like a German folk-music ensemble, as the following events will show.

Just as a reminder, there was no democratic civil liberty in the Soviet Union in 1972. Under Leonid Brezhnev the CPSU ruled every aspect of the people's lives, right down to the most private areas. Freedom of the press and the right to travel were forbidden, and anyone who wanted to visit the Soviet Union could only do so in organised travel groups in clearly defined regions. There were no Western products, and even the most trivial everyday items – like ballpoint pens or socks – were prohibitively expensive luxury goods for Soviet citizens. And so we arrived in a country that was firmly in the grip of a ruthless dictatorship.

A total of 20 concerts in four weeks had been planned. Tbilisi, Leningrad, Kiev and Moscow were our destinations. Our mood was soon dampened by the Aeroflot flight to Tbilisi in Georgia: it was a tiny machine with low seats, bare light bulbs and luggage nets as in third-class train compartments. That's where the chickens were put. There was a dreadful smell of oil and petrol, and during takeoff the rear door opened. The pilot turned back without a word, managed to get it shut, fastened it in a makeshift fashion and the journey continued in the same aircraft.

Then there was the hotel in Tbilisi, a faceless prefabricated building with doors hanging off their hinges, water running down the walls and everything dirty and dilapidated. To make matters worse, Günter's organ and the music stands hadn't come with us, ostensibly because they didn't fit into the small plane. Although the tour was sold out to the last seat, I decided to cancel the first concert, since all our equipment hadn't arrived. I felt sorry for the many disappointed Georgians who, without a word of complaint, made their sad, quiet way back home, but I wanted to show the Soviet authorities right from the start that we wouldn't just put up with everything.

When we had all our equipment, nothing more stood in the way of our first performance in Georgia. At the request of our hosts, I had included many German and Russian folk songs in our programme – but the audience didn't respond to these songs at all. It wasn't until our first international repertoire section that the Tbilisi audience finally thawed and the excitement rose with each new tune. I should have realised that what people wanted to hear was the sort of music practically forbidden in their land – Western pop. So I decided to change the programme, removing the folk-song section. In Tbilisi and Leningrad – St Petersburg today – that was barely tolerated, but the authorities repeatedly tried to interfere, demanding we dispense with certain songs. The pressure on me became more and more severe.

Every day some bigwig's deputy sat backstage on the phone with his big boss in Moscow getting the OK for our programme. 'Let the Sunshine In' was tellingly forbidden, as were songs by the Beatles. 'Nyet!' was the constant refrain.

One time we asked if we were allowed to play 'Na Na Na Na, Hey, Hey, Kiss Him Goodbye'. The apparatchiks didn't know that one, so Moscow approved it. But when the 5,000 people in the hall began singing along, our watchdog rang Moscow again: 'The people are all going mad here, they're singing along!' That wasn't on, so we weren't allowed to play that one any more.

But then I remembered the trick we played at the music school in Bückeburg: giving German names to 'decadent' songs when we weren't permitted to play jazz. So we wrote simply 'English folk song' on the sheet music and that way we were able to out-manoeuvre Comrade Nyet and smuggle a Beatles song into our programme.

But news of the Western band that got the atmosphere going in their concerts spread like wildfire. We played four or five days in Kiev, in the Ukraine, where people were scrambling in through the windows in the hall because it was so full that the authorities wouldn't let anyone else in. Then things really kicked off.

In front of us, below the stage, they had erected a grating. This was ostensibly to protect us, but we felt like we were in a zoo. 'As long as the grating is there,' I said, 'we won't start.'

It grew quieter and quieter in the hall, because the audience realised what we wanted. The band sat on stage, but didn't make a sound. Our super-communist was soon on the phone again. 'You must start. Music!'

'Nyet! Not until the grating is gone.'

Finally, they removed it and we began to play. The people were in high spirits, singing and clapping, and, as the end of the concert approached, some wanted to approach the stage to hand me flowers and a small hand-painted jug. But the watchdogs and functionaries dragged them back by the hair and bludgeoned them with their boots and fists. I wanted to stop the senseless brutality, but I didn't stand a chance. Everyone on stage was appalled by these events. I decided to simply keep playing and so we delivered the concert of our lives to the people of Kiev: every musician gave more than 100 per cent. We returned to our hotel exhausted and thoroughly depressed.

It seemed like a confrontation with the authorities was becoming inevitable. And I was right – the following day a delegation from the Ministry for Culture turned up in the hotel, demanding programme changes. I tried to turn the tables by insisting that, if such brutal beatings occurred again at one of our concerts, I would break off the performance on the spot. The gentlemen remained unimpressed. 'Mr Last, by the time you reach Moscow, you must change your programme.'

This demand was even supported by a telegram from the German Embassy in Moscow. '…Embassy requests that you give the comments of the representatives of the host country the attention that they deserve…' I thought that rather strange, as I thought the embassy was supposed to represent *our* interests.

In the Soviet capital it finally came to a showdown.

Power to the People

The 'Finale Furioso' actually began in an amusing manner. At our performance we met a very nice cloakroom attendant, who I invited to visit us in Hotel Rossiya. Suddenly, there was a knock at the door. 'We have come on behalf of the Minister for Culture. She wishes to speak to you.'

'I'm afraid that's inconvenient. I have a guest. I wasn't expecting you.'

'Yes, but she is only a cloakroom attendant, and outside the people from the ministry are waiting for you!'

'Oh, and I thought that here all people were equal!' I retorted. 'I think it would be very impolite to leave my guest in the lurch.'

Then things got tougher. There was a serious disagreement about the concert programme, which I finally ended by saying, 'Good, if you want the Western newspapers to announce "CONCERT CANCELLED BECAUSE OF HUGE SUCCESS". I decide the programme and no one else.'

around the world

By special order of the Minister for Culture we were permitted to play our programme as it was, but there were still some unpleasant surprises. The climax to our tour was two concerts in the Moscow Sports Palace, each to an audience of 15,000. When we arrived for the sound check, we saw that police and military in uniform were doing a seating trial. One of them was sitting in the aisle at the end of each row. They were in uniform for this trial, but of course in the evening they wouldn't be. But everyone knew where he should be seated. And only officials sat in the first row.

No sooner had we begun to play than they closed ranks so no one could come forward towards us. People in the Moscow audience wanted to bring us flowers too, but they wouldn't let them. Finally, the audience could not contain their feelings any longer and made a rush towards the stage, hugging me and my musicians warmly. My eyes filled with tears of joy. The music had won in the face of the pigheaded intolerance of the bigwigs. As an encore, I had the idea of taking a little musical revenge. We began the first few bars of 'Power to the People' – which led to the authorities promptly turning off the power. But we played on through to the end unplugged – without electric amplifiers but amplified 15,000 times by the voices of our audience.

The tour lasted four weeks and we were all more than relieved when we finally set foot on 'Western' soil again in Helsinki. The diplomatic embroilments surrounding our guest performances even found an echo in the foreign affairs section of the German dailies. Under the headline 'JAMES LAST STRAITJACKETED', the *Weser-Kurier* newspaper of 5 July 1972 reported:

The coming into force of the trade agreement between the Federal Republic and the Soviet Union is a further step towards normalisation of their relations. Now a cultural agreement remains to be negotiated ... but this is likely to prove far more difficult and time consuming due to the vastly different positions of interest. ... The most recent example of a collision of interests was the tour of West German James Last dance orchestra. The state agency Gosconcert ... interfered massively in the programming and only the threat of breaking off the concert altogether brought James Last some degree of freedom of choice with his music. The Soviets feared that the unfamiliar Western music could heat up their comrades too much.

On our departure we took a grim little revenge on our watchdog, who had got on our nerves during the whole tour with his constant 'nyets'. Although he was faithful to party principles, he had wanted one of our records right from the start. Well, he'd get one. I got hold of an album with boring, endless speeches by his big boss Brezhnev, stuck the red Polydor label on it, and put it in a *Beachparty* cover. At the airport I ceremoniously handed over this original James Last LP. I wonder how great his joy was when he listened to the album back home.

The Russian tour also had a sequel. One of our interpreters was Nadia, 26 years old, small, red-haired and temperamental. Nadia desperately wanted to get out of the Soviet Union, and the only way seemed to be to marry a Westerner. Dieter Kock, one of our trumpeters, was about to marry his girlfriend in Hamburg, but he postponed his plans for a year and was prepared to travel back to Russia to marry Nadia *pro forma*. All her family came to the wedding, bringing every last rouble and chickens and eggs to give to Nadia. After an infinite series of dreary formalities, Nadia Kock was allowed to leave the country. After a long delay Dieter eventually married his German girlfriend, who tragically died during the birth of their daughter. Dieter left the band in 1976 and opened a dental surgery near Hamburg. He remarried and died under mysterious circumstances after he'd been in a coma for a long time.

Nadia still lives in Germany, has a good job in Düsseldorf and sometimes comes to our concerts. Many of the songs on the LP *Russland Erinnerungen* (Russian Memories) I owe to Nadia, who found the scores to these old Russian and Ukrainian folk tunes. She also contributed many ideas to my last classical album, *Classics from Russia*.

Hits and Flops

It is an indescribable moment as a musician when you unexpectedly encounter one of your own compositions somewhere in the world. About 35 years ago I was in Beverly Hills, Los Angeles, with Polydor boss Heinz Voigt, and he had invited me for a drink in a particularly luxurious hotel. We were heading towards the hotel bar – dignified atmosphere, business people engaged in small talk, several couples in love – and exactly the second we entered the bar, the pianist struck up 'Games That Lovers Play'. It was sheer coincidence, but it was one of those magical moments when a tingle goes down your spine. 'Games That Lovers Play' is one of my greatest international successes. Still, for a good song to really become a hit, the wheel of fortune has to land exactly at the right spot, and sometimes there has to be someone who will help to stop it for you.

The first song I wrote myself that was ever played by an orchestra – even if only just once – I composed during my time as a bassist in Hans Rehmstedt's orchestra at Radio Bremen. Almost all of my colleagues turned up with a homemade opus at some stage. We would put it on Rehmstedt's music stand without comment and wait for him to pass his judgement. Naturally, I wanted to follow suit. After all, if you want to be a real musician, you have to write your own music. Besides, if one of your pieces got played at a performance, that meant royalties – on one hand quite gratifying, but on the other a cause for niggling jealousies.

My 'Opus no.1' was a lightly swinging, jazzy number with room for bass improvisation. It was simply called 'Melody' and I had worked on arranging the strings and horns for many evenings. I now knew how strenuous and demanding arrangements for a large orchestra were – but also how pleasant. One lovely day I was satisfied with my piece and trotted off to the radio station full of hope. Nervously, and not at all sure of success, I distributed the notes to the musicians. To play down my nervousness, I also passed a bottle of cognac around – a ritual when one of us turned up with a new piece.

Finally, Rehmstedt opened my score, studied it for a few minutes and finally gave the signal to start. The orchestra let it rip, but what came out was far from what I had imagined. This wasn't due to the musicians, but to my arrangement. It was dreadful, a failure. I gathered up my flop of a 'Melody' with my tail between my legs and left the studio with the firm intention of never writing another note.

Composing is like many other things in life: when you are caught up in the middle of it, often you can't see the forest for the trees. It can be very difficult to recognise whether a piece is of any worth, let alone whether it has the makings of a hit. Sometimes you need outside help from someone who is not so caught up in it and thus has a clearer view of things.

My first big hit, 'Games That Lovers Play', really needed that kind of impartial ally. I had originally written it under another title for a gay Dutch duo to sing, but their voices were too small and 'Games' sounded more like child's play. In any case, the record company thought the song was just poor, so it ended up in a drawer.

Then, when we recorded 'Lara's Theme' – Maurice Jarre's worldwide hit from *Doctor Zhivago* – as a single, we needed a number for the B side. The music publishers Francis, Day & Hunter said, 'If you use one of your own songs and publish it with us, that would be more lucrative for everyone.' That's when 'Games' came to mind again. I rearranged it, changed the vocals to two trumpets, and my composition was released as 'Eine ganze Nacht' (An Entire Night) on the flip side of 'Lara's Theme'.

Even that wasn't enough to make it a hit. Then fortune came to my aid – Billy May and his orchestra were in the USA to do studio recordings with Eddie Fisher. The singer was going through a slight dip in his career at the time and, worse still, he and Liz Taylor had just divorced. Fisher and May heard the number by chance – I still don't know how it happened – and Eddie said spontaneously, 'I'd like to sing that!'

Eddie Snyder, who had written English lyrics for Frank Sinatra's version of 'Strangers in the Night', composed some new words and the song became a hit all over the world. There are now hundreds of cover versions, from Connie Francis to Mantovani, and recordings in dozens of languages. When I play 'Games' at our concerts, the audience still loves to join in, even after almost 40 years. So a song my company didn't want at all, and then became a B side, ended up as a huge success just by chance. I feel I should be thankful to those two Dutch boys. After all, if they had actually sung 'In my heart I feel our love is meant to be...' who knows what would have come of it?

I have always been particularly critical of my own compositions, but when you've been working till three or four in the morning on little sleep because you've been doing so many things at once – and you have to be in the studio again at eight – your judgement can be impaired. That was the sort of nerve-racked state I was in when I tossed a score I considered a failure into the wattled black wastepaper basket next to my desk.

Luckily I had played it once already to Waltraud and, when she came in to try to tidy up my study a little, she found the music in the bin. 'Throwing that away is just out of the question,' she declared firmly. 'Something has to be done with this piece.'

'OK,' I said, 'if you believe in it, then it's your song. You can open your own publishing company and see what comes of it.'

And that's exactly what Waltraud did. Together with her friend Lilo Bornemann, who sadly died far too young, she founded Panorama Song Verlag publishers, and all of a sudden the song 'Happy Heart' was a worldwide hit. Andy Williams, Petula Clark, Peggy March and many, many other great stars have recorded it. When I received all the single samples – 'Happy Heart' in Italian, 'Happy Heart' in Japanese, 'Happy Heart' in Swedish – it dawned on me that I had created something that spoke to people in many parts of this world. That was, and still is, a great experience for me.

Once I experienced that high very personally on a flight from Fort Lauderdale to Los Angeles. I was sitting in the first-class lounge near a blind man with a dog. Now I am not a great dog lover, so I was secretly praying that this man and his dog wouldn't be sitting next to me on the plane. Needless to say, that's exactly what happened – the guide dog and its owner ended up right next to me. Slightly put out, I was sipping at my gin and tonic when the man spoke to me, introducing himself. '...and what's your name?'

'James Last.'

'What are you doing?'

'I'm going to LA to record some music.'

'James Last? Music?' And then he quietly began to hum the melody of 'Happy Heart', including a perfect key change. Once again that tingling sensation!

'I love it!' he said, and we spent the rest of the flight chatting about music.

But the success of 'Games That Lovers Play' and 'Happy Heart' caused some difficulties at my record company, since neither song had been published with a Polydor company and consequently Polydor earned nothing from the royalties. If you are tied up with a record company, they naturally want to benefit from the publishing rights as well. They want to have your songs, which they record, published by their own houses, and they're in quite a position of power, because they can say, 'We'll only release your compositions if we can have the publishing rights.' This practice is very common. So that you don't give up everything to the label, you found your own publishing company, in which the artist and the record company have fifty-fifty shares.

There is incredible pressure put on people in the music business, and that is why it is so hard for young people to assert themselves. The Beatles recognised that problem in time and had their own label, so they kept many of the rights. Back then I hadn't thought into the future and just accepted this rule of the game. Polydor told me what percentage I would receive, I said yes to everything, and we founded Happy Music publishers. I had yet to write the song with this title, but at that time that was the only way German publishers could make a name for themselves – with an English name.

To be perfectly honest, I still don't completely understand how publishing rights work. Despite innumerable recordings, the author's international rights to a big hit have made me relatively less money than, for example, the arrangements for the LP *Ännchen von Tharau*. The main reason for that is because in the USA the royalties are not paid directly to the composers, as is usually the case in Germany, but indirectly via the publisher. A fellow musician once said to me, 'The publishers in the USA have sticky fingers – it all stays stuck on them.'

Now I feed my songs to a new publishing company of my own, with the profits going to my second wife, Christine. And, by the by, we put the song 'Happy Music' back into our tour programme in 2002.

People often ask if I have a favourite among my own compositions. 'Music from Across the Way' and 'Fool' are two that I am very fond of. 'Fool' was recorded by Elvis Presley, although I didn't particularly like the way he interpreted it. 'When Snow Is on the Roses' received an award as Best Country Song of the Year, but perhaps my most frequently played title is 'Happy Luxemburg'. This was for many years the signature tune of Radio Luxemburg, from which the private television station RTL later emerged.

One very successful composition at the end of the 1970s was 'Der Einsame Hirte' (The Lonely Shepherd). I originally wrote it for an idea that never got off the drawing board – an LP called *Film Music without Films*, which was to consist entirely of my own compositions. The song was eventually released on my second Russian LP, *Russland-Erinnerungen* (Russian Memories).

Our tour promoter at the time, Hans-Werner Funke, also had the Romanian pan-flute soloist Georghe Zamfir under contract. I heard Zamfir in the Hamburg Concert Hall, complete with his gypsy orchestra, cymbal and dulcimer. I thought he was great, and I had the idea of having the theme of 'Shepherd' played on the pan flute. On the spur of the moment, I asked Zamfir if he felt like joining us in the studio, as I had a number for him.

Georghe came by, listened to the piece, played around with it a bit and then said, 'OK, let's record it.' In next to no time, we had it on tape and Georghe got his money, not really knowing *what* he had actually recorded there.

We mixed the song, cut it, and only then did we realise what great potential it held. Two weeks later we were doing a live TV show in Brunswick. I tried to get hold of Zamfir to ask if he would play with us. The record had already been pressed, but Zamfir was not under contract to Polydor – he was with Phonogram. After tedious negotiations it was agreed that we would have the LP rights and Zamfir the single rights. We played 'The Lonely Shepherd' in Brunswick, and the single shot up the charts like a rocket. In 1977, the highpoint of disco, it was in the hit parade for 13 weeks. Zamfir had recorded all over the world, but that was his breakthrough. As a result, all his records were re-released, and on all of them, contrary to our agreement, the first track was 'Shepherd'. In Australia there was even a TV series that used 'The Lonely Shepherd' as its theme music.

Georghe came with us on tour in 1978, and, during our visit to Manchester, his daughter was born. We congratulated him heartily: 'Fantastic, you're a dad! Let's drink to it!' But he didn't pay for a round.

We took our revenge at the next concert. We had a song in our programme called 'L'Alouette' (The Lark). For this Georghe imitated different birds with his pan flute, but, as he was twittering along, the shrill quack of a duck came from the auditorium. Our pianist, Günter Platzek, pulled out a gun from beside his concert piano and shot the imaginary bird, whereupon an endless stream of feathers poured down over our pan-flute conjurer. We had taken them from our hotel pillows, put them in a bag and hung them among the stage decorations above Georghe.

Unmoved, Georghe played on till the end, but his microphone got bigger and bigger as its electrostatic energy attracted more feathers. So by the end we had not so much a lonely shepherd as a feathered one. Zamfir didn't find our joke particularly funny, but he is a great musician. He can even play on a cola bottle and it sounds great.

In 1989, we re-recorded several of my compositions for my 60th birthday, and I wrote introductions for all of them. I still think of the album as 'the introduction CD'. When we'd finished mixing the album and I was at home listening to it, the introduction to 'The Lonely Shepherd', played by our solo trumpeter Derek Watkins, sounded so good I threw open the window and turned the volume up full blast so he could be heard all over the Outer Alster lake. I wanted to play it to the whole world!

In the summer of 2003 I learned that 'The Lonely Shepherd' had even attained an honour in Hollywood – the director Quentin Tarantino used it on the soundtrack to his film *Kill Bill* with Uma Thurman, David Carradine and Samuel L. Jackson. Annoyingly, on the *Kill Bill* CD it says that Georghe Zamfir produced the track. But at least – albeit 25 years late – this composition finally did end up on a film.

Today it is almost impossible to write a song 'on spec' for a particular singer. Most artists are tied to particular composers over long periods of time, because there's more money to be made working that way. A few years back I tried to do something new for various German groups, from the very popular folk group Kastelruther Spatzen (the Sparrows of Kastelruth) to the boy band Echt and the dance-singer Loona who had two number-one hits in 1998. I composed several songs, recorded demos and met up with people – but nothing came of it in a market that's deaf to music.

For instance, for the Sparrows – who are from the German-speaking part of alpine Italy – I wrote 'Sehnsucht nach den Bergen' (Yearning for the Mountains). They changed the lyrics, recorded the song and wanted the publishing rights for themselves. Since I thought my composition was strong enough to run elsewhere, I insisted on retaining the rights with my own company – it was my idea, after all – and so it came to nothing.

I didn't even get an answer from other producers. Take Ralph Siegel, for example, who won the Eurovision Song Contest in 1982 with his protégée Nicole singing 'A Little Peace'. I wrote a song for her with lines like 'You drank and you stank, but I loved you all the same' – she's old enough for lyrics like that now – but I received no response. I hope Ralph didn't take the lyrics too personally. Strangely enough, Nicole brought out a CD in 2003 with the title *Frauen sind kleine Schweine* (Women are Little Hussies). My thoughts on the subject of an image change were apparently not so far off the mark.

All these stories show how hard it is for new people to break into the market. I can only advise young newcomers to stay true to themselves and never let anyone impose a style on them that they don't feel comfortable with. People can't lie to themselves for a whole lifetime. If you can show your real self, you'll have the best chance.

Sing Along – the Super-Parties

Hamburg taxi drivers still talk about our famous carnival parties, which we held for years in the Ernst-Merck Hall. When we went on stage for our last set at half past three in the morning, the giant hall would still be as crammed as it was at ten in the evening. The people really partied and there was hardly a sober spectator in the building.

It all began in February 1972 with the *Voodoo-Party* LP – a very contemporary choir album for which I dived into the wave of Latin-rock started by Carlos Santana. We had a top-class rhythm section enhanced by drummer Rolf Ahrens and jazz vibraphonist Wolfgang Schlüter and we played songs by such artists as Santana ('Get Ready'), Sly & The Family Stone ('Everyday People') and Marvin Gaye ('Inner City Blues').

A special event was organised to advertise the album – a concert without seats so the audience could really get dancing. Since we were shown on the cover wearing peculiar Tarzan costumes and it was carnival time in Germany, the slogan for the party was: 'Carnival, costumes and – coconuts!' The marketing department at Polydor had the unfortunate idea of letting coconuts rain down in the hall as a gimmick – with the result that three audience members were slightly hurt. Nonetheless, the event was a big hit – and not just because of the coconuts. Several thousand delighted fans joined in our voodoo magic and the dance concept caught on.

So there was no reason why we shouldn't repeat this party every year. All we needed was the right mix of music. For the new series, which we called *Sing mit* (Sing Along), I arranged a mix of German pop hits and nonsense songs, with a German choir and the same party sounds as *Non Stop Dancing*. Except that, instead of playing Slade, Gary Glitter or Tina Turner, we played hits in German by such people as Chris Roberts, Michael Horn and Daliah Lavi – after all, *everyone* was supposed to be able to sing along. The albums appeared each year at carnival time, ten volumes in all, and every year we organised an appropriate sing-along carnival dance party.

The programme would start at 8pm and rarely end before four in the morning. We played anything and everything from our dance repertoire, and every half-hour we alternated with various guest stars. Over the years we had, for example, Baccara, Hubert Kah, Silver Connection, Alvin Stardust, Mr Acker Bilk and once, in honour of my student years, the Bückeburger Jäger – the Bückeburg Hunters.

Hamburg people have a reputation for being stiff and formal, but they came in the wildest costumes, and the Ernst-Merck Hall bubbled over with party spirit more and more every year. Although we played up to three nights in a row, the concerts would still sell out, with about 7,000 enthusiastic guests each time. All of a sudden it was considered the in thing in Hamburg society to be at our sing-along parties. Ticket prices climbed and they were sold at many times their face value on the black market. When the promoter really hiked the prices one time, I stood at the door and personally poured each of my 7,000 guests a glass of schnapps. Although I earned next to nothing from these events – the expenses were far too high – as the host I felt obliged to compensate a little for the high entrance fees.

An article in the *Hamburger Abendblatt* newspaper in January 1978 described these parties rather well:

When Germany's Party King strikes up, the enthusiasm knows no limits. Thousands of jubilant Hamburg people party till four in the morning. ... Wild partying under five tons of crepe paper hung from ten kilometres of cord, with two carousels, shooting stands and stalls for beer and sausages. ... No chance to catch a breath on the dance floor, and no drop of sweat manages to reach the floor. You can forget waltzes with full turns here. And it isn't only young couples who enjoy the involuntary intimacy – it's carnival, after all! A pirate embraces a blonde angel. Melon men and squaws jostle each other into the right mood. A longhaired Lorelei, a mixture of paprika and seduction, bounces across the dance floor. James Last and his musicians alternate every half-hour with the jazz combo of Mr Acker Bilk. By then their throats are dry, but the fluid stocks are gigantic...

There was plenty of fluid back stage as well. It was actually intended for the thirsty throats of my musicians, but often our backstage bar was drunk clean by dance-mad Hamburgers. The enormous success of the sing-along parties led to us appearing in other cities with our dance nights, in Munich, Cologne, Dortmund and Innsbruck.

The concerts were a tough job for the band: three evenings in a row, eight half-hour sets and always the full big-bang programme. But there was a particularly pleasant pay-off to the sing-along parties for the musicians: it was the best and easiest way to meet the prettiest girls in Hamburg. Everyone in the band – only those who were single, of course – had plenty to do for the next few months as each one of them had a long list of telephone numbers to work through. And, to be honest, I too enjoyed the intimate atmosphere to the fullest. In the course of one of these evenings, dozens of girls who wanted to party on afterwards would gather backstage, and who could say no to that! So usually the day had well and truly begun by the time I finally fell exhausted into bed.

Many fans may have a rather hazy recollection of one party where our pianist, Günter Platzek, had to leave early, since he had to play at an NDR harbour-side concert that started at five or six on Sunday morning. 'So, folks,' I announced, 'since Günter has to go down to the harbour, anyone who wants to go with him should just go along.' One hundred and fifty people didn't wait to be told twice! So there we sat – in full costume, fully made up and with no sleep – among the freshly groomed early-risers of Hamburg. The harbour concert was being broadcast live on radio, so the audience was expected to behave 'appropriately'. But we were totally boisterous and burst into a polonaise through the middle of the NDR Orchestra, barging our way between wobbling microphones. Luckily, no one took it amiss.

Incidentally, it was at one of these carnival concerts that one of the stars of my band made his debut, our trumpet and flugelhorn soloist Derek Watkins, from England. I asked Bob Lanese to take 'the new boy' under his wing – 'Let him stand next to you so he gets the hang of the phrasing.' But my concerns were groundless. Derek had picked up our style in less time than it takes to play a quaver in the 'Orange Blossom Special'.

Over the years, Derek has become an essential mainstay in the orchestra, not just because of his brilliant musical abilities, but also because of his personal qualities. Although all of my musicians receive the same money, I wanted to make an exception with him and offered him a special fee. But Derek refused to take it. 'Perhaps I have a little more talent than some, but the others give it their best, too, just like me.'

Derek can do anything, the highs, the lows, the feeling, anything. When he stands at the edge of the stage during our concert to play his big solos, I get a tingling sensation down my spine. He is also fantastic in the studio. When we were recording 'My Way', we were listening from the control room as his big solo was being recorded. When Derek had finished his part, there was an awestruck silence in the room. We were in raptures. When Derek came out of the studio and the recording was played back to him, he said, 'I don't know... somehow there's something missing at the end.' Another musician, John Barkley, said jokingly, 'That's easy, just add another octave.'

Derek simply nodded, went back into the studio and added the octave. All of us sitting in the technician's room looked at each other in disbelief. That cannot be – what he just did is physically impossible. But for Derek nothing is impossible.

Perfectly Normal Madness

Sing-along parties, concert tours, arranging, studio appointments, TV appearances and PR obligations – today I can hardly imagine how I managed to fit all that into 365 days. A glance at one of my old appointment diaries shows what a 'perfectly normal' James Last year was like. Take 1976, for example...

January

Two new albums are released in Germany, *Non Stop Dancing '76* and *Sing mit 4*. I have just finished mixing them and they shoot straight into the Top 20.

In Holland a new tulip species has been named Party King in my honour, so I have to go to a ceremony in Amsterdam.

At night I am writing the arrangements for the folk song LP *Freut Euch des Lebens* (Rejoice in Life).

Preparations for a spring tour of Great Britain are in full swing. Our British promoter, Harold Davison, notifies me that most of the concerts are long since sold out.

February

The strenuous sing-along parties are on the agenda. We play in Hamburg, Berlin, Munich and Innsbruck.

The arrangements and compositions for the new album *Happy Summer Night* have to be finished. At the end of the month we will record it and *Freut Euch des Lebens* with the band and choir. I am finding it a little difficult to get the right feeling for a 'Happy Summer Night' sound because of the inclement weather.

March

We finish mixing *Freut Euch des Lebens* and *Happy Summer Night* and release them, with both reaching the Top 20.

In Great Britain, three albums are released at the same time – *Non Stop Dancing '76, In the Mood for Trumpets* and *Classics up to Date, Vol. 3* – so I have to make a quick PR trip there.

On 26 March, we start our fourth tour of England, Wales, Scotland and Ireland, so I quickly write a new arrangement for this tour.

April

The sold-out tour goes on until mid-month. The last three concerts are in Dublin.

On the long bus journeys through England I work on the arrangements for a new LP which I am supposed to record right after our return.

Back in Germany we go straight to the studio. We have to record the new arrangements that I wrote on the bus for the charity LP *Stars im Zeichen eines guten Sterns* (Stars under a Lucky Star) to benefit the German Cancer Foundation. The stars I accompany with my band are Wencke Myrhe, Karel Gott, ABBA and Freddy Quinn.

I receive my 147th gold record.

On 30 April and 1 May we give two concerts in Dortmund and Munster, 'Dancing into May'.

May

I am writing again – this time the arrangements for *Non Stop Dancing '76/2*. The album has to be recorded this month.

Afterwards we go on a short holiday. After all the stress of the last few weeks, I have invited the entire band on a week's holiday to Spain.

June

Non Stop Dancing '76/2 is released, but I am already writing again – the arrangements for *Happy Marching* and *Classics up to Date, Vol. 4* are next in line.

July

A quiet month. *Rock Me Gently*, a choir album originally made for Canada, is released in Great Britain. I like this production so I'm glad to hear this.

We record the LP *Happy Marching* – not exactly my favourite project. Afterwards I finally go on holiday with Waltraud and the children to our house in Fort Lauderdale.

August

We go on a short concert tour of Scandinavia. After this we go to Bremen for *Starparade*, then there is another concert in Denmark.

Happy Marching appears in the stores.

Last preparations for the big autumn tour.

September

We give a concert in Hanover that is broadcast live on NDR, then we start our big German tour. Nineteen concerts in three weeks.

October

The tour is barely over and I'm back in the studio recording *Classics Up To Date, Vol. 4.*

At the same time I am writing the arrangements for the new *Non Stop Dancing.*

The next *Starparade* is coming up, this time in Vienna. Since we're going to be in Austria, we tack on two concerts in Vienna.

Next year's UK tour is already as good as sold out.

November
Classics up to Date, Vol. 4 is released. *Non Stop Dancing '77* is recorded.

December
Non Stop Dancing '77 is released. *Sing mit 5* is recorded.

What clearly didn't receive enough attention in all this was my family life. Waltraud was able to cope with my frequent absences, but it was much more difficult for my children, for Ron and Rina. But I'll let my daughter tell you that for herself...

Caterina

It's typical of our dad to give us the opportunity in his autobiography to present our view of living with him. He and Mum made every effort to bring us up as freely and easily as possible. He had no secrets and never tried to force his or any other opinions on us.

We – my brother and I – soon realised that our father obviously had a rather exciting job. My room was next to Dad's study, so I often listened to music late at night. It was great when he played the piano or put on records. There was an English singer called Alma Cogan who I liked a lot. She had recorded a German song called 'So fängt es immer an' (It Always Starts Like That) which is hardly remembered today but I loved it.

I vaguely remember my dad's first record using the name James Last – I could barely decipher the handwriting back then – but I still recall how surprised we were when this first *Non Stop Dancing* record was played in our home. Then there are the faces I remember: Katja Ebstein, the Norwegian singer Wencke Myhre, or Freddy Quinn. Freddy was a fixture in our house because Dad had written songs for him before he became James. Freddy did not come by often, but we once went past his boat – he was hanging about in the yards, doing his seadog thing. We were standing below and said, 'Oh, look at that guy up there – we know him! Ahoy, Freddy!'

'Ahoy, sweetheart,' he shouted, 'there you are, then.'

That was it, but for us kids this was exciting because Freddy was a star and yet everything was free and easy. Or the first tour with Katja Ebstein: we could only see the concert in Hamburg, since we were still school kids, but I remember the phone calls with Dad: 'How's it going?'

'Oh, very well. Katja's singing beautifully, everything's great. Last night we had oysters for dinner, a tremendous feast for Katja.' These are the little episodes that have stayed in my mind.

My father's rising fame was relatively unproblematic for my brother. Every now and then he'd give interviews in our busy father's place or accept an award on Dad's behalf at an important gala. I, however, had a hard time with this celebrity hype. I found it very irritating. There is a photograph of me with Andy Williams, the American singer, and it's clear that my smile is forced. I didn't like these PR things – I wanted to be left alone and just be a kid like all the others. But that was not possible, so I had to pretend.

Dad's celebrity status made itself felt even at our school. When I was 13 or 14 – it was the era of hippies and the Flower Power movement – there were many passionate discussions about ideologies and revolution, Marxism and capitalism among teenagers at my school. Dad was always portrayed as being the supreme capitalist, which was nonsense – he was just a musician. There was no logic in comparing him to big business, but perhaps these insights come later when you're older. At that time, however, I always felt I had to justify myself. My peers also rejected Dad's music – none of them would have listened to James Last. They didn't know that at home we always listened to the latest records and not *Ännchen von Tharau*.

There never was this dramatic conflict in our family between youth culture and adult culture, because my parents listened to exactly the same music as we did: Cream, Procol Harum or Blood, Sweat & Tears. Mum and Dad took us to discos before we were even teenagers, and also went to rock concerts with us: Santana, Led Zeppelin, The Who. I bet that didn't happen in many families.

All the *Non Stop Dancing* albums were discussed at home: which songs should be used? Which ones will still be up-to-date when the album is released in two months? Which titles might still make it into the charts by then and should therefore be recorded? We all discussed these questions, but especially Mum, Dad and Ron. We regularly read the trade journal *Billboard* because most hits came from the US singles charts, so we were always very well informed about the American and international music markets.

Of course it felt great when one of Dad's titles turned up in *Billboard*, either for entering the Top Twenty or for getting nominated for some kind of award, like his composition 'When the Snow Is on the Roses' for which he received the Country Western Award in Nashville in 1972. If you read something like that in black and white, you know, even as a teenager, that's a huge success.

As kids we were at many of the parties in the studio, at the *Non Stop* events, at home or in Fintel. At that time, the parties did not necessarily start at midnight. Often these celebrations began in broad daylight, which is why we kids could go, too. That was a lot of fun. We often went to the *Sing mit* parties as well, but by then Ron and I were already teenagers.

Once, after a fancy dress party in Hamburg, I had the difficult task of getting our father home and into bed on time because he had a plane to catch the next morning. There were dozens of girls trying to pick him up but I intervened. 'Rina, you're spoiling all my fun!' grumbled Dad. But I was unwavering.

The other side of the coin was definitely that Dad was away so often. When I was a teenager, he was practically never at home. We rarely saw him because he was on tour for weeks. Mum took care of everything. When Dad came back, he was agitated and restless, stayed up all night and drank enormous amounts of alcohol. We had to get his feet back on the ground slowly. After touring for so long, he could not come to terms immediately with the daily routine at home, with its school and family problems. Maybe he even felt like an intruder at that time, as Mum, Ron and I were always together and he was the one who just turned up every now and then.

When Dad wasn't on tour, he often had workaholic periods. He'd disappear into his study in the basement to do some arranging. As soon as he was done, he'd drive to Studio Hamburg and spend the rest of the day there, sometimes well into the night.

Dad worked incredibly hard and very, very intensely, putting all his love and his entire heart into his work. There was an album review once in which the critic called it 'music for the toothless', which doesn't do him justice. I can't imagine anyone putting more thought into every single note he ever wrote. I feel he made his best albums whenever he was able to realise his own ideas. When he produced albums using mostly material or ideas suggested by his label, it was his good nature at work, if you ask me. He had a contract guaranteeing him the right to choose his own projects, but again and again he let others tell him what to do, maybe because he was sometimes insecure.

Sometimes I wished that Dad had not become famous. When

we walked around Hamburg, it wouldn't be two minutes before people were shouting, 'That's him! That's James Last!' And then off we'd run, taking cover, so to speak. Dad quite liked being recognised everywhere but I thought it was annoying.

Another down side was that we never had Dad to ourselves, not even on the holidays in Florida. Our house was always full of people and often there was lots of alcohol involved, which to me was very irritating. Alcohol changed his personality and sometimes he did or said things that hurt.

He could also be real male chauvinist, although he certainly didn't mean any harm. When I had to repeat a year at school, he tried to comfort me by saying, 'If school doesn't work out for you, you can always find a husband to take care of you.' Those words did the trick! My ambition to finish my A-Levels was back immediately.

Once I even went to Alcoholics Anonymous with my girlfriend because I was worried about Dad's drinking. I had no idea how bad things really were. This incredible celebrity hype that had hit him so suddenly – everyone thought he was great, everyone wanted something from him – had to be dealt with in some way. At the same time he suddenly had lots of money, which gave him the feeling he could take all kinds of liberties.

On the other hand, Dad's popularity brought me many unforgettable moments, privileged events for which most people of my age – and not only them – would probably envy me intensely. Once, Harold Davison, Dad's concert promoter in England, invited us to London for a Frank Sinatra concert. The big surprise came after the fantastic show: we were to have dinner with Frankie boy himself. I was a huge fan of Sinatra; I had all his old albums of the 1950s at home and had spent many nights listening to *Only the Lonely*. So having dinner with him was definitely one of my life's great highlights. Cheekily I asked

Sinatra why he hadn't performed 'Angel Eyes' on stage; he looked at me and lied charmingly, 'Because I didn't know you were in the audience, honey!'

Flying to Florida for holidays isn't exactly typical for the average family either. In the 1970s there was a non-stop flight from New York to Hamburg-Fuhlsbüttel, landing at six o'clock in the morning. That meant that Ron and I could be at school at eight, so, on Sunday, the last day of the summer holidays, we'd board the plane in New York in the afternoon, arrive early on Monday morning, and rush straight off to school.

On one occasion the tour operator who also organised Dad's concert tours surprised us with tickets to fly to New York on Concorde. The flight attendants wore designer dresses, we were offered champagne before we even boarded the plane, and we had dressed up for the occasion. Travel was really exciting for us teenagers: first-class flights, the delicious food and, of course, there was a big difference between spending your holidays in a caravan on Sylt and flying to Florida and your own residence.

Mum tried to keep our feet on the ground and, all things considered, she was very successful. She also courageously turned a blind eye to Dad's tour romances. 'JAMES LAST: I CAN'T BE FAITHFUL' was a headline in some tabloid once. And that was true, in a way. Dad didn't make a big secret out of it. In the late 1970s I studied in Munich, and, when Dad had a concert in Nuremberg, I visited him and afterwards travelled on the band's bus. He was smooching with a girl right in front of me. When I later tried to talk to him about it, he just said, 'That was nothing, really, it didn't mean a thing.' Somehow Mum was able to deal with that: she would never have got a divorce.

When Ron and I had grown up, there was no doubt for Ron where he wanted to spend his life. The ink on his school-leaving certificate hadn't dried when he took the first plane to Fort

Lauderdale to enjoy his freedom. In Florida, he had his first flat, his first house, his first marriage – for him, Florida is home, too. Today, Ron lives only a few miles away from Dad in Palm Beach Gardens. In 2004, he married for the second time – his long-time girlfriend Silke.

I, however, stayed in Hamburg, where I live with my husband and our two sons Jeremy and Leonard. Every year we spend our summer holidays in Florida with Dad and Christine, at last having Dad and Grandpa all to ourselves. And that's really wonderful.

part five:
Island Memories

Rule Britannia

In 1971 we toured Great Britain for the first time. Our first concert in London was on a modest scale, in a converted cinema and with no choir or strings. The British press was nonetheless impressed and surprised, too, by our concerts. 'I had never imagined I would ever hear a German band playing "Rule Britannia" – but James Last performed the anthem, even making it swing,' wrote one critic.

Another added, 'This was James Last's first visit to Great Britain – and with five encores at the end of the concert it is obvious that he will soon have to come again.' I didn't wait to be told twice.

Two years later, in 1973, we returned with the full orchestra, including choir and strings. This time, however, our venue was to be the Mecca of the pop world, the Royal Albert Hall in London (named, incidentally, in honour of Queen Victoria's German husband, Prince Albert of Saxe-Coburg and Gotha). No sooner had the first tour poster gone up than the concerts were all sold out, in less than two hours in some cities. One journalist observed, 'On the black market, you could perhaps get a ticket for the World Cup final or an invitation to the Queen's garden party, but definitely not a ticket for a James Last concert.'

For me, a concert at the Royal Albert Hall has always been something special. All the pop and rock greats have performed there, from the Beatles and the Rolling Stones to the Who and Fleetwood Mac. And then we come along, a German orchestra barely 25 years after the war, and get to play there, too! I was indescribably nervous when I was about to go on stage for the first time in the giant oval hall. I was trembling from top to toe and wanted to flee. I was on the verge of giving up and I very nearly did.

To reach the stage of the Royal Albert Hall, we all had to clamber up a tiny ladder then climb through a small door. It took forever to get 40 musicians on stage. We were not allowed to go around the outside to get on stage. No, we had to go that way and no other – an eccentricity even the British sometimes find amusing.

Anyway, I had time to think and let my stage fright get the better of me. How would the audience react? Would the people loosen up or would they remain stand-offish? Could I get them to their feet or would they leave me in the lurch? It was clear to me that a lot was at stake that night. If you can make it in the Royal Albert Hall, you don't have to be afraid of any concert hall in the world. And we were a hit – a big hit! When I climbed up on to the stage at eight o'clock, I was welcomed by a whistling, clapping and stomping crowd. It took less than three numbers to turn the Royal Albert Hall into a giant party hall. You'd be hard-pressed to find an audience anywhere in the world as enthusiastic as the one this historic venue attracts.

Some have even rented their own boxes for life. A small brass plaque on a door might say: Lord and Lady Hamilton. There'd be a butler in front of the box, and inside there'd be a champagne reception – but at the end of the concert even these ladies in their gorgeous, expensive dresses would be up on their feet, dancing exuberantly to the music, their mink stoles thrown into a corner.

In such a magical place, I wanted to prove we had more to offer than our *Non Stop Dancing* party feeling. The concert numbers were therefore very important to me in our programme – and this music was also very well received. After the concert all those who wanted to congratulate me squeezed into my dressing room, and I had to sift through a whole stack of telegrams from wellwishers. Afterwards there was a big party in a London hotel, which was attended by two giant names of jazz: Count Basie and Stan Kenton! On one occasion Oscar Peterson was in the audience, another time Paul McCartney – they came to the Albert Hall because they knew that, if you performed there, what you did couldn't be all that bad.

I experienced some very special, emotionally charged evenings at the Royal Albert Hall. For my 50th birthday, for instance, my son Ron had prepared an incredible surprise. I had already noticed that a grand piano was standing to the right of the stage – that was unusual, since we only needed one piano and that was on the left, where Günter Platzek sat. I asked Conny Güntensperger what the extra piano was for, but received only a blank-faced shrug of the shoulders. The same thing with the musicians. No one appeared to know what was going on.

At the start of the second half of the concert, I went on stage, gave the cue – and nothing happened. Except that a spotlight lit up the second piano – and there sat Ron. What's he doing here?

I wondered. But then he began to play, then the band joined in, then the strings... and together they played in honour of my birthday. Ron was 21 at the time and had never before appeared in front of such a large audience, not least because he – like me – rattled with stage fright. But there he sat now at the piano, in front of 7,000 people, singing 'Photographs (Bring Back the Memories)', a song that we had written together, with my orchestra... I stood there listening in awe – absolutely fantastic.

Later Ron told me that he had invited our mutual friend the American composer and pianist David Foster to play the piano, but he'd had to cancel at the last minute because of an important appointment, so Ronnie had to play the piano himself. He was in a cold sweat, but he played three pieces and the audience erupted, and once again I had that tingling feeling!

The fans also sang in my honour. The whole hall started singing 'Happy Birthday' – 7,000 people suddenly singing for me! Again a shiver went down my spine. At the back of the hall, the middle door opened and in came eight people carrying a giant birthday cake, as big as a coffin. It had been baked by Tony Milner, a London baker who is a big fan of my music and who'd been coming to my concerts with his wife since the year dot.

We couldn't take that huge thing with us on the bus, so we loaded the cake back into Tony's van and I rang the children's hospital saying we had a rather large cake and asking if they were interested in having it.

'Is there alcohol in it?' the sister asked.

'Probably.'

'Well, bring it over and we can all sleep well tonight.'

I also bought a few children's bicycles and some toys so we could have a proper party at the hospital. When we turned up with all the surprises, it was like Christmas and Easter rolled into one for the children – and me.

island memories

In 1977 I risked a very unusual experiment for the first time. Since my British fans flipped out so much at our sing-along parties in Hamburg, I thought about putting on one of these parties at the Royal Albert Hall.

The seating of this time-honoured hall had never been removed before, let alone the space made available as a dance floor. But we succeeded in sweeping away all the misgivings and our enormous success proved us right. The Brits learned quickly, and very soon these parties became a big event there. From then on a London visit consisted of three 'normal' concerts with two Dance Nights tagged on afterwards – and every concert was sold out.

David Longman, a critic for the trade magazine *Music Week*, wrote of the first Dance Night,

For nearly five-and-a-half hours James Last and Mr Acker Bilk played on stage at the Royal Albert Hall last Thursday for their evening of dance music. The hall, with the central area converted to a dance floor, was a mass of colour and lights with coach loads of Last fans travelling from as far away as Sunderland to share in this evening. ... Acker Bilk opened the evening ... [and] the change over to the Last orchestra was accomplished with clockwork precision. The lights were turned up and the volume increased and the evening was really beginning to warm up. It would be impossible to pick the best songs from James Last, as he's such a seasoned performer and his orchestra exacted every note with such clarity. It was a glorious evening and all the performers honestly deserved the standing ovation.

Whenever we perform in London, many of the band members bring their families along, so our parties end up being quite large. After one particularly successful concert, we had a party at Trader Vic's in the Hilton hotel with over a hundred people all drinking Mai Tais. It was still required to call time back then, so a waiter came round ringing a bell and calling for last orders. So I ordered, 'One hundred and fifty Mai Tais, please.' The waiter just laughed. 'I'm not joking! I'd like one hundred and fifty Mai Tais.' The poor bartender was still shaking drinks at three in the morning.

There's another unforgettable spine-tingling occasion I associate with the Royal Albert Hall. Normally, our humming choir, the Bergedorf Chamber Choir, could not come with us on tour, since it was financially impossible to take 40 extra people. But, on the special occasion of my 60th birthday, I invited them all to London, to a concert in the Royal Albert Hall.

It was the end of a tour and the band had long since established a perfect routine, but the choir was to go on stage for the first time. Hellmut Wormsbächer likes to do things properly and not leave things to chance, so he appeared punctually for the sound check in the hall, excited and nervous. 'Hansi, let's get going! We need to rehearse!'

After four weeks on the road, the musicians were all completely relaxed. 'Take it easy, Hellmut, we'll be fine.'

I knew him well enough to know that the choir would be more than prepared. And I was right. We played the slow section of 'Rhapsody in Blue', the choir joined in and then the strings – in this hall! It sounded magnificent. My God, what a sound! Incredible! At moments like this, tears come easily to my eyes.

After the concert we all went for a meal together and ended up at an Italian restaurant where Frank Sinatra occasionally twisted his spaghetti on a fork. Our troupe descended like a plague of locusts – there were 120 of us – but it was already late in the evening. There was only one late-night couple there, a black man with a big cigar and a lady who appeared to be an escort girl.

They were both clearly put out as our noisy horde took over the establishment, but the concert had been a complete success and we were in high spirits, looking forward to a good meal.

After a little while Hellmut Wormsbächer tapped his glass and all the choir members took up their positions on the dance floor and began to sing, in Low German, 'Dat du min Leevsten büst' (You're the One I Love Most). The black man came over to me and said, quite moved, 'I have seen so many things in my life, so many orchestras and choirs, but I will never forget this evening. That was the best choir I ever heard!'

I also celebrated my 70th birthday in the Royal Albert Hall. After the concert we hired an entire restaurant, a TGI Friday ('Thank God It's Friday'). I got a red-and-white-striped TGI uniform, stood at the bar and mixed drinks for everyone. More and more fans wanted to come in and we let them join us. Finally, the place was so full we could hardly breathe – but it was a fantastic party for me. Someone had had the idea of bringing along an aquarium with wind-up fish. I had it filled with champagne, added straws, and it made the rounds of the bar with everyone taking a drink. At some late hour I decided I should open my own bar, DSI Monday – 'Damn Shit It's Monday' – but somehow I still haven't got around to it yet!

In the long years of my relationship with the British public, I have toured England, Wales, Scotland and Ireland with my band so often I could probably fill an entire book with memories. We toured the British Isles every year, in contrast to Germany, where there were times when no concert promoter would risk putting on a James Last tour. Between our first concert in 1971 and our last to date in 2004, we have been on tour in Great Britain approximately 25 times. I can only review this almost unbelievable period of time in the form of snapshots of sorts...

Port Talbot, for instance, is a small town in South Wales. Towards the end of one tour, at a time when golf fever had broken out in the band, it was a magnificent day there, so of course almost all the boys signed off to play golf. I, too, felt the pull of the first tee. Only our tailor Charly Cisek, Tommy Eggert, Stefan Pintev and two or three others stayed behind. Come 6pm they were waiting, as arranged, outside the concert hall, where we were due to sound check. However, they were the only ones who were there at six. The rest of us, including me, were miles away. We'd had a super day playing 18 holes of golf followed by a particularly intensive meeting at the notorious 19th hole – the clubhouse. All of us completely forgot about the time.

When we finally arrived at the hall just before the concert was to start, admission had long since begun and the rows were already filling up. Without a care and not so sober, I strolled backstage. Tommy Eggert raced over to me in alarm. 'My God, Hansi, where have you been? What about the sound check?'

'Rubbish! Sound check? To hell with it! We're just going to go out there and play. What do we need to practise for? Are you a pro or a wimp?!!'

The sober non-golfers looked at me aghast. They had probably never seen me like that, and they all knew about my usual stage nerves. But that day they had disappeared, thanks to that intensive meeting at the golf course.

Ole Holmquist, our trombone soloist, was so drunk he couldn't appear in the first half of the concert. During the first half, Charly had to treat him with ice-cold showers and leg compresses to get him fit enough for the second half, because he had a big solo in the Beatles' song 'Michelle'. Finally, he was shoved on stage, with an empty bucket nearby, just to be on the safe side, and the totally inebriated Ole delivered a fantastic solo, full of feeling. No one noticed. How is that possible? Must be a matter of practice.

Two of the most unusual places we ever performed at were on the Channel Islands of Jersey and Guernsey. We arrived on Jersey in good weather and played our concert, with everything running smoothly. But the next day a hurricane swept over the islands. We were supposed to take the ferry over to Guernsey, but that was out of the question. There were huge waves with furious, foaming crests, so the ferry service was cancelled. Someone managed to find a mad private pilot with a six-seater who said he would fly us over, so we all headed to the airport but the hurricane was so wild that the trees were bending like matches. It's simply impossible to take off in this weather, I thought to myself.

One half of the band, those with the weak stomachs, dulled their nerves with gin and tonic. The braver ones... did so, too. Then we set off, the pilot flying back and forth several times, each time with three passengers and instruments. Below us in the Channel the ferries sloshed back and forth, unable to dock. We could only see churned-up foam all around us but our pilot stayed cool. In the end everything worked out all right and our concert on Guernsey was able to start on time.

In some British cities we were actually able to contribute to improving the venues' facilities. Among the places we'd had to play were cattle-auction yards, beer tents and dilapidated municipal halls. In some cases they were so filthy that our stage clothes were black after every concert, because no one had even thought of dusting the seats. The sanitary facilities consisted of two toilets for 3,000 people. Poor Charly Cisek had to set up our wardrobe in dingy cellars where it seemed inevitable that a rat would poke its head around the corner at any minute.

One day I said, 'That's it. This is not on. If you want us to come back, you have to renovate the places properly.' And what do you know? The following year a number of the places had been really spruced up.

I particularly remember our night journeys to Scotland. We usually drove on towards Glasgow after our last concert in the Midlands. At the beginning of the journey everyone would still be hyped up from the show so there was a lot of activity in the bus as we laughed and drank and fooled around. Then, after an hour, quiet would descend and the bus became a sleeper-car. The lights went out, the conversation died down and here and there a snore could be heard. I would sit at the front next to the driver as the journey took us northwards. In the early morning, as we reached Scotland, the sun would rise slowly above a magnificent landscape and we'd put quiet music on the radio to wake the others. Then we'd open the window to smell the sea – wonderful.

In 1984 I made a special album of Scottish tunes for my fans there, *James Last in Scotland*. On it I tried to reproduce exactly these impressions of moor land, old castles, the lochs, the cliffs, the rolling hills, the luscious greens, the leaden sky, and at the same time the exuberance and cheer of the Scots.

Of course, the world-famous golf links of Scotland are fantastic. It was Terry Jenkins, who took over from Barry Reeves on drums in 1978, who gave the band the golf bug. Today almost all of my musicians and tour attendants are mad about the sport. We stay in golf hotels – or at least near golf courses – whenever possible and every morning you'll find the Last family on the links. For us Scotland is simply paradise with its ancient golf courses and carefully preserved traditions. It is overwhelmingly moving when at sundown, before a course closes, the pipers appear and play 'Scotland the Brave' to the blue evening sky.

Irish Stew

No tour of the British Isles would be complete without a few concerts in Ireland. Audiences in Dublin are very special: nowhere else do the people go so berserk, and nowhere else – apart from China – are our audiences so young. And the Irish can sing, really sing – not just shout. When you play Irish music in Ireland everyone joins in, and you can really conduct them. When we played the song 'When Irish Eyes Are Smiling', for example, we had a *fermata* – a tiny pause – in the music right near the end. The audience watched me, took a deep breath and waited for the precise moment to resume their singing.

In 1986 we gave an open-air concert in front of the Bank of Ireland in the middle of Dublin. That was the only place big enough to cope with the anticipated mass of people. The entire city centre was cordoned off, and for weeks the newspapers were full of announcements, diversion routes and warnings about the barriers. And all because of us… When the big evening arrived, it was pouring with rain. The streets, however, were still absolutely packed with people. Sixty thousand came to see us; nobody was put off by the bad weather. We performed one half of the concert with Irish musicians before playing our usual programme in the second half. On the next day the Irish daily newspapers' headlines were 'LAST SOUND STOPS A CITY', 'DUBLIN DANCES IN THE RAIN' and 'THE NIGHT DUBLIN TURNED INTO A THEATRE'.

The Irish really do have a big heart; once you've got them on your side, they remain true to you. After our concert, the people just didn't want to go home; they carried on singing and dancing. On one occasion the police had to clear the stage five times in quick succession. The enthusiasm was unbelievable and I've never forgotten it. In Ireland I also had the feeling that I knew everyone personally. Wherever we went, whether it was a bar or a golf club, we were welcomed and immediately offered hospitality.

The many invitations we received were also to blame for my band almost disappearing in the midst of Ireland's green hills one day. We were travelling from Dublin to Cork but after half an hour one bus broke down. I got into the second bus and carried on my journey with the string section, but the band was stuck and had to wait for a replacement bus. Things being the way they were, they didn't just hang around at the roadside; they disappeared into a pub. There they got a big welcome: 'Ah, the James Last band's here!' To make the time pass more quickly as they waited, they played some music, sang and drank lots of draught Guinness. When the replacement bus finally arrived three hours later, the lads in the band were already pretty drunk. One more swift Guinness and the journey to Cork was resumed. In the next town there was a collective cry of 'Stop! There's a pub! We've got to stop, we need a beer!' The entire journey proceeded in this fashion and it was long after midnight, on Easter morning, when they finally arrived in Cork – where I was waiting for them.

Only once was the Irish hospitality of a rather idiosyncratic variety. In Dublin there was a really swish restaurant. The owner drove a luxury car, and how he could afford one became clear to me when I was presented with the bill: I had to pay several thousand pounds, which was a bit much even for my almost inexhaustible patience. The owner, though, had the bill printed in a newspaper – and before long the dear man had a tax audit to contend with. But our problem was at least as serious: we had all fallen ill. Some of the owner's wickedly expensive oysters had probably been less than perfect. Our solo violinist Stefan Pintev was suffering so badly that he had to pull out of the next concert.

We also performed in Belfast, although the circumstances surrounding our visit were somewhat eerie. We were taken to the concert with maximum-security precautions: police in lead-weighted jackets, an armoured scout car ahead of us, then the band's bus, then another armoured scout car, then the string musicians' bus: that was how we arrived in Belfast. The members of the audience were searched for weapons as they entered the hall and the authorities' fear of a terrorist attack was palpable.

Then came the concert. We began with a slow prelude, the start of the song 'How High the Moon'. At the point when the wind section came in, a rocket whistled through the hall and 'exploded' on the stage. That was part of the regular show: the 'rocket' was attached to a fine wire cable. I had thought long and hard about whether it might be better to do without our explosive effect in this particular case. I stole a glance at the soldiers posted at the hall's entrance doors: hopefully they weren't drawing their carbines... Luckily, nobody was bothered by our little explosive interlude.

I suppose that has something to do with the distinctive dry humour that the people there can call their own. For example, there's a golf course in Ireland where the players have to hit their drives over a graveyard. The inscriptions on the gravestones' in this God's acre are full of witty word games involving golf terms: 'This is his first honest lie', 'As always, out of bounds', and 'In his deepest divot' are just a few of the epitaphs there.

All in all, I have devoted three albums to Irish music. The first, *The Rose of Tralee*, appeared in 1984. The Rose of Tralee is a festival at which Irish beauty queens from all over the world come together and are celebrated with a grand parade. We performed in a football stadium; it had rained all week, but after our second number the clouds dispersed to reveal a wonderful sunset and 30,000 people began to sing. The audience was very young, and the girls sat on the boys' shoulders – just like at a pop concert. Everyone partied along with us, and I'm sure there was hardly a musician who remained untouched by the fantastic atmosphere. At the parade afterwards we had our own truck and the people cheered us like princes. The album *The Rose of Tralee* went platinum once and gold ten times over in Ireland.

I recorded one of my Irish LPs in Dublin, and I invited along Comhaltas Ceoltoiri Eireann, a traditional Irish folk troupe with a fiddle, concertina, a variety of whistles and flutes and several stringed instruments. After two or three songs I said, 'Now we'll have a short break. Let's have a drink, then we'll carry on.' That, however, was a cardinal error. Break? You can't do that in Ireland. I had to prise each and every one of those musicians out of the pub individually. They simply sat there contentedly with their dark beers, not giving the slightest thought to getting back into the studio. All in all they were a lively bunch, and a real friendship developed between us during the time we worked together. They all came from the same school of Irish dancing and folk music. Even if you walked past the school building at night, the sound of the heels clacking and the music playing carried as far as the street.

I feel that the music and the landscapes in Ireland go particularly well together: the old forests, the castles, the meadows – I'd like to make music about ancient trees. Their knotty trunks, thick bark, tangle of branches – bizarre figures emerge over time, furrowed faces, mysterious shapes... You could tell whole stories about giant, weather-beaten trees like that.

For a while I thought about buying a house in Ireland but my enthusiasm for the Emerald Isle might have ended fatally. After a concert in the coastal town of Cork, we were sitting in a pub with friends, partying the way the Irish like to party: with plenty of Guinness. I was talking about my fondness for the country, and then one of the lads stood up and said, 'You haven't been to Ireland unless you've put your foot in the Irish Sea!' OK, fair enough. Together with the whole horde I set out, in the middle of the night and a bit merry, but determined to rectify my omission.

Unfortunately, the Irish Sea didn't do me the favour of waiting for me on a nice sandy beach. On the contrary, it clearly preferred to defend itself against my entry with steep rocks. In my elated mood, I wasn't going to let that stop me. As I started to climb down the rocks, I came within a whisker of plunging involuntarily into the sea surging far below me. But then St Patrick – or at least one of my Irish friends – held out his protective hand and I escaped with a few grazes.

One of the absolute highlights of my career was a Christmas concert that we gave in St Patrick's Cathedral in Dublin, as a benefit for a home for physically handicapped children. St Patrick's is more than 800 years old and is the biggest church in Ireland. The first Irish university was established there, and its history is associated with many famous names. I felt that doing justice to this important symbol of the island's cultural and spiritual heritage – and its wonderful historical setting – was a special challenge and a duty. So, instead of having the musicians in our usual concert formation, I arranged them in the style of a symphony orchestra: the violins front left, the cellos in the middle, the violas and basses on the right – and the wind section behind the strings, fortified by the presence of Manfred Zeh on the oboe. The rhythm section – bass, guitar and drums – sat directly in front of me.

Then we played pieces from our classical repertoire – Haydn, Vivaldi, Grieg, Schumann – plus a number of traditional Irish Christmas carols. The orchestra was supported by the St Patrick's Choir and the Monks of Glenstal Abbey Choir – a combination of Protestant and Catholic that was by no means a matter of course in Ireland. A guest appearance was made by the folk singer Noirin Ni Riain, who had made a big name for herself with her interpretations of old Gaelic songs. St Patrick's was full to overflowing, and the concert was broadcast by Irish television and shown on giant screens in the square in front of the cathedral. In the front row Protestant and Catholic bishops sat next to each other in peace and harmony. The occasion and the performance resulted in an LP which I regard as my best Christmas album and which I still enjoy listening to on Christmas Eve.

Toshi San

The album at St Patrick's Cathedral and many of the other Christmas albums I have produced over the years were outrageously expensive luxury productions that no company would finance today. Whether it was the *Festliche Weihnachtskonzert* at St Michael's in Hamburg or *Weihnachten mit James Last*, featuring my own compositions around the theme of church bells, we had a huge orchestra in the studio each time – the full string section and additional woodwind and horns. In short, that kind of quality costs. The clarinettist Nothart Müller, now concertmaster for the NDR Symphony Orchestra, would come over especially from Berlin. He was always enthusiastic: 'My clarinet never sounds as lovely as it does here. I feel like I am in a musical bed here.'

It is arranging this kind of music that gives me the deepest satisfaction. The strings have always been important to me – after all, I am a string player myself. The string instruments are the nearest in sound to the human voice, so they should also be treated in that way. That is what is special about my style of arranging the strings: I use the same phrasing and the same breathing patterns as for singers. We all have to breathe and, if this is ignored with the string instruments, the music just drones along, lacking spirit and intensity. I let the lower voices ring out longer than the actual note value, so that above the melody there is a harmony that is carried on in the bass, for instance. This gives an echoing effect, which is not the result of spatial acoustics but the score. This is characteristic of the Last sound and is what makes our strings so distinctive.

This method of writing for the strings also works very well with the recording technique of Peter Klemt, who places great importance of achieving a spatial sound.

I used to have double basses, cellos and violas in the orchestra when we went on tour, but have long since had to leave them out. The double basses are rather difficult to transport and can be replaced relatively well by synthesisers. I've also done away with the violas in favour of a deeper violin sound: instead of four violas and twelve violins I now have sixteen violins with a virtuoso character. What I really regret is that because of the cost we had no cellos for a while: the cello is one of the most beautiful and elegant of instruments and cannot be replaced electronically. On our tour in 2004, however, we had at least one cellist in the orchestra, as we were playing several quartet passages again.

It would be impossible to go on tour without strings. With our kind of music, audiences do not expect to hear half-hearted synthesiser sounds coming out of the speakers, and our stage appearance is associated 100 per cent with a large panorama of musicians. If the money were there, I would love to work with a giant group of string musicians, just as I did back in the days of the arrangements for Harry Hermann.

At the beginning of my career I used the string players of the NDR Symphony Orchestra. They tended to be older, more serious gentlemen. Today, I have young, talented people who want to have fun, and that's why our string section is so lively on stage. The head of this group is Stefan Pintev. He started with me when he was 17 – alongside his father, and they both still play in my orchestra. Stefan is excellent: even though he comes from a classical background, he can also give his violin plenty of jazz. Because of this he has just the right grasp of the sort of pieces we should offer our audiences.

The distinctive string sound of my orchestra was probably also the essence of our success in Japan. The market in Japan is big and orchestra music is well loved there. My first encounter with Japan was when I still worked for Alfred Hause and I rearranged a series of well-known Japanese melodies in his tango style. From this experience I knew the Japanese audiences particularly liked a wide-ranging, luscious carpet of sound, so, before we set out to conquer the Japanese concert halls, I produced an LP that was certain to get a good reception there: *Violins in Love* – rich string arrangements of great pop titles.

The idea of the James Last Orchestra touring Japan had first buzzed around the heads of Polydor Japan as early as 1968, when I recorded the LP *Sekai Wa Futari No Tameni*. It wasn't until the mid-1970s, however, that plans were put into action. When Alfred Hause toured Japan with his orchestra in 1964, I had not been allowed to go. That had hit me hard, not least since my arrangements had contributed to his success in Japan. But now at last I could catch up on what I had missed. In 1975, we travelled through the Land of the Rising Sun for three weeks before flying on to Australia, and in 1979 we followed that up with a four-week tour.

But, before we reached that point, we had to overcome some tedious hurdles. The greatest problem, of course, was the enormous costs for our large orchestra. European instrumental music has always been very popular in Japan – the French musicians Paul Mauriat and Richard Clayderman, for example, performed there regularly – but their stage shows were nowhere near as elaborate as ours, and as a result their tours were significantly cheaper than our giant troupe.

It wasn't easy to carry out negotiations with the Japanese and there were long, tough talks. On one side of the conference room sat our people with a huge blackboard and on the other the Japanese with another huge blackboard. First the Japanese wrote something, then there was murmuring, then lists of figures, then head-shaking, then everything was crossed out and the process started again. Then it was our turn to write, murmur and calculate. That went on for four or five hours and then, at last, lunch! Fantastic, I thought, it's over. Not by a long shot. After lunch we had to return to the conference room, the boards were wiped and we had to start again.

Once we'd finally succeeded in getting the concert trip sewn up, everything ran like clockwork. The halls were smaller than those we were used to in Europe, but they were acoustically excellent and fantastically equipped. The concerts always started on time, at 6.30pm, since a lot of people lived outside the cities due to the expense and bus services didn't run outside the cities at night. That was quite convenient for us, since that way we had a chance to experience Japan in the evening after the performances.

I opened the proceedings with a tranquil piece, since I knew the Japanese were keen on that, and the auditorium grew completely quiet as everyone listened reverently. Then a more lively number followed and suddenly the Japanese shot out of their seats on to the stage, danced wildly and were thoroughly exuberant – but no sooner was the title over than they were sitting quietly in their seats again as if nothing had happened. That was quite a surprise because we had been expecting a more subdued audience.

We also played some numbers from the *Beachparty* series and to underline the theme visually we had a campfire on stage. There was a large pan in which the fire flickered, and around it sat the choir singing 'Sitting on the Dock of the Bay' and 'Shangri-La'. The campfire, however, was strictly forbidden in Japan. Every evening the promoter came and complained, 'That's enough. You can't do that. It is forbidden!'

But it created such a lovely atmosphere I didn't want to give up. So our roadie, Jürgen Mayer, lit his campfire over and over again – and every time we had trouble.

Of course, there were huge difficulties in communication, because we were completely unfamiliar with the very different mentality of the people in this land. For example, because of the cost we didn't have our own string musicians with us and had hired local musicians from the New Japan Symphony Orchestra instead. At the first rehearsal I gave the sign for them to enter, but nothing happened. So, politely, I tried it again, 'We are now starting with the "Romance in F minor". At my signal!' The concertmaster stood up, bowed deeply and nodded obligingly. Once again I signalled them to enter, but no one started. I tried a third time and again the same ritual. Finally, someone explained: Japanese musicians are accustomed to having their note-folders opened for them, otherwise they don't play. No note-opener, no tone!

Even the technical rehearsal created amusing misunderstandings. During the first bars of our opening slow number I particularly wanted a darkened stage, so I asked Conny Güntensperger, our stage manager, to sort that out. He grabbed the head lighting technician, Toshi San. Neither of them spoke perfect English, so a comic dialogue ensued:

Conny: 'At the beginning we need no light.'

Toshi San: 'Yes, Mr Conny.'

But nothing happened and the stage remained brightly lit.

Conny: 'Toshi, we need no light.'

Toshi San: 'Yes, Mr Conny.'

Still the stage remained brightly lit.

Conny tried again, gesticulating wildly: 'No light, Toshi. NO light!'

Desperately, Toshi San turned to me. 'Mr Last, very sorry, we have red light, we have blue light, we have yellow light. But we do not have NO light!'

Communication outside of the concert halls was even more difficult. We travelled from performance to performance by train, and, since hardly anyone understood English and we couldn't read Japanese lettering, we had cards hung around our necks showing the place we had to travel to. We were standing around at the station waiting for our train when stage technician Dieter Ruge said he was just popping off to buy a magazine. He went off, came back with his magazine, joined the group with its violin cases and trombones, and started to read. He hadn't looked very closely, though. When they all embarked, he suddenly realised that they weren't his lads – quite by chance, another orchestra had been waiting for the train as well!

By then, however, we'd switched platforms because our train was now departing from a different one. Dieter hadn't noticed this and all the station announcements were in Japanese. Then he saw our train speeding away from the platform, and that was that. Dieter didn't speak a word of English, so his travails were the same as those of Conny Bogdan in Canada: he had no money and no train ticket. In the end he took a taxi to the Japanese TV station NHK, which was promoting our tour. There he was given a guide who finally took him to the right destination. From that moment on there was a mandatory triple check every time the heads were counted.

Towards the end of the tour, Swedish ball of lightning

trumpeter Lennart Axelsson caused quite a stir. He suffered terribly from the fact that there seemed to be no aquavit anywhere in Japan. That's a disaster for a Swede. No aquavit for four weeks! Lennart's elixir of life! Then we went into a bar in Osaka and Lennart's joy knew no bounds. Right up on the top shelf was a full bottle of aquavit. Lennart went into raptures: 'Hey, is that real?' He ordered a glass, and the barman came back with a little shot glass. Lennart just laughed and asked for a water glass. The barman poured a double, but Lennart signalled 'More, more!' until the glass was full. Then our sturdy Swede downed the whole glass in one. Then he passed out. The barman, not Lennart! It was just too much for the poor fellow. The sons of Japan even find it hard to understand how two people can finish off a bottle of rosé between them. I've never seen wine glasses as tiny as those in Japan. And now such a huge dose of spirits!

What stunned us were the amazingly high prices. A steak would set you back $85. If you were invited somewhere, you brought the hostess, say, half a melon, instead of flowers because everything was so incredibly expensive. It beggared belief!

Even today, 25 years after those tours, I can hardly believe we were able to enthuse so many people on five continents, in countries so different and with cultures so contrasting, with our music. But despite the many international successes that I have experienced with my orchestra, there remains one country I've not yet managed to conquer, despite several attempts. To my regret it is, of all countries, the 'land of opportunity'.

part six:
Go West!

Sleepless in New York

The fact that the USA has remained a blank area on the map as far as my tours are concerned is by no means a matter of indifference to me. Firstly, I live there. Secondly, I have always found it particularly stimulating to work with American musicians. Thirdly, my very first listeners were Americans – the GIs in Bremen's jazz clubs after the war. In addition to that, I believe that some of my best recordings were done in the USA.

My first visit to the United States was in 1964, when I went to Nashville to do some recording with Brenda Lee. I was immediately impressed by the professionalism of studio work in the USA, and even then I felt a desire to record an album of my own in that country some day. I had to wait a decade, however, before the opportunity arose.

I returned to the USA in 1967, shortly after Eddie Fisher had

173

had a hit with my song 'Games That Lovers Play'. I was accompanied by Heinz Voigt, who was my manager at that time, and we wanted to use the momentum to get my name established in the USA. Besides, Heinz wanted to show me New York, its music scene and its shows – the big wide world, in other words. We stayed at the highly luxurious Hotel Americana and, as I looked out from my room on the 48th floor, the New York night spread itself out before my eyes. Heinz, who'd been familiar with this view for a long time, looked at me expectantly: 'So, what do you think of that?'

'Well, it's pretty big' was my less than enthusiastic reply.

My curiosity wasn't really aroused until we were sitting in the hotel lobby shortly afterwards: Caterina Valente was singing in the ballroom and, quite by chance, Bert Kaempfert strolled past our table. Now I, too, was impressed by New York.

Klaus Ogermann was one of our first contacts in the city. Previously a pianist and arranger with the bandleader Kurt Edelhagen, Klaus was a man of great talent. Heinz and Klaus knew each other from those days, when Heinz had been Edelhagen's manager. The plan was for Klaus to receive the publishing rights to some of my songs and then make sure that my albums were released in the USA.

Klaus was making it big as a producer and arranger, working with such major stars as Barbra Streisand, Frank Sinatra, Connie Francis and Sammy Davis Jr – he is still a highly successful arranger to this day. His scores sounded great but were written in an entirely chaotic way. He was certainly a colourful character.

So Klaus was to represent James Last in the USA, and a number of albums were indeed released, including *That's Life* under the title *The Big Brass of the American Patrol*. After that, unfortunately, our plans fell through because Klaus had too many other things going on.

go west!

My first attempt to establish myself in the USA, then, came to nothing, but I had still got to know a host of interesting people. These included the Ertegün brothers, founders and chairmen of the jazz and R&B label Atlantic Records, who produced such great stars as John Coltrane, the Modern Jazz Quartet, Ray Charles, Roberta Flack, Aretha Franklin and later Dire Straits. I also met Jerry Leiber and Mike Stoller, whose office was on the same floor as Klaus Ogermann's. They had written such famous numbers as 'Spanish Harlem', 'Charlie Brown' and 'Stand By Me', as well as 'Hound Dog' and 'Jailhouse Rock' – two big hits for Elvis Presley, the King himself. The meeting with this sought-after duo was to have a totally unexpected outcome six years later. Jerry Leiber had kept a few of my songs, and so it came to pass that in 1973 Elvis recorded my composition 'Fool'.

Although I associate my first stay in New York with all these positive events, there was another incident that made me very sad. We accompanied Klaus to a very famous restaurant called the River Boat, not far from the Empire State Building. There we encountered one of the true greats of jazz, one of the idols of my youth: the unforgettable Count Basie! But Basie wasn't there for dinner: the man who had shaped a whole new genre of jazz, whose recordings had influenced one generation of musicians after another, was striking up a dance tune in front of a few dozen diners! I had already made Count Basie's acquaintance as a young bassist when he presented the awards for the Jazz Poll in Hamburg, which I won on several occasions. Now he came to our table and said, 'I know you – you're the guy from Hamburg.' As delighted as I was that Basie recognised me after 15 years, I was deeply distressed to see such a significant musician playing his terrific music in front of a few bored guests in a half-empty restaurant.

A Phantom Concert

Even at that early stage, long before we'd even been on tour in Germany, we began to talk about touring the USA. In 1969, two years after the trip to New York, we gave our successful concerts in Montreal, which naturally revived the notion. As a first step, my interpretation of the musical *Hair* was released in the USA, complete with a rather too psychedelic cover, which strangely depicted a single giant eye. After that I produced an album specifically for the US market: it featured songs by Bob Dylan, Peggy Lee, Jimmy Webb, the Leiber/Stoller song 'Is That All That There Is' and four compositions of my own. This record was deemed unsuitable by our American partners, however, and they never released it. Some of the numbers finally ended up on other records, but some remain dormant in the archives.

Within the individual departments at Polydor there were widely varying opinions on the type of music most likely to help me achieve a breakthrough in America. Because of the large numbers of Americans with German origins, some people thought polkas and German folk music offered the best prospects of success, but other decision-makers saw such music as too 'continental' to be popular in the USA. To be quite honest, compared with the Canadian branch of the company, Polydor USA seemed to be less active in promoting the US.

The fact that our productions certainly were of interest in America was shown by an episode that a Canadian radio man reported from New York. He visited a big hi-fi show there and, quite by chance, had one of our *Trumpet à gogo* albums with him. In one projection room, some songs or other from the Polydor repertoire were being played without arousing any great interest. The Canadian pressed our record into the DJ's hand and said, 'Come on, play "La Paloma".' When he passed the room again an hour later, our music was still blaring out and the audience was jammed up against the loudspeakers. It is said that all our import records in New York sold out soon afterwards.

We tried again during our long Canadian tour in 1973: four performances in the USA were planned, including one in New York's famous Carnegie Hall. The American concert agency had organised PR spots on the popular Johnny Carson talk show, press conferences were arranged, an expensive insert for the trade journal *Billboard* was produced and some good promotional posters were distributed: the project had made a pretty good start. Not until we'd been touring in Canada for some time did I receive the news that the concerts in the USA had been cancelled.

The reason given for this was that the promoter and Polydor USA had disputed the fees due to the notorious US musicians' unions. These unions demand that, for every foreign musician who performs in the USA, an American musician must be hired as well – even if he never plays a note!

Remarkably, articles about our cancelled concert in New York appeared in the German press, telling of a sensational success and even letting it be known that Connie Francis and Eddie Fisher had been sitting in the front row of this phantom concert and were inspired by it. A great bit of research!

Made in the USA

In 1975 I decided to experiment: I wanted to record a complete album in the USA with a very modern, jazzy sound, using only American studio musicians. Firstly, I simply wanted to try out something new, and to gather some ideas away from the well-worn path at Studio Hamburg. But we also wanted this record to penetrate the US market.

For our producer we managed to secure Wes Farrell, who had just caused a sensation with the TV series *The Partridge Family*. When I met him to give him my scores so he could start preparing, I asked whether he needed anything else, whether we should provide any demos... I wanted to make everything as perfect as possible. Wes was totally calm: 'Don't worry, your music's in safe hands here. I'll see you in a few days in the studio.'

Finally, the first day of recording arrived. A handful of easy-going, relaxed black and white musicians drifted into the studio, the Record Plant in Los Angeles, and, after a brief welcome, right away they were sitting at their mikes playing the first song. I didn't recognise my own arrangements; it was fantastic. Wes had assembled a group of jazz musicians who were all leading lights in American music in their own right – Max Bennett on bass, Larry Carlton on guitar, Larry Muhoberac on keyboards, Tom Scott on flute and two-times Grammy winner Ernie Watts on saxophone. Quincy Jones happened to be present, listening, in the central control room. He, too, seemed electrified. My music sounded completely different from the other James Last albums, and that was exactly how I'd wanted it. I called my family in Hamburg every evening and played the tapes down the phone to them: 'Listen to that, how it sounds. I wrote that!'

The album was called *Well Kept Secret* and contained eight numbers, ranging from a very funky version of Ravel's 'Bolero' through Cole Porter's 'Love For Sale' to the gentle Moody Blues hit 'Question'. The songs had been chosen on the basis of the probability of their receiving airplay on mainstream American radio stations.

The album's release was accompanied by a pretty elaborate marketing strategy. The folding cover showed the construction plans for a biplane, I had to pose in flying gear like the Red Baron at the controls of an old Fokker, and it was all bound in sacking to underline the mystery of the title, *Well Kept Secret*. All this was backed by a costly advertising campaign, but, even though the American critics were very kindly disposed towards it and Polydor made every effort, *Well Kept Secret* failed to produce the hoped-for commercial success in the USA.

For the German market, on the other hand, it was too jazzy: the public there expected more popular styles from me. On top of that, Polydor in Germany was not particularly thrilled that I'd produced the album in the USA, thereby evading their direct participation. The LP's performance in Europe therefore lived up to its title. But maybe, too, I was just a step too far ahead: *Well Kept Secret* has now achieved cult status in record exchanges and on Internet auction platforms. One curious detail is that this LP, produced for the USA, was also released in the USSR under the title *Big Secret*!

Despite these small defeats, I regarded my expedition into American studios as an enrichment and an expansion of my horizons – and it left me wanting more. Plans and discussions on the subject of 'Last in the USA' emerged time and again, and one such session was even held in my house in Florida in the presence of Polygram president Coen Solleveld. Projects were developed and abandoned, there was discussion and criticism, and finally some test recordings were made with David Foster, one of America's top pianists and producers, and musicians from the group Toto, such as Jeff and Mike Porcaro. But this project never reached fruition either, due to organisational reasons. One of its songs, however – 'Piece No.1', a composition by Ron – did appear on another album, *Classics up to Date, Vol. 5*.

Then, at last, something turned up which everyone thought could finally earn us some *succès d'estime* in the USA. The composer and Oscar-winner Giorgio Moroder, originally from South Tyrol, had written an excellent soundtrack for the Richard Gere film *American Gigolo*. Its main theme was 'The Seduction', and around it Ron and I composed eight more songs that tell an entire story: a hot summer night, two people meet … come-hither looks … a flirt, sexual tension … erotic touching … urgent desire, a pulsating love act … and the feeling of blissful relaxation afterwards.

We recorded the title song in New York, in a studio on the second or third floor of an old building. The elevator was tiny, with just enough room for the big drum, so it had to go up and down a lot before all the musicians and their instruments were safely in the studio. For the saxophone solo in 'Seduction' I was hell-bent on getting the US superstar David Sanborn, who around that time had contributed the most beautiful sax solos for many different artists. But David was under contract to another record company, which he forgot to remember. But we made a discreet enquiry – and he actually turned up for the recordings. When we were finished, and the cramped elevator was on its way down again, David was a little uncertain: 'I don't know, I think I've made a mistake. I'd have been better off recording that thing for myself.' But David had been paid – $5,000 for one number, not a bad fee – so there was no going back for him.

The single was released and made it into the Top Ten. David's record company were unhappy and started to cause a fuss; they wanted to sue us.

We were supposed to record the rest of the album in Los Angeles, but then we – Ron and I – were informed that we had to get out of California because there were going to be legal proceedings on account of this business with David Sanborn. As our record company obviously wanted to avoid a situation where I would have to make a statement in court, this led to a game of

wo Norwegian stars: Wencke Myhre and Anita Hegerland (famous for the song
t Is Beautiful To Be In The World'), who later married Mike Oldfield.

Above: With Astrud Gilberto, of 'Girl from Ipanema' fame.

Below: Ron and Astrud perform a duet on a Dutch TV show.

Above: With Karl-Heinz Hollmann, Wencke Myhre, Rene Kollo and Udo Lindenberg in my native Bremen on my 60th birthday.

Below: Berlin, two years before the collapse of East Germany.

In the studio recording *New Party Classics*: a world-class line-up. (*From right to left*) Bob Coassin, Chuck Findley, Derek Watkins, John Barclay and Stuart Brooks.

Florida in the 1990s – these should have
been the best years of our married life.

My wife, Christine – we have been married since June 1999.

Above: Christine and I walk together in the mornings to keep fit.

Left: With my grandchild Jeremy on my 70th birthday.

On the eve of my 77th birthday, 16 April 2006.

cat-and-mouse that could have come straight from a movie.

Since every state in the USA has its own jurisdiction, Polydor decided to send us to Nevada, where we would be safe. Although Ron and I were officially staying at the Los Angeles Sheraton, we were actually taken to a different hotel. There we were picked up during the night by a big, bald, black guy, who drove us straight to the airport in a huge stretch limo with darkened windows. From there we flew to Las Vegas, where the next limousine was waiting; it chauffeured us to Caesar's Palace. There I was given an apartment the size of an indoor swimming pool with every imaginable manifestation of luxury.

During the day I carried on working on my arrangements, and in the evenings we went down to the slot machines. Ron discovered that one particular machine was quite consumer-friendly and spewed out no end of winnings: ten champagne buckets full, in fact. The dining table in our living room was absolutely covered in small change.

After two days we were able to return to Los Angeles, as the court proceedings had come to an end. The two record companies had come to a reasonably amicable agreement, and we were allowed to carry on recording the rest of the album. The Sound Lab studios were officially unavailable because Barbra Streisand was recording her LP *Guilty* there with the Bee Gees – and, when superstars like that are at work, mere mortals have no business being there. But they let us in, probably because we knew the Gibb brothers and their production crew. Barbra roamed around the studio in white knee socks, lobster in one hand and champagne in the other, and we were very impressed. Then the musicians who had just been playing with Barbra came into our studio and carried on playing with us during their breaks.

I had really fantastic people for this production, and I was proud that the elite of American session musicians didn't consider it beneath them to play for a German bandleader. That might sound a little strange; after all, the guys earned just as much money with us as they did with the big American stars. All the same, it was a very special experience for me to record an album with such icons, guys who could really pick and choose their work.

The attitude they showed to their work was quite different from that shown by most of their colleagues in Europe. The keyboard player Michael Boddicker filled the whole studio with his synthesisers, Lee Ritenour arrived with 17 guitars, and Richard 'Slyde' Hyde brought four different trombones covering every register. When I looked at all this quizzically, they just said, 'When you book us, you get the whole programme. Before recording starts, you never know what you might need.'

That made me think of the trombonist in the NDR Orchestra, the union man who had reprimanded me so sternly many years ago with his remark about bassists having no say. He would have demanded extra payment for every semitone below the low E-flat that he had to play.

Above all, we had an unbelievable brass session. Its intended members were the trumpeters Jerry Hey, Gary Grant and Chuck Findley, already a world-class team. But who did the three of them have in tow? Our solo trumpeter Derek Watkins! Derek hadn't even been booked; he was on holiday and just came along for a laugh. What we didn't know was that he was one of Chuck Findley's best friends; Chuck even named his son after him. We were delighted to see each other again, and the three Americans invited Derek to join the session. In 2002, when Derek was unable to come on tour with us because of a persistent leg injury, Chuck stood in for him and played a wonderful solo in 'Nature Boy'. That's how the wheel turns full circle…

Right after our recording work in Los Angeles, I invited Chuck, Gary Grant, Jerry Hey and the great Slyde Hyde to come to

Britain with us that same year (1980). In this way we had – together with the regular team – seven trumpeters on stage for some numbers. Incidentally, Slyde Hyde and I have an instrument in common: the tuba. He had played it on the Supertramp LP *Breakfast in America*, and now he was dead keen on unpacking it for our recordings as well. Sitting on the forestage, he let his legs dangle over the side and played the 'Adagio' theme from Dvořák's *9th Symphony* in bass register – totally bonkers!

Not the least of the pleasures of working in Los Angeles was that it enabled me to make a youthful dream come true – a dream that had nothing at all to do with music. When I was still a jazz musician, I once saw a photo of the great bandleader Woody Herman. It had been taken in a studio in LA and showed Mr Herman at work – with fresh prawns in his hand. For me at that time, this was the epitome of success: making music with terrific musicians in a superbly equipped studio in America, while enjoying the small comforts of life – I too wanted to experience this feeling.

So that's precisely what we did. The studio is very close to the famous Farmers' Market, which I had been crazy about for a long time; I had even immortalised it with a short composition on a *Non Stop Dancing* record. It offered every conceivable delicacy: the freshest fruit, the freshest oysters, salmon, crunchy vegetables, aromatic bread rolls. For breakfast we strolled from one stand to the next, with paper plate in hand and a bottle of champagne – to me it felt like paradise. It was a fantastic time in the truest sense of the word, because I was experiencing something that had been fantasy for many years.

The work we did in the USA also helped me musically in a particularly important phase of my career. Once a certain level of success has been reached, it becomes more and more difficult to renew yourself and develop further. It is always very tempting to just let things carry on as usual. You develop a routine, take the path that involves the least work – and suddenly you're just repeating yourself all the time. To avert this danger, I asked myself specifically, 'Where am I going? What do I want to do next?'

The *Seduction* album had been aimed at the American and international markets. This direction, however, didn't seem to work for the record company: Polydor Germany didn't really appreciate such records. Clearly, the LP didn't fit into the conventional picture of James Last as it wasn't anything like *Ännchen von Tharau* or *Polka Party*. It was 1980 but they had fallen behind the times a little and hadn't noticed that the TV news programme *Tagesschau* had a new theme tune and the sports programme a new fanfare.

In my view, though, if someone was producing six to eight albums a year, it was fine if one of them didn't always comply with broad popular taste – particularly if the main purpose of such records was to learn new things and gain input for future projects. And, even though the *Seduction* album wasn't the big breakthrough we'd hoped for, the single taken from it reached the Top Ten in the USA, which was surely more than just a *succès d'estime*. If the *Well Kept Secret* and *Seduction* albums had been more successful in Germany and the USA, perhaps I would have composed differently from then on. Who knows how my career would have developed? Perhaps it would have shifted more towards America. Perhaps I would have been finished long ago. Who can possibly say?

But one thing that has never materialised, unfortunately, is a tour of the USA. After the ill-fated attempts in the 1960s and 1970s, concrete plans were made for 1989 – a performance in Carnegie Hall in New York was discussed. The next attempt was in 1994, and finally live broadcasts of our concerts in 2000 (*Gentleman of Music*) and 2002 (*A World of Music*) by the US television channel PBS was proposed as the prelude to an American tour. This dream, however, is still waiting to be fulfilled.

New Tones

At the beginning of the 1980s we recorded several more albums in the USA. In addition to *Seduction*, we recorded two *Non Stop Dancing* records and the reggae LP *Caribbean Nights*. During this period I intensified my work with my son, who was ultimately – many years later – to become my regular sound engineer.

Ron had started to work for me when he was still a teenager. As Rina has told you, before I recorded a new *Non Stop Dancing* LP, we as a family discussed the choice of songs – and this was how Ron developed an ever-improving instinct for potential hits. He also became more and more interested in the musicians behind those hits.

In our house in Hamburg we had a small indoor swimming pool with a bar and an improvised disco, where the latest LPs piled up week after week. That was Ronnie's favourite place for doing his homework: he listened to the latest records as background music while he was studying. In doing so, he always paid close attention to the individual musicians' names on the sleeves: if a solo or a riff particularly impressed him, he noted the name of the person who played it. This finally resulted in a long list containing the best studio musicians in America. As I was putting together the initial plans for the *Seduction* album, he thought about which musicians could best provide the style I had in mind. He assembled three different rhythm sections for me, believing that musically they would function well together. We talked about it, and then he called Kathy Kasper in Los Angeles and suggested these people.

Kathy was our contractor; her job was to select and book musicians for the studio dates. She probably had no idea that she was speaking to such a youngster over the phone and assumed this brash, confident caller was an experienced producer. Ron read her our lists, and then Kathy gave her expert advice on his suggestions: 'It'd be better not to take this pianist, as you never know whether he'll turn up completely sober. Those two guitarists have never played together, and I don't think it'll work' and so on. But Ronnie never wavered. He just said, 'What the heck – let's just give it a try. Book them!'

This led to some very special combinations, as when we put rock guitarist Waddy Wachtel together with Lee Ritenour, who was more of a jazz guitarist. Kathy was highly sceptical about whether the two of them would blend, but, lo and behold, it worked.

All of these people were real perfectionists with an incredibly professional attitude. Lee Ritenour, probably one of the ten best electric guitarists of all time, turned up with more equipment than most studios had ever seen. As soon as he'd set up his various electronic magic boxes, he began demonstrating an endless range of sounds, even in stereo – it was truly fascinating.

Since my life's centre of gravity was shifting more and more towards America, I decided to set up my own recording studio in Florida. As one of the leading studio-equipment suppliers had its headquarters very close to our house in Fort Lauderdale, Ronnie and I paid the company a visit. We did a little shopping and shortly afterwards converted two of the guest rooms into a small recording studio. A multi-track machine, a mixer unit – plus an ever-greater variety of state-of-the-art options for the electronic instruments – and my universe had already expanded by another galaxy, one that freed me from the restrictions of studio dates in Germany.

go west!

Now, though, I had to make sure that there was someone in addition to Ronnie who could handle this new world of wonders. That person was to be Tommy Eggert.

Tommy was Ron's school friend from their grammar-school days in Hamburg. Even as a teenager he knew how to handle synthesisers. This was no simple matter in the late 1970s when, long before synthetic sounds could be retrieved by pressing a button, every sound had to be put together laboriously. Tommy knew fairly exactly how these electronic sounds came into being: he knew how to create vibrations and he understood the physical interrelations, which meant that he could create quite specific sounds. As I needed special sounds time and again for a variety of *Non Stop Dancing* songs, I finally hired him – still a teenager – in 1977 to help with studio recordings.

When Ronnie and Tommy had successfully passed their final exams, I invited Tommy to stay with us in Florida for three months. At that time I had two domestic staff, an elderly Italian married couple. The husband, Dan, was the chauffeur and had to look after the cars, which were always freshly polished and tanked up in the garage. To give the boys a treat, I had them picked up from the airport by Dan in a white convertible. Tommy was thrilled, and even today he goes into raptures about his first impressions of Florida: sunshine, palm trees and the open-topped car – with its marvellous stereo – in which they whizzed down wide, almost empty highways to our house. He was just stunned.

I let the two of them laze around for six weeks – they had genuinely earned it – but then we got down to business. 'Right, lads, you've done enough partying – now let's get to work.'

Ronnie then organised a studio technology course for Tommy and himself in Ohio. As a graduation present I'd given Ronnie a Jeep, and this was what they used to negotiate the long, long journey up to Dayton. On the way they stopped off in Nashville and had a look at the recording studios Kris Kristofferson and Elvis Presley had used.

Tommy Eggert was just the right man for the job. In Hamburg he had always been keen to watch the mixing work in our productions and anything technical fascinated him; he was the perfect complement to Ron. From around 1980 he was a regular presence in the studio, and out of this developed an intensive cooperation. Tommy always brought the latest equipment along. Whenever he saw something new in a trade journal, he always said, 'Hansi, there's this fabulous device – we've just got to have it!' to which I would reply, 'Fine, let's get it then.' Again and again he'd sit with a new synthesiser, day and night for weeks, examining it down to the last detail. Maybe I found his enthusiasm infectious; at any rate I became fascinated by the possibilities offered by the synthesiser, even though they were still pretty limited. This intense involvement with new sounds inevitably culminated in a number of synthesiser LPs, although they weren't really planned in that form.

Equipped with lots of these newly acquired electronic miracle boxes, we set to work in Florida. The working atmosphere was extremely creative: we tried things out, experimented and looked for possible new sounds. In order to get the right tones out of these imperfect devices, it was necessary to configure the electronics separately for every new sound: every tone had to be formed out of various modules and brought to life. As a result, it could take as long as two hours before a single bass sound was just right.

At first, the only works created in my little studio were layout productions – templates for future recordings in the main studio. In 1982 we recorded the bulk of an LP in Florida for the first time, and the title track was to be one of our biggest hits: 'Biscaya'.

Most of the compositions on this album were by me, Ron and

Tommy, and production was finished after six weeks. It was our first accordion LP and turned the spotlight on a musician who was responsible for many wonderful, emotive solo moments in my concerts: Jochen 'Jo' Ment.

'The last time I had sex, a litre of petrol still cost 43 pfennig!' Jochen was well known and popular among the band members for such cracks, which he would come out with quite unexpectedly. We knew each other from our days working together at NDR, and Jo actually started out in my band as a saxophonist. This first phase of our musical cooperation didn't last very long, however, as Jo was himself making records of a very similar style with Teldec. Despite our friendship, I didn't want to serve him up our latest tricks on a plate. Jo didn't return to my orchestra until 1980 and this time he was playing an instrument that suited him much better: the accordion. His mastery of this instrument could really produce moving results. There may be virtuosi who are more spectacular or technically brilliant, but Jo's ability to get deeply soulful and lyrical sounds out of his accordion was unequalled. His solo phrasings in the Bryan Adams song 'Have You Ever Really Loved a Woman' or 'The Way We Were' brought tears to my eyes.

The oldest member of my orchestra, Jo died at the age of 78 in October 2002. Since then we have refrained from playing the song 'Biscaya' at our concerts.

Two years after *Biscaya* we produced another accordion album, *Paradiso*, although this time with rather unconventional way of working. I put the accordion down on a table in front of me so I could plays the keys like a piano, while Ron and Tommy had to operate the bellows – just as choirboys used to do at the pump of a church organ.

Paradiso was followed by *Paradiesvogel*, another album strongly influenced by electronic sounds, although this time the focal point was the pan pipes. As Zamfir was not available, Horea Crishan, a violinist from the NDR Orchestra, took on the part. Polydor was not keen on this album at all, believing there was too little Last in it. However, despite all prophecies of doom, *Paradiesvogel* – under the title *Bluebird* – sold very well, particularly in China and Japan.

Despite the success of the single 'Biscaya', the new electronic sounds were getting me criticised, sometimes quite severely: In earlier interviews I had repeatedly stressed that everything about our sound was 'hand-made' – in other words there were no electronic instruments – so this change of direction took many of our fans by surprise. But I have never hidden behind the endless regurgitation of some successful formula; without constant development 'James Last' would probably have faded away long ago.

I have often been asked – and still am – what is the secret of the 'typical Last sound'? I have never really been able to connect with this notion of a 'typical Last sound'. What does a *Classics* album have in common with a *Non Stop Dancing* LP? Or a *Polka Party* with a *Beachparty*? Which of these is the 'typical Last sound'?

The only 'secret' is that I have always written down what I felt at that moment. It has always been my feeling, but of course it has changed continuously. My arrangement of 'Granada' on the first *Trumpet à gogo* LP from 1966 sounds very different from the same song released ten years later on *Happy Summer Night* or 35 years later in our concerts. The journey from the 'bowling-club sound' of the first *Non Stop Dancing* album to the arrangements on *Seduction* has been a long one – and it's still far from over.

part seven:
Starparade

Astrud, Wencke, Milva and Co.

In the mid-1980s, Polydor appointed a new head of music who remembered my jazz past and thought that jazz with a bit of a Latin sound might produce an interesting combination. The production was to be called *Plus*, this being a reference to my wonderful colleague Astrud Gilberto. The 'Queen of Bossa Nova' from Brazil hadn't recorded a new album for ten years, which meant that the planned cooperation was a pretty exciting affair for both of us.

Astrud was viewed as being extremely cautious, probably because she hardly saw a penny from her first global hit, 'The Girl from Ipanema', which she had recorded as a young girl with Stan Getz and her husband João Gilberto. The laurels for this song, which won a Grammy, also went to others – at the time, Astrud didn't even get a mention on the record cover. So, when

Ronnie and I met up with her in New York, I had been warned. The conversation went well, however, and we quickly agreed on the album's concept: the songs were to be provided mainly by Antonio Carlos Jobim, his son Paolo and Astrud herself. She was also very keen to have her own additional musicians in the studio; they would be responsible for the rhythm tracks. I arranged the orchestra, and everything seemed to be going excellently.

The recordings in Fort Lauderdale, however, turned out to be anything but simple. We did 30 or 40 versions of one number, and there was always something that wasn't quite right. Astrud's son Marcelo was playing the bass, and he wasn't exactly a world champion. On the other hand, she had brought along a percussionist of exceptional class: a Brazilian by the name of Café. He lugged a vast number of crazy instruments around with him, and even had a singing saw in his luggage. I was so taken with him I invited him to go on tour with us afterwards. He came, and played a different solo every day.

One of the compositions on the album, 'Listen to Your Heart', was written by Ronnie. As soon as she heard the demo in New York, Astrud said, 'I've got to sing this number together with Ron.' When we finally recorded it, Astrud was quite sure that 'Listen to Your Heart' was a potential hit: 'It's going to make Ron a star.'

When the production was finally finished, the album was to be released in the Netherlands first so we had to appear on Dutch television, again at the *Grand Gala du Disque*. The show featured an outstanding spectrum of performers, including stars such as Paul Young and Tina Turner. Astrud was supposed to sing 'Listen to Your Heart' together with Ronnie, and the rehearsals went off without a hitch – except perhaps for the usual rivalries that may be inevitable when two divas like Tina Turner and Astrud Gilberto cross paths.

On the day of the live broadcast, however, Astrud, who never drank alcohol, was completely 'indisposed'. 'I don't know what's wrong with me, but you'll have to sing for two today,' she said to Ronnie just before the programme started. So he performed the lion's share of the 'duet', while Astrud exercised great vocal restraint.

This incident, although not even noticed by the television audience, had a pretty major impact at the record company. It had been intended that we would promote the number on a large scale in Britain, with TV appearances and all the rest. Astrud's indisposition, though, spelled the end for these plans. Despite excellent reviews, the album was hardly promoted in Germany and was not released at all in Britain.

That was a bitter disappointment for Ron, not least because the number's potential was shown in the fact that 'Listen to Your Heart' spent six weeks in the Top Twenty of Radio London's listeners' charts, even though it wasn't available in the shops. That surely didn't happen often.

Astrud Gilberto is just one of many singers with whom I have worked quite intensively. In the 1960s, my band accompanied an artist who came to Germany as a young girl and rose to stardom there in a flash: Wencke Myhre. The whirlwind from the far north was just 17 when she came to Germany in 1964, labelled 'Norway's most popular songstress'. The Hamburg-based producer and drummer Bobby Schmidt took her under his wing for Polydor, but after a not particularly successful debut single I was asked to take on the role of musical director for her first LP.

At that time Wencke was chaperoned constantly by her father. The only place that stern Dad didn't accompany her was Hamburg – presumably he thought that two such honourable gentlemen as Bobby Schmidt and Hansi Last would make sure that little Wencke didn't get up to any mischief. It wasn't quite like that, however. After spending her days hard at work in the studio, she was really keen to experience life in the evenings and immediately dragged us to St. Pauli, Hamburg's red-light district. But, as Bobby and I grew more and more tired, Wencke was just starting to wake up. She wanted to see everything – and in St. Pauli that was quite a lot, even in the mid-1960s...

Only a year after her first tentative steps in Germany, Wencke won the *Schlagerfestspiele* pop festival in Baden-Baden with the song 'Beiß nicht gleich in jeden Apfel' (Don't Bite Every Apple) and from that moment there was no stopping her career in German-speaking countries. We recorded many of her most successful songs together, notably her huge hit 'Er hat ein knallrotes Gummiboot' (He Has a Bright Red Rubber Dinghy) and my compositions 'Jägerlatein' (Hunter's Tales) and 'So eine Liebe gibt es einmal nur' (Music From Across The Way) for her first German feature film *Unsere Pauker gehen in die Luft*.

Our work together finally came to an end as my life became increasingly drawn towards Florida. Even today, though, there remains an indirect link between Wencke and me: her current partner Anders Eljas, formerly the keyboard player with ABBA, played for our orchestra for a while.

George Walker was a Canadian singer who represented a very different type of music: his style could be termed classic American. He was recommended to me by Polydor Canada; one of the company's bosses had heard him in a bar and, since we were having such great success in Canada, they hoped that they could ride that wave to make him popular there. In 1968 we produced an LP together – *James Last Presents George Walker*. George sang a mixture of my compositions, such as 'Games That Lovers Play' and 'Who Are We', and established classics like 'The Sound of Music' and 'Plaisir d'Amour'. We recorded the LP in

Hamburg and, when George arrived at the airport, he wanted to know how many musicians would be in the studio; he probably thought we were a small combo of seven or eight people. When I explained to him that an orchestra with 40 musicians was waiting for him, he was shocked: he hadn't reckoned on that.

In the studio, George was always beating out Spanish rhythms on the drums – 'Hey, you like Spanish music?' – so I sat down for a whole night and arranged a Spanish song for him: 'La Malagueña Salerosa'. Despite everything, however, the album was not a great success and that was the last I heard of George Walker.

In the same year I took on the role of producer for a German beat group: five lads who called themselves Wonderland. The band had been put together by *Bravo* magazine and its readers had chosen their name. But this was not just a boy band: Wonderland were real musicians from the Hamburg scene. Achim Reichel, Frank Dostal and Dickie Tarrach had previously played with the highly successful Rattles, a German version of the Beatles. Helmut Franke also played guitar in my band, and finally there was a young Englishman, Les(lie) Humphries, then completely unknown.

They were great lads, really prepared to work hard for success. Les – still a couple of years away from forming his own group – was very eager to learn. He nurtured arranging ambitions and often called me late at night: 'Say, how do you transpose a horn? How do you set the cellos? How do I get this or that sound effect…?'

The first song we produced together was called 'Moscow' – a number in typical 1960s style that Wonderland immediately made popular. Their first concert was held in the main lecture hall at Hamburg University, with Joe Cocker and Barry Ryan also on the bill. It was promoted by the *Hamburger Abendblatt* newspaper, and it was not particularly well organised. The changeover from one group to the next took too long, the audience became increasingly restless and started to boo, and finally some of them tried to invade the stage. The person in charge then came out from behind the curtain to mediate, but our roadie didn't know who he was. Assuming he was an angry member of the audience, our man gave him a real sock on the jaw, sending the poor guy crashing from the stage. This, while unfortunately laying out the promoter, clearly served as a deterrent to the rest of the audience: things then calmed down and Wonderland were able to perform.

The group didn't stay together for long: as is frequently the case with test-tube bands, personal differences quickly emerged and they split up. Shortly afterwards, Les Humphries founded the Les Humphries Singers and dominated the hit parades of Europe for a long time with his gospel-beat sound: 'Mexico' and 'Mama Loo', for example, were absolute mega-sellers. When Les married the singer Dunja Rajter, my wife Waltraud and I were witnesses.

One problem I have observed during many productions is that record companies rarely allow their artists any scope for development. Wencke Myhre, for example, is a versatile woman with comedic gifts; it was a pity she had to sing in the 'Knallrotes Gummiboot' style for so long. Everyone involved has their say – except for the artists themselves. This means many talents were – and still are – misjudged, overlooked or pretty much flogged to death: if a singer has success with a particular type of song, the producers want them to carry on in that same style. They don't recognise the person, the artist, behind it. It would be far more helpful – and even more valuable for the labels – if they had stars who changed and were encouraged to develop: independent people with whom you can work for a lifetime, people who become personalities and don't remain children.

One such personality is the Italian diva Milva, 'La Rossa'. Milva never allowed herself to be tied down to a particular style or cliché: she sang Bert Brecht as naturally as she sang Robert Stolz's Austrian operettas, German pop songs or French chansons. She played under the direction of the Italian theatre and opera director Giorgio Strehler; she was fêted in the Olympia in Paris and New York's Madison Square Garden alike and she acted in films alongside Michel Piccoli and Michel Serrault. She played the role of Prince Orlofsky in *Die Fledermaus*, and she appeared in the tango opera *María de Buenos Aires* by Astor Piazzolla. She was an absolute world star – and in 1994 we were supposed to make a record with this multi-faceted artist!

We had first got to know each other in 1982 when La Rossa recorded the song 'A Ship Will Come' by the celebrated Greek songwriter Manos Hadjidakis. The idea for my new album *Dein ist mein ganzes Herz* (My Heart is Yours Alone) had come from Metronome, a Polydor subsidiary to whom Milva was under contract. It was some time, however, before the project took on a concrete form, but when things finally got moving – what an experience! What a marvellous woman! I could have fallen in love with her on the spot.

For this production I had rearranged a number of classical songs, such as 'Concierto de Aranjuez', Bizet's 'The Pearl Fishers' and Tchaikovsky's 'Chanson Triste', and written a very unusual arrangement for the title track, Lehár's 'My Heart is Yours Alone'. Ron contributed two beautiful compositions, and finally Milva sang a fantastic version of my song 'Fool' – the one that Elvis had reeled off somewhat unlovingly more than 20 years earlier.

When the orchestral recordings were finished, Milva got in touch and said that she would be coming in the following day. 'Tomorrrow I'll come to the studio, just to hearrr it!'

Milva had a reputation for being very difficult: it was said she'd come into the studio, listen to the backing tapes for three days and then, maybe, start to sing.

I have often heard well-intentioned warnings of this kind, but have never allowed them to worry me unduly. We do our part of the job as well and as conscientiously as possible: the backing tapes are mixed in such a way that the soloists are handed everything virtually on a plate. All the singer has to do is add his or her vocal ingredient to the dish, and Ron knows exactly how to make a playback sound so a singer feels comfortable with it. This creates a positive atmosphere from the start.

So now here was the diva, sitting in the control room, her red mane carefully tied into a knot, headphones on, listening to our playback tapes. First song, second song, third song – then she jumped up and, with that untamed Mediterranean spirit, shouted, 'Wonderrrful! I want to sing! Rrrright now!'

The recordings were finished in just a few days. When we told the people at the record company, they couldn't believe it all had gone so quickly and smoothly. For that Ron can take much of the credit: one of his specialities is ironing out the soloists' mistakes before they get to hear the recording, whether it's Milva, Céline Dion or Derek Watkins. The best way is to leave him alone, and the number will soon be clean. So, when Milva came into the control room and demanded, 'I'd like the first take up to the 12th bar, the second version up to the 25th bar and then the close from take one again', Ron had long since prepared it and Milva was happy.

With typical Italian exuberance, Milva always called me 'Maestrrro!!!' with at least three exclamation marks at the end. She was extremely taken with our communal lunch breaks: I had hired a chef especially for the purpose and every day he conjured up superb delicacies for us. We'd stop work in the late afternoons, but instead of going to some restaurant we'd dine together, the whole team, in the studio. Those were wonderfully friendly, pleasant moments of great human warmth, which I remember with pleasure to this day.

The result of these joint endeavours was a wonderful CD: I believe Milva's big, warm voice is particularly well suited to our music. Recently, she phoned my son and said what a shame it was that we'd never gone on tour together. The songs that we'd recorded on this CD, she added, were of timeless beauty and would have been ideal for the world's major concert halls: maybe she's right.

Also in 1994, I produced a Christmas CD in London with the British entertainer Engelbert Humperdinck. We were sitting in Olympic Studios waiting for him, but he didn't turn up. Not at ten o'clock, not at eleven and not at twelve noon. Suddenly, at three in the afternoon, there was a collective yell from the engineers: 'He's here!'

A gold Rolls-Royce came around the corner, Engelbert got out and, with a very hoarse voice, said, 'Really sorry, folks. I had to sing in Dubai for two weeks, and my voice has totally gone. We can't do this today.'

Fair enough; we just postponed the recording.

'But listen,' he continued, 'I've heard that Ron's an excellent golfer. As I'm here, maybe he could show me how to draw or fade a golf ball?' So he had his clubs brought from the gold Rolls, and there he was – in this magnificent recording room – with his golfing gear, and this was where my son explained to him how to play a hook and a fade.

A week later, after the songs had been recorded and we'd returned to America, Ron and I were watching the news on the sports channel ESPN. Among the reports was one about a golf tournament involving professionals and famous stars. The winning pair had gone round the course in 69, the second-placed in 71, and finally the commentator said, 'There's no way we're going to forget Engelbert Humperdinck, who took 123 shots to play his round! He should have stayed at home!'

Engelbert was the second big-voiced singer with whom we'd produced an album. Five years earlier I had recorded a CD with the tenor René Kollo, featuring interpretations of classics. René, who always wears a white scarf as befits a famous tenor, is a very pleasant colleague. Perhaps he is a little too cautious, however, in not wanting to hurt anyone's feelings.

Not long before East Germany collapsed in 1989, we gave a joint concert at the Semper Opera House in Dresden. When we arrived there, the house choir was rehearsing *Nabucco*, an opera about the liberation of a people. Visually, the stage set bore an astounding resemblance to the Berlin Wall. This had a clear implication: if the state Opera House was allowed to make such allusions, the regime would probably be unable to survive much longer.

Since we also had 'Flieg, Gedanke', the prisoners' choir from *Nabucco*, on the CD with Kollo, it seemed obvious we should play this piece in the evening, preferably with the Opera House Choir. I invited them to perform with us, but their official escorts were on hand straight away, forbidding them to have any contact with us. René Kollo was holier than the Pope: he refused to sing the song because he didn't want to do anything inflammatory. That evening, after the joint section with Kollo, we returned to our normal tour programme for an hour. At the end of the concert I announced where we would be playing next, and somebody in the audience called out, 'It's easy for you to go there, but we can only go via Hungary!' That was pretty courageous, despite the radical changes that were just around the corner.

The atmosphere during this performance was markedly

different from that which prevailed the first time we were guests in the GDR. After several attempts and prolonged negotiations, it finally happened in 1987: we were able to go on a five-day concert tour of East Germany. At that time, Honecker's SED (Socialist Unity Party) still had the country firmly under its control, and wherever we went we were left in no doubt about who the masters were in this state. If someone wanted to make a phone call in the hotel, it was always 'Not possible!' Twelve hours later, at three in the morning, the phone in the room would ring: 'But you wanted a connection to Hamburg...' It was pure chicanery.

Our concerts in East Berlin, on the other hand, were a wonderful experience and the audiences reacted fantastically. It seemed to me that the people were glad to experience a small piece of Western normality.

We did three evenings in East Berlin's Palace of the Republic, and all three concerts were recorded as co-productions by GDR television and edited in Otto Waalkes's mobile recording studio as soon as the last one was finished. The CD was released only a few days later; it was to be one of our best live recordings. To this day I feel a very special warmth from the audiences at our concerts in the former East German states.

At around this time, the late 1980s, I recorded an album with the Dutch flautist Berdien Stenberg. I had got to know Berdien three years previously, and even at that early juncture we toyed with the idea of cooperating on an album with a semi-classical repertoire. Eventually, under the title *Flute Fiesta*, it turned out to be a very cheerful, romantic LP with a Mediterranean touch – and a horribly kitschy cover on which I gaze lovingly at Berdien, surrounded by palm branches.

Berdien also accompanied us on our five-week European tour in 1988. During this tour she had to make an awful lot of phone calls, but not to her husband or a friend: no, at the other end of the line was her dog.

When Berdien minced around the stage in her coquettish little dresses and suits she always seemed a little affected, like a living doll – something my musicians, with their ribald sense of humour, soon seized on. I had to act as a brake on the band throughout the tour, but on the last evening nothing was going to stop them: as Berdien was stalking around the stage in her light-blue frilly dress, the musicians stalked behind her, imitating her. I'm not sure if Berdien really found that amusing, but she had the right response ready prepared: after the concert she gave everyone involved with the tour a little decorative flute as a memento.

Our collaboration with the French pianist Richard Clayderman stretched over several albums. Monsieur Philippe Pagès had been accompanying a number of French chanson stars such as Michel Sardou and Johnny Hallyday before he was discovered by Olivier Toussaint and Paul de Senneville. This composing and producing duo had already had a huge hit with 'Dolannes Melodie', and in the mid-1970s they were looking for a suitable interpreter for a nice little piano melody. The friendly Pagès seemed to be the right man; his name was changed to Richard Clayderman, and the tune – 'Ballade pour Adeline' – was a massive international hit.

Richard and I met for the first time in 1981 when he was a guest on *Showexpress*, which had taken over from *Starparade* the previous year. We couldn't record together then because Richard was under contract to the 'wrong' company, but, after his switch to Polydor's subsidiary Decca, Polydor's managing director Götz Kiso suggested a joint project. The idea was that 'Richard is successful in France, James Last in Britain, and if we team them up they can strengthen each other.'

So I sat down in Florida and composed, Olivier Toussaint and

Paul de Senneville did the same in Paris, and the resulting 12 numbers were released on the album *Dream Melodies*. It sold excellently, so we followed it up with *Serenades* a year later. The latter even included a very old song of mine, 'Maracaibo', which I had composed for Harry Hermann in the 1950s. *Serenades* did even better, especially in Britain, so we released a third album, *In Harmony*, in 1994.

The procedure was the same every time: we recorded the backing tracks in Hamburg, then Richard added his piano part in Olivier Toussaint's studio in Paris. So we didn't actually meet at all, and didn't even appear together until various TV programmes and a TV commercial were recorded. On that occasion we were working in London's legendary RAK Studios, with huge, hanging spotlights completely obscuring the ceiling. Richard was practising an excerpt from a piano concert when one of these spotlights came loose at the other end of the room. It was still hanging from a cable and it swung like a pendulum straight towards Richard's head. There was a great shriek from everyone in the room, but Richard just bent forward slightly and the spotlight missed him by perhaps 20 centimetres. Even more amazing was that he didn't even play a false note. He is exactly the way he plays – calm, elegant and friendly – but many people underestimate him. As a pianist he is capable of far more than he is usually allowed to show.

Sadly, one of my favourite ideas has never come to anything: I would have liked to make a record with Barbra Streisand and Gidon Kremer. That would have been a synthesis of three wonderfully compatible worlds: Barbra's marvellous voice, Kremer's solo violin and our string sound. Polydor's people, however, thought that something like that would never happen.

In Front of the Camera

Television has always played a very important role in my work. At the start of my career it was, first and foremost, the legendary *Starparade* music show that became an important platform for my orchestra. We appeared on the programme for the first time on 9 March 1968. Charly Cisek had cut brand-new made-to-measure suits for the band and dressed me elegantly in black. Thus attired, I launched my television career by snapping my fingers to the pop song 'Judy in Disguise'.

It was always very important to me that we played the songs on *Starparade* live whenever possible. Although that was more expensive than using a taped recording, I was – and remain – convinced that the audience notice the difference. Most of the singing stars, however, just mimed to a tape, so when there was 'singing' we could take a break. To prevent the TV audience noticing this, the taped playback performances always took place in a different corner of the hall. Occasionally, however, my musicians couldn't resist joining in. Only the studio audience saw and heard this, of course; all the viewers at home got to hear was the playback.

Sometimes the band gave a wonderful impromptu performance to accompany a song, while on other occasions they just fooled around. On one occasion, Mireille Mathieu, the little Frenchwoman with the powerful voice, sang 'New York, New York' and the band overdid the whole thing, miming comically. Derek Watkins grabbed a saxophone and pretended to play it, really hamming it up. Then the musicians all swapped instruments. The studio audience were transfixed by all these shenanigans and enjoyed it hugely. The show's editor, however, was completely humourless: from the next programme onwards a wall was put up in front of us when we had a break.

starparade

Even so, we usually had a fair amount of fun on our many shows, even if the staff didn't always appreciate our sense of humour. When Caterina Valente performed the song 'Frutti di Mare', for example, she was given a basket of plastic fish to illustrate the song's title. Just before she was due to go on, we replaced them with real fish, well past their sell-by date. Now poor Caterina was standing on stage with these foul-smelling 'fruits of the sea', trying discreetly to hold the basket as far from herself as possible – although that didn't do her much good. To her great credit, she steadfastly completed the song without letting anything show.

The great thing about *Starparade* was its musical diversity. The spectrum ranged from T. Rex to the sentimental German pop of Rex Gildo, from ABBA to the heavy metal of Roy Black, so we were able to try out lots of different styles. Often I wrote special arrangements for the show that never appeared on any of our LP productions – slow preludes, changes of rhythm and short soli.

It was my opinion that you had to offer something special for such a great TV programme, partly to give the director scope for spectacular shots of my musicians, and partly to show the audience musical sides of ourselves that they might not know. After all, on *Starparade* we were playing in front of our biggest audience. There were no commercial TV channels in those days, so an average of 15 million people gathered in front of their TV sets to watch the programme. Ratings like that can only be achieved in Germany today if the national football team reaches the World Cup final – and perhaps not even then.

Time after time, however, my efforts to give German television audiences really special arrangements were thwarted by the constraints of television. The producer used to go around the studio with a stopwatch around his neck, insisting that this or that song could last only 3 minutes 25 seconds, as this was all the time we had. The number's original version may well have been, say, 4 minutes 55 seconds long, which meant I often had to sit down at night, rather annoyed, to write a new arrangement.

Incidentally, in 2004 a compendium of our appearances on *Starparade* was released in a number of German-speaking countries. I was called *Die James-Last-Show,* although I only found out about it accidentally, and the four DVDs contained our appearances from 1968 to 1980. For our Charly Cisek it is a great showcase for his tailoring business; for me, on the other hand, it is a condensed documentary of my band's ever-changing styles.

Starparade was discontinued in 1980, and in the autumn of that year we began with the successor programme, *Showexpress,* presented by Michael Schanze. This programme was not quite so successful, however, and it was dropped in 1982. The opportunity to play regularly in front of such a big TV audience was a very important factor in our success, so I very much regretted the loss of this platform – especially when I see what's par for the course these days.

Previously, the TV channel paid you for making an appearance; now you have to stump up money for the privilege because 'It's advertising for you!' This only pays off, though, if a singer appears alone and mimes over a playback: with one person the costs can be kept down. If a 40-piece orchestra has to come into a TV studio, it becomes impossible: each musician has to be paid, whether they play a note or just pretend to. In any case only rarely would we be allowed to play live, as the technical efforts required are generally now too costly for TV companies. For this reason, most music on TV these days involves silly pseudo-performances, with five musicians doing a bit of posing with their instruments and that's it.

I'm not surprised when viewers are disappointed by 'shows' like that, particularly since we could do it a lot better. In the autumn of 2004, just before our tour, we performed for a whole week on Stefan Raab's show *TV Total*. There, for the first time in many years, we actually played live in a television studio.

The *James Last Specials*, which concentrated on our LP productions, were something else entirely, and there were some highly successful shows that were also very popular with television viewers: *Viva España*, *James Last spielt Bach*, *In Scotland* and – recently – *Mein Miami*. The filming usually lasted several days, and the individual scenes were split up into many short takes and recorded in turn, as with a feature film. One of the most successful of these programmes in Germany was *James Last im Allgäu*. We played a variety of German folk songs and I brought in a few specialists for the 'Allgäuer G'stanzln' and 'G'strampften', including the zither player Alfons Bauer and Friedrich Finkel with his accordion. They were joined by special guest singers Vicky Leandros and Karel Gott; Ronnie had written two very nice songs for them.

On one of the filming days, the plan included close-ups of the individual musicians. We were shooting high up on an alpine pasture and it was a terribly cold morning, so I organised a big barrel of mulled wine to raise the temperature and our spirits a little. Without anyone noticing, though, our Swedish trumpeter Hakan Nyquist had enhanced the mulled wine by pouring a whole bottle of cognac into it. It was nine in the morning, and since we were all freezing we had a hearty drink or two. Our mood improved noticeably as the director worked his way through the close-ups, until finally it was drummer Terry Jenkins's turn. Takes like this were filmed using a playback: Terry had his own recording played back to him and then he faked it along to the music. Now the sound man was obviously feeling the benefits of the cognac, because he deliberately made the playback run faster, then slower, and so on. Terry had terrible problems keeping up with the ever-changing tempo, and, while he groaned and wheezed trying to find the right rhythm, the rest of us were bent double laughing. What a pity that wasn't filmed!

I often invited our British fan club to film projects such as this. Our British friends can always be relied upon to generate a real party mood, and their good cheer is reflected on the TV screen and spreads to the viewers at home. The 'Brits' often combine this kind of opportunity with a few days' relaxation 'on the continent' and a group of them had come to see us in Allgäu, too. They clearly enjoyed the trip, for just a few weeks later I got a lot of pleasure from reading the report by their 'chief' Peter Boosey in the club magazine:

> *"James Last in Allgäu" was the motto of a five-day mini-holiday for 103 of our members, who will probably never forget this trip. ... Hansi welcomed us when we arrived in Kempten, and he suggested that we come to his hotel after the concert. ... On Friday evening the concert began at around eight o'clock, 65 minutes were recorded, and then, after a short break, Hansi upped the ante and played the highlights from his last European tour. This continued until after eleven, and then we drove to the Allgäuer Berghof, where Hansi greeted every one of us and thanked us for coming. The orchestra, the choir, a few friends, and us – he invited all of us, about 180 people. We ate and drank for two and a half hours before returning to Kempten at three in the morning.*

The most accurate impression that TV audiences can get of my music and me is through edited versions of our concerts. The benefit concert in front of Schöneberg town hall in Berlin in 1974, the show at the Royal Albert Hall in 1978, the concert at Berlin's Waldbühne in 1982 (where we appeared with Freddy again for the first time in many years), my 60th birthday concert in front of Bremen city hall, the broadcast from St Patrick's Cathedral in Dublin and many other performances all over the world – these show the undiluted James Last, performing the way I like it best.

We have also done several concerts – conceived especially for television – to tie in with a new record. Examples of this are The Rose of Tralee in Ireland or a Beatles concert in Liverpool. These performances were particularly demanding for my musicians, because in addition to songs from the new LP I also wanted to offer the live audience our usual concert programme. It was by no means rare for one of these concerts to last for about four hours. If there had already been a TV rehearsal that morning, my musicians would be reaching the limit of their capacities; for the wind players in particular, a marathon like that is an enormous strain.

The concerts in Zwickau and Bayreuth that we recorded for American television in 2000 and 2002 went particularly well. The direction, art work and sound recording at both concerts was virtually perfect. But they were also hard work and very expensive: eight articulated trucks were needed to cart the stage, lights and sound equipment to the venues, while 40 engineers, 30 television staff and 30 assistants were required for the work in Bayreuth's Oberfrankenhalle. Recording began without an audience at nine in the morning; then the close-ups were recorded for integration into the video later Shooting continued until five in the afternoon, then the concert proper followed in the evening, with the cameras recording our show in a packed hall – on two consecutive days. And, after 12 hours, you still have to lift people's spirits and look good.

Behind the Camera

I got to know cinema and television from a different angle – behind the camera – through my work as a composer.

My first experience of working on film music came in the late 1960s. Theo Hinz, who later achieved fame as a producer with the film-makers' cooperative Filmverlag der Autoren, was chief press officer with Constantin-Film at that time. He had the idea of asking me to compose the music for a film based on Eric Malpass's witty family novels, and in 1968 *Morgens um Sieben ist die Welt noch in Ordnung* (Morning's at Seven) hit the cinemas of Germany. The story of rascally little Gaylord and the Pentecost family attracted a total audience of more than three million, for which it received a Golden Ticket. Since it was so popular, a sequel was produced the following year: *Wenn süß das Mondlicht auf den Hügeln schläft* (At the Height of the Moon).

I tried to contrast the boisterous action of the film with rich tone colours. Together with the sound engineer Peter Klemt, I tried out a few distancing effects, and the mood of the ten pieces of music ranged from cheerful to melancholy. We play the two title melodies in our concerts to this day: when the trumpets from the main theme from *Morgens um sieben* ... enter and the flutes add their distinctive ornaments, audiences are as enthusiastic as ever. The films were forgotten long ago, but the melodies live on. That makes me proud.

In the 1980s I wrote the music for a number of some very popular German TV series, such as *Zwei Münchner in Hamburg*, with Uschi Glas and Elmar Wepper, *Grenzenloses Himmelblau*, a TV film with Inge Meysel, and *Der Landarzt* – where the harmonica theme in the title melody is played by the great Toots Thielemans. The most popular series, though, was *Das Traumschiff* (The Love Boat) with its many exotic backdrops from Brazil to Bali, and these gave me the opportunity to let off steam musically in every direction.

The stimulating part lies in composing precisely to fit a set length: feelings and moods have to be expressed or effects created with very few bars, sometimes even a single chord. This kind of work is very much suited to my natural instincts for music – in my thoughts, everything is immediately linked with music, whether I am seeing an extraordinary landscape or a remarkable face, or ruminating over a special memory.

I would have loved to compose for Rainer Werner Fassbinder. That would have been a most fascinating task, as some idea or other occurs to me immediately for all of his films. Such a cooperation, however, never took place.

With most of the TV series, I did not write the music until the episode had been filmed and edited. With *Lorentz & Söhne*, however, I was integrated into the preparations as early as the script stage. This meant that I was able to allocate each important character his or her own musical theme, thereby creating a more coherent atmosphere. We were also allowed unlimited resources in terms of musicians, with tubas, clarinets, oboes and a contrabassoon at our disposal. The result was a full, highly luxurious, almost classical orchestra sound.

Lorentz & Söhne was all about a wine-growing family from Baden and their intrigues, passions and tragedies. In a variety of ways, my private life in the 1980s would have fitted in quite well with the sometimes tragic, sometimes absurd stories – except that I never became a wine grower...

part eight:
Rollercoaster Rides

Christine

We all know what it's like: there are times in one's life when everything happens at once. Quite unexpectedly fate will dish up a wild series of ups and downs and we find ourselves on a crazy rollercoaster ride of events and emotions. This is what happened to me in the first half of the 1980s.

It was inevitable that during my tours I would occasionally get to know attractive women. Waltraud must have guessed this and of course did not exactly approve, but she also didn't really want to know about it. This was very generous of her; I don't think I would have been as magnanimous if it had been the other way round. But she was basically right; these tour romances were nothing more than an itch, a flirtation, where I was playing with fire on a low flame. I have to feel something for the person I go to bed with. Sex without emotion is a merely mechanical and ultimately uninteresting exercise.

Only once did Waltraud do anything decisive – no doubt she sensed that this time the affair really was serious. We were playing one of our sing-along carnival parties in Munich. After the concert, when I was standing in my dressing room soaked in sweat, Conny Güntensperger brought along a young blonde woman he'd picked up behind the stage and simply said, 'Look who we have here, this is Christine from Munich.'

This Christine had been going round dressed as a lady-in-waiting with a group of girlfriends from a Munich carnival society. She was definitely pretty, but this did not arouse me at all at that point; after all, girls often came backstage. Without thinking I invited her to the after-show party: 'We're going to the Hilton afterwards. Do you feel like coming along?'

At the party our conversation became very intense and that's when we suddenly clicked.

Next morning Christine called me. 'Did you sleep well?'

'Very well. Shall we have lunch together?'

But I first had to go to an interview at the Bavarian Broadcasting Commission, and she agreed to pick me up there. She drove up in her car, a rusty wreck full of holes, but she'd stuck flowers in all the holes. What an idea! I was enraptured; after all, I'm a true romantic! During our lunch I already realised that I felt very close to this young woman: with her everything was so completely different.

From Munich we went on to Nuremburg and our next concert. Bob Lanese had invited some friends from Munich to go to this concert, so I asked Christine if she'd like to follow later together with Bob's friends. She said yes, and so began a three-year love affair that ran the whole gamut from wonderful shared times to telling lies to my wife.

rollercoaster rides

When everyone knows who you are, this kind of thing can quickly go wrong. I once flew from Hamburg to Munich for the night to see Christine. When I came home the next day I told my wife I'd been drinking all night with colleagues after filming a TV appearance. Waltraud simply held up the morning newspaper. A reporter from the *Hamburger Morgenpost* had seen me at the airport and next day my picture was in the paper with the caption: 'JAMES LAST ON HIS WAY TO MUNICH'. This was the first and last time in our marriage that Waltraud was annoyed: 'What do you find so fascinating about this woman? Is it her youth? Or sex?'

I was 53 and Christine 24 when we first met. My wife and I had been married for over 25 years by then and sex had not played a role in our lives for a long time. Yet over the years our marriage had also developed into a fantastic, supportive partnership. Need I say more?

Our children Ronnie and Rina, both pretty much the same age as Christine, reacted very differently to their father's affair. My son and Waltraud were very close and, because he sensed how terribly hurt she was, he was very angry with me. With my daughter it was different. She understood me, we talked about it, and I said, 'Look how amazing it is when an old tree blossoms again.'

Waltraud knew she didn't want to lose me – and I realised that Christine and I could never be happy if my family suffered. So I had to make a choice.

I drove up to Sweden with Christine for four days to play golf. In the car on the way home I explained to her, and probably also to myself, that things couldn't go on like this. I heard Christine swallow. We talked a long time, and finally Christine accepted the end of our relationship – for all time, as we thought. The LP *Erinnerungen* (Memories) resulted from our time together. I wrote the song 'Unvergessen' (Unforgotten) for Christine; it was my gift to her.

But the affair with this young woman was just one side of the coin, the exciting and – in spite of all the problems – the good side. It was the upward ride of the rollercoaster, and the down side came all too soon.

At the same time as I got to know Christine, around 1982, she noticed that there was something wrong with the skin on my back and urged me to consult a doctor. The diagnosis of Professor Nasemann was shattering: 'Mr Last, you have skin cancer.'

'Is that really necessary?' Back then I was still in my prime, so I pretended to take the diagnosis with a pinch of humour. But in reality I felt quite panicky on hearing what sounded like a death sentence. Like any other person, I too asked, Why me!? At the time I didn't know how many people in the world suffer from cancer.

Of course, I had to have an operation as quickly as possible. The date was fixed, the necessary preparations made – and, when the time came, I was sent home without anything being done. The night before, I had drunk heavily to give myself Dutch courage – so heavily they couldn't give me the anaesthetic because I had too much alcohol in my blood. The operation was carried out at the second attempt, with seven areas of skin being removed. After the operation the doctor asked me if I had strong nerves.

'Sure,' I replied. 'Why?'

'Take a look at this thing!'

He showed me what had been cut out of my body; one growth was as big as a tomato! I had been incredibly lucky.

Later, however, I also had melanomas – on my nose and behind my ear – which were malignant and very dangerous, but these too were recognised in time and removed. In all, I have had to undergo dozens of operations where bits have been cut away – and inevitably you always look a little strange after these operations. You might have a black eye or big bandages, but with a bit of humour you get over these things. If I turned up in the studio with my head in bandages and there were people there who didn't know what was wrong with me, I'd just say, 'Hell, I really had a rough time down in the red-light district last night...'

Really terrible, on the other hand, were the ridiculous headlines in the press, when you learn of your imminent demise from the papers. Heading the tabloids was of course the *Bild* newspaper. The reporters pestered me for days outside my home, which was worse than the illness itself.

As if that wasn't enough, two deaths in the family occurred about the same time. In July 1982 my brother Werner died at the age of 59 and three years later my brother Robert died of a heart attack. This made me the last remaining member of that mad group of musicians from 33 Helmholtzstrasse in Sebaldsbrück.

Father and Son

Although my son Ronnie was becoming more and more closely involved in my work, he too provided me with a number of rollercoaster rides. As our spring tour of Great Britain in 1983 came closer, I wanted to persuade him and his friend Tommy Eggert to come with us. I always enjoy the company of young people, but I also wanted them to become familiar with concert life on tour as well as giving them a chance to earn some money. I knew that Ron didn't much like the stress a tour caused, so I had to resort to a trick to motivate him.

'Listen, I don't know how long we'll still be able to do these big tours,' I told him. 'Who knows, maybe this will be my last concert tour of England. It might even be the very last tour I'll ever go on – but it's such a fantastic feeling. It's something you've got to experience, so won't you come with us?'

Ronnie and Tommy talked it over, then they both agreed to come. I rearranged a few songs so that two synthesisers could have important backing roles, we prepared all the sounds in Hamburg, and after three weeks we were ready to leave. We flew to Dublin for our first concert, which was a great success. We played to 5,000 people in a huge cattle-auction hall made of timber, with a brightly decorated stage. The fun-fair atmosphere was simply fantastic! About two-thirds of the way through the concert we had to stop because the stage was full of fans. They kissed and hugged us, danced and thanked us for the music – it was unbelievable!

Ronnie and Tommy were overwhelmed. They had never experienced anything like it. They both did their work extremely well and I was truly happy. It was easy to imagine things would continue this way and that in future I would go on tour regularly with my son – and who knows what might come later? Perhaps Ron would one day follow in my footsteps... perhaps.

When the tour was over I asked the two young men if they would come on tour again next time. Tommy immediately said yes – he'd tasted blood. But Ron refused. He said it was difficult enough to measure up as the son of such a father in the same business and to be taken seriously, without having to stand beside me on the same stage as well.

No doubt he was right, but at that moment – after our successful concerts and my dreams of the future together – I felt he had let me down. That was probably also the reason why my reaction was so harsh: I accused him of being lazy, of not being interested in my work. One thing led to another and the altercation ended up being a full-blown quarrel. Looking back, I'd say that for him it was the classic situation of cutting loose and emancipating himself from his 'old man'. This is a problem many parents have to deal with, but, when the father casts a particularly long shadow, then the son's reaction is bound to be particularly strong. Maybe Ron's negative attitude to me was also influenced by my relationship with Christine.

Be that as it may, after that I was busy for some time in Germany and when I returned to Florida a big surprise awaited me. During my absence Ron had got married, without having breathed a single word of it to me. Apparently, someone had advised him to get married immediately. After the two had apparently not been able to get hold of me, they decided on having the wedding without family or friends. Whatever the reason, Ron presented me with my new daughter-in-law, Cheryl. I was really annoyed this time. It took me a long time to get over what he'd done. If it was Ron's intention to hurt me, he had certainly succeeded.

After this business we didn't talk to each other for some time. Of course, I was unhappy about the way things had turned out – any father in my position would have been. However, I'd always believed that my children should be allowed to make their own decisions, and even now I had no intention of forcing my son to do anything he didn't want to. Deep down, I also knew that this rift would not last forever. Nevertheless, a little nudge from outside was needed for us to make it up again.

In the end, we only got together again when I suggested we form a business partnership with Polydor. I wanted him to take over most of the organisation, to coordinate the recordings and to look after the whole of the production side of things. Ron agreed to do it. I realise that it was only possible for him to take this step because he had consciously decided to put his own artistic ambitions on ice. He signed a contract with the company and took on the task with great enthusiasm. We have been making music together ever since. Apart from being great fun, it gives us the opportunity to get to know each other in a very interesting and intensive new way.

When computers entered the studios and drastically changed the work of the sound engineers, Ronnie gradually took over the work of Peter Klemt, who found it difficult to accept the new technology. It's been quite a while since we gave up working with 16 and 24 tracks: now we use Pro-Tools, which has 96 channels. The TV show *A World of Music* was recorded entirely at this desk. Every instrument has its own track and can therefore be listened to individually – every violin, every trumpet, the whole lot. That's the moment of truth for every musician: it isn't possible to hush up anything during a concert and no one can hide behind a fellow musician any more.

Since the mid-1990s, Ron has been at the mixing desk for all our productions. Two years ago, using the pseudonym By 4, he produced an album called *Elements*. It includes a few of my old songs, which he sampled and remixed with new sounds. *Elements* has turned out to be a good CD production, and his second wife, Silke, designed a fantastic cover for it.

I didn't interfere in his work in any way. I neither criticised anything nor did I try to give him any advice – the album was completely his baby.

Going Bust

Regardless of all my private ups and downs, if all my business affairs had been well ordered, I would be rolling in money today. Oil wells in my name would be bubbling out barrels of oil, there'd be a Pinot Noir pressed in my own vineyards, and whenever I had a little pain I could be cured in a hospital that I had helped finance myself. Unfortunately, this was not the case.

It took me a while before I realised this, but eventually it became clear to me that as a businessman I was a dead loss! I had never had a manager in the real sense of the word. It was only a few years ago that my friend Dr Bodo Eckmann – a Hamburg doctor and president of the German Boxing Association – took over this post. When you suddenly earn a lot of money in a very short space of time – as was the case with me – it doesn't take long for all sorts of people to try to give various forms of advice.

One of these was a tax consultant in Germany. When the concerts became more and more successful and the royalties were really rolling in, he recommended various companies in which I should invest my money so as to avoid paying excessive taxes. For example, he told me to invest in clinics and rehabilitation centres. As I couldn't possibly spend all the money I had earned, I allowed myself to be persuaded by all the talk about 'safe deals' and 'fantastic investment opportunities' and did as I was advised. No doubt this advice was well intentioned and given in good faith.

Everything seemed to be going well, because after a while he said the time was now ripe to invest on a larger scale: Germany was no longer suitable and we should enter the US market. He recommended an American financier who suggested the most incredible deals. On his advice I bought oil wells in Wyoming, vineyards in California and cotton fields in South Carolina. All, of course, easy on the taxes. So he said.

In fact, it was all an enormous bubble and in 1985 it burst. One day I decided to take a look at my fabulous Californian vineyards and experience the pride of ownership, but not a single vine could I find on my property, not even an empty wine bottle.

Worse still, the name of a completely different owner had been entered in the land register.

All the other projects turned out to be castles in the air, too. This meant that virtually all the money I had ever made had gone west.

What's more, the FBI suddenly paid us a visit, asking me all about my relations with my so-called consultants. As if this weren't enough, I suddenly had huge tax debts, because, as none of the investments had been real, tax deductions had not been possible either. My losses were therefore double: I had been strung along for 15 years and now I also had to pay millions of marks to the state. But where was I to get all this money? I was bankrupt, plain and simple!

The feeling that overwhelmed me at this debacle reminded me of an experience I'd had when I was a young pup of 18 or 19. At that time, at the end of the 1940s, I had been sometimes responsible for arranging our appearances at the Yankee clubs. This work provided me with a couple of hundred marks. The person who completely ruined my pleasure at having earned my first money was a certain minor public servant at the Bremen tax office. He repeatedly summoned me to his office and, using all the power of his position, made me stand in front of his desk while he proceeded to tear strips off me. I was just a young fellow and, although I hadn't done anything wrong, he treated me as if I was the most despicable tax evader of the district. He simply wanted to exercise his power, although like a good boy I had paid my few marks in tax. I was at the mercy of the apparently mega-powerful Mr Redanz and, trembling with rage and helplessness, I felt I had been treated badly and humiliated. That's exactly how I felt four decades later when it became clear that I was bankrupt.

For a while I seriously considered selling my shares in the record company to pay off at least part of my huge debt.

Fortunately, my children prevented me from doing such a stupid thing – we would manage somehow. I took out an enormous loan from the Hamburger Sparkasse bank, and over a period of more than 15 years I succeeded, year by year, in paying back a total of one million marks – a very considerable sum of money. Shortly before my 70th birthday I had done it – the loan was paid off, the deficit gone and I could begin again at zero.

To make the new start a little more pleasant for myself, I applied for a new loan of one million marks. The icy response was, 'Sorry, Mr Last, but you're too old for a loan as high as that.'

Of course, the loss of my assets was a depressing business. However, I only had myself to blame. When such large sums of money are involved, it is nothing other than unforgivably stupid to trust one or two people as unconditionally as I had. While I am convinced – now as then – that with my German tax consultant it was essentially carelessness and lack of experience that cost me my money, in the case of the American finance consultant it was clearly a case of fraud. However, no court in the world will ever be able to prove this: the man died shortly after the matter became known.

Since this whole business was not generally public knowledge, another series of clever advisers lined up after the reunification of Germany, all wanting to convince me to invest in East German projects. But by that time I was, thank God, a bit smarter. In spite of these setbacks, my life has always been pleasant from a financial point of view. Regardless of occasional losses, or when something had not been billed correctly, or when taxes were due, my family and I were able to live comfortably. The mentality of wanting 'bigger, better, harder and faster' things never suited my character.

My music allowed me to earn a lot of money, but I also spent a lot of it. Maintaining such a big orchestra is expensive. It's my most luxurious madness, my most expensive hobby – but it's also my biggest and greatest pleasure.

Just think what it costs when a troupe like this flies to Asia. No promoter could afford to pay so much, so I always ended up paying extra out of my own pocket. That is why I never really made any profit on these tours in the early days, not even at the height of our popularity.

But all the musicians travelled like kings. They were and still are like my second family, so it was only natural for me to always pay for everything. The money was there, and the main thing was to have fun. For example, on one of our last tours, when I was in our hotel in Düsseldorf after the concert, I felt a great urge to drink some really fine red wine, so I ordered a bottle of the best. One of our violin players happened to pass my table and said, 'Hey, can I have some wine too?'

'Sure. Waiter! Another bottle, please.'

Then the next table asked, 'Could we have a bottle, too?'

After having brought five bottles, the waiter got worried: 'Mr Last, do you know the price of these bottles?'

'No idea.'

'Two hundred euros!'

Well, I just laughed, because there was no point in being annoyed.

Things like that over the years have cost me many millions of marks and euros. But, if I think *I* can afford something, why shouldn't the others have their share? I'd hate to sit all by myself in a corner, taking the occasional sip, because then even the most marvellous wine wouldn't taste any good! That's what I'm like, and I have never changed in this, not even when I was paying off my huge debts. I've always said that, when I can no longer lead my life with my orchestra in a way that is enjoyable, I'll have to stop. Then I'll sit down at home and write.

I used to donate quite a lot of money to charity – 100,000

marks here, the net profits from record sales there. But only seldom did I get any reaction. For example, at Easter 1974 we played a benefit concert in front of the Schöneberg town hall in Berlin, in front of 65,000 people. The musicians played without getting a fee and every penny from the proceeds of TV and record sales were donated to charities. But the only acknowledgement I ever received was an official letter stating, '…the event has been concluded; therefore no further claims can be submitted.'

That's why today I much prefer to give something to beggars in the streets because then I know where the money has gone. Just recently I saw a girl at Hamburg's Dammtor station sitting on the ground and holding a sign: I'VE GOT AIDS. I walked past her and drove home. But I couldn't forget her. When I see someone sitting there looking so miserable, I can't be cheerful. I couldn't enjoy my dinner, so I got in the car again, drove back and gave her some euros.

In my opinion, we can't always just look away. I think these small gestures often contribute more to the way we live together than big promises and empty speeches.

What I absolutely can't stand are politicians who just jump on a bandwagon. We were having a meal in Isernhagen near Hanover when a group of children stormed into the restaurant; they had seen me and wanted my autograph. The women in charge of them also came in and apologised profusely, but I didn't mind at all. 'It doesn't matter in the least,' I said. 'Let me get everyone a Coke.'

One perky little girl said, 'We're from the orphanage just across the way. Would you like to come over and have a look?'

'Right you are. I will.' The whole band marched over with the kids. We saw the way these children had to live: damp walls, old furniture and lumpy beds.

In the day room stood a television set and the girl said,

'Unfortunately, we can't watch *Starparade* because the TV is broken.'

That was enough for me. I took our tour manager Conny aside. 'Can you spare some time? Then come with me.' We drove 20 kilometres to Hanover where I bought a brand-new television, a video recorder and some records and took the lot back to the orphanage. The children were thrilled. Then the woman in charge approached me saying, 'I've organised something. Can you wait a moment?'

After a few minutes the mayor of Isernhagen and the *Bild* newspaper appeared. At that I really let loose. One of the officials in particular caught the brunt of my anger: 'How dare you turn up here just at this moment! Why haven't you bothered to visit this place before? Then you would have seen the conditions these children have to live under!' The *Bild* reporter also got what was coming to him: 'If a single word about this appears in the paper, I'll take everything away again and it will be your fault. You are not to take a single photo or write a single word about this.' This happened a long time ago: today the children from the home have children of their own, and many of them still attend our concerts with their families.

While I certainly am a politically minded person, I have never allowed anyone to use me for their ends. Nowadays, however, we should all think more than ever about the direction in which our society is going. It really makes me very sad that it is becoming more and more brutalised and is in danger of losing its ethical basis. You find this on all social levels – whether it's violent videos on mobile phones, politicians who try to exploit their positions economically or in some other way, or businesses that announce profits of millions of euros and then – almost simultaneously – say they are cutting thousands of jobs.

As far as I'm concerned, we're all in the same boat and

therefore ought to make sure it doesn't sink, rather than trying to poke holes in the hull. And we're all equally responsible. But I also think that the politicians should set an example. When I was younger I never expressed my views on these matters. I never spoke much on stage anyway. Nowadays, though, I do feel the need to comment on these things during my concerts, to counteract in some way the negative mood that has been spreading during the past few years.

In 2004 we had a very free interpretation of Haydn's *The Emperor Quartet* in the programme. In the second movement the melody of the German national anthem is played. I called my arrangement 'Germany is beautiful' because that's exactly how I see the country – with a sense of pride and several years of experience behind me. Even if it is 'only' music, it has perhaps helped to give some people the courage to speak of Germany once again with admiration.

Some Kind of Dinosaur

From the mid-1980s onwards, it became very noticeable what happens when the people in a company no longer have the same goals. Heinz Voigt had left Polydor years earlier, and then Ossi Drechsler and Werner Klose left too, so our successful quartet was reduced to a solo performance. The new bosses were not particularly interested in promoting the James Last product on the same scale as their predecessors. It was obvious I wasn't someone with whom you could create a striking new image – I was almost part of the furniture. The company had gone through countless bosses in the past 30 years so the only constant figure was this Last person. Admittedly, he had for a long time been one of the economic bases of the company but one with whom they didn't quite know what to do now. I guess I was something like a dying species, a dinosaur.

Incidents both big and small revealed that my albums were no longer considered as important as in the past. After the company moved, my office suddenly disappeared. Gold discs, which had previously been presented at official celebrations, now simply came by post. Suddenly there was a lot of back-stabbing, with comments like: 'Last just isn't what he used to be.' No wonder then that they also reduced my budget. As a result, we had to reduce the broad range of styles with which we had been able to reach different target groups, and naturally sales dropped.

Success is like an avalanche. It grows and develops a momentum of its own and mows down anything that gets in its way. It's the same the other way round; your success can disappear again just as quickly if it is not constantly nursed, groomed and cultivated. Not doing this will cause sales to drop *because* fewer albums are produced, but this doesn't really seem to interest anybody. And of course, once you have been enormously successful, being 'only' fairly successful is seen as being relatively unsuccessful.

At that time Polydor was uncertain which of the many different styles in which we had played should be considered our flagship. While the *Classics* had all sold over a million copies each, sales had taken place over a longer period of time. By comparison, every new *Non Stop Dancing* album had sold 250,000 records within two months. As soon as the company was no longer sure how to continue with this series and what marketing strategies to adopt, there was a marked decrease in sales in general. This was very disappointing: if I'd had my way we should have continued to produce *Non Stop Dancing* albums every year up to the present day.

The mid-1980s might have been the right time for me to switch to another record company. I certainly considered taking this step, although it would have been difficult to move on against Polydor's will, since the legal position regarding rights and contracts was not as clearly in favour of the artist as it is today. On the contrary, the company held most of the aces. Today the law is interpreted as follows: since the product is the intellectual property of the artist, he therefore owns it. Using this argument the back-catalogue – all previously issued recordings – at least could have been shut down. What happens when an artist is at odds with a record company can be seen in what happened to the Kelly Family. When the father of the Kelly clan moved to a different label, Polydor reacted by reissuing their back-catalogue, thus making it more difficult for new Kelly Family recordings for quite some time. Considering the enormous productivity I had developed between 1965 and 1985, it is easy to imagine what could have happened had I decided to change.

Even so, Polydor, in my opinion, didn't help the situation for me in the 1990s due to the huge number of reissues they brought out. When CDs began to appear on the scene, Polydor brought out a vast number of compilations from old recordings, making large profits by recycling these old tracks two or three times without spending much money or effort. So it's understandable that they didn't feel it necessary to bring out anything new. The track 'Biscaya' was, I think, included on about 50 different CDs. Even on my 75th birthday, when the album *James Last Gold* was brought out, this track was included.

In theory, the record company was supposed to get my OK before every reissue, but, as a result of the very large number of albums that were produced over the years, it's almost impossible to check everything. What's more, the fact that I didn't have a manager until a few years ago also made things difficult. The kind of job that Bodo Eckmann now does didn't exist then; a contract was extended with a handshake. It often happened that

Polydor's people simply turned up at the studio with a paper for me to sign when they needed my approval for a new compilation. Obviously, though it was done in good faith and well intentioned, when I'm in the studio my head is full of other things: 20 musicians might be sitting there waiting to play, with various technicians rushing around and me with a stack of sheet music in front of me that I'm about to record. Then three people rush in with some piece of bumph for me to sign. Nowadays, this would be unusual, but it was common practice in the industry for many years.

In addition, the people I had to deal with were constantly changing. Projects by the dozen were planned, developed and then rejected. A Gershwin CD was to be produced... or perhaps Beethoven actually... Tchaikovsky wouldn't be bad either... but it might also be good to do *Non Stop Dancing*... or maybe better a South American disc... But in the end none of these ideas would be realised, although they cost energy and nerves, and so a great deal of creativity ended up being wasted.

I was confronted with similar problems concerning our German tours. Although we gave occasional performances in Germany between 1987 and 1996, it wasn't possible to arrange a longer tour. Promoters were suddenly afraid of the risk involved in sending our expensive orchestra – expensive because of its size and presentation – on tour without a popular singer as an added attraction. They didn't think the takings would cover expenses if I toured on my own. But I was not willing to tour the country as a supporting band for some singer who was unlikely to be compatible with our sound anyway. This was the reason there was no James Last tour in Germany for ten years.

In Great Britain it was a totally different matter. We toured there almost every year during that period and were always very successful.

Computer Capers

In the 1960s and 1970s, whenever we were recording a new album, I'd arrive at the studio with a stack of sheet music. The musicians would have a look at the number and I only got to actually hear my arrangement when we had our first rehearsal. Gradually we went over to making so-called demos: I would design the arrangement on the computer and we'd produce a rhythm track that would serve as a reference track for the following recording. This track is then used when the band is actually recording the number. The advantage of this procedure is that later editing, such as the post-synchronisation of the strings, can be done more easily and precisely.

But nowadays it isn't quite so easy to find suitable premises in which our orchestra can record. Around 1990/91, Studio Hamburg in Rahlstedt, which had always served us well, was closed. The operation was no longer profitable and too much money would have been needed to invest in new technology, so they turned it into a TV studio. The SAT 1 football programme *Ran* (On the Ball) could be said to have been our successor.

However, the precise rhythm tracks with which we were now working caused a problem. When making the actual recording, the rhythm track from the computer had to be replaced by a real instrument. But Terry, our drummer, wasn't able to achieve the same precision. This wasn't a problem during our concerts, but in the studio everything had to be absolutely exact. So the drum track that Terry recorded had to be arduously edited and stretched, beat by beat, until the timing was completely precise. The only other alternative would have been to replace it. As this editing was very time-consuming, I tested several new drummers but I wasn't really satisfied with any of them. Ron took over percussion several times, but this wasn't a practical solution because of his ever-expanding responsibilities in the studio – he was more important to me as my sound director than as a drummer.

So sometimes we had to use beats from the computer. It was not the best solution, but it wasn't until 2002 that I was able to find a drummer who completely fulfilled my present-day expectations and needs, even when compared with the guys we worked with in Los Angeles. Stoppel Eggert is that man. He has the precision and at the same time a feeling for even the smallest nuances, and that's what I need.

The possibilities opened up by working with a computer fascinated me so much that I desperately wanted to learn to use this new technology myself. Tommy Eggert was to be my teacher. 'I want to be able to use the computers that we have in the studio at home as well,' I told him. 'You have to teach me!'

Tommy looked at me sceptically. I could tell what he was thinking by the look on his face: What's he on about? He can't learn all this new stuff at his age! He tried to talk me out of it, but he didn't know what I was like. We bought the best equipment you could get at that time and set up this magic new world in Florida. Tommy was convinced that within two weeks I would be totally fed up with all the digital stuff, but I was fascinated and really got into the new challenge. Every 15 minutes I'd dial Tommy's phone number: 'Listen, how do I save this sound?'

'You have to press such-and-such a key.'

'OK, thanks. Ciao!'

Next phone call: 'Hey, how can I call up this other program?'

That's how it went for weeks, or rather months, but I refused to be put off. Step by step I learned to use the technology. Just recently I installed a brand-new program that once again opens up a whole range of new perspectives. Once again I'll have to practise day and night until I have everything down pat.

rollercoaster rides

Just how vast the possibilities offered by this new technology are can be seen in two numbers from the album *Classics from Russia*. 'Lichtertanz' (The Bridal Dance) from Anton Rubinstein's opera *Feramors* and the first movement of Sergei Rachmaninoff's second piano concerto are both very demanding pieces for any pianist. I practised playing them myself, one part at a time, and then with the computer set each note exactly as I imagined it should sound. However, I was careful not to reveal the name of this 'secret' soloist in the CD booklet; otherwise somebody might have had the bright idea of wanting me to play it live to demonstrate my skills as a pianist. And so the piano virtuoso thought it better to remain anonymous...

Working with the computer has also changed my arrangements and the style of my music. The musicians in the studio have fewer liberties than before, but I get exactly what I have written down and the basic structure of a number is more stable. We don't sound as lax, since we now play with marked precision, and this makes the sound more aggressive, more modern. But this also had an effect on our live performances.

For the album *Viva España*, which we recorded in Barcelona in 1992 on the occasion of the Olympic Games, I was looking for a musician who could play the Spanish guitar. Eventually I came across Erlend Krauser in a Hamburg nightclub, and he seemed to be the right man for the job. I hired him for the production and then the whole band flew to Spain, where ZDF recorded a very extravagant special for *Viva España*. I was really impressed by the way Erlend played, both in the studio and for these TV recordings, so I asked him if he'd be interested in joining us on our upcoming tour of England. He accepted the offer and that was how I came to have one of my severest critics in the band. Immediately after our first concert, he complained,

'Hansi, what's going on? The band should be playing with much more precision!'

What did that mean? Weren't we in fact known to sound exactly the same live as on record? At first I refused to listen: 'What do you expect? This is live music. We're not machines, you know.'

But Erlend is a fanatic and he didn't let up. 'Hansi, I've programmed so many cool sounds with fantastic effects for myself which will only work if we play the exact same tempo every single night. Otherwise you can forget it.'

'Well, all right,' I said, giving in. 'What do you suggest we do?'

'Very simple. We need a rhythm track on stage as well.'

Erlend was right. Because of modern production methods, audiences have become used to a very precise mode of playing. Quite unconsciously, they expect the same sound at a concert. But, with so many musicians playing, a turmoil of emotions is automatically created – and every person thinks *he* is playing the right way. A song only really sounds light, swinging and groovy if all 40 people are fully disciplined in their music and that's why consistency is so important. I therefore decided to introduce a click track, a kind of electric metronome that gives the musicians the tempo via headphone.

There was a lot of resistance to this in the band. In particular, some of the old hands feared their individuality would be lost. As a result, a generation change in who played some of the instruments gradually began to take place. This, however, would not be complete until several years later, causing a big row.

Taking Risks

Ten years had passed since our last tour of Germany. Then one fine day in 1995, a young man turned up in the office of Liz

Pretty, who worked for our English concert agent. The man wanted to know if it would be possible to book the James Last Orchestra for a series of concerts in Germany. This bold fellow was only 23 and he introduced himself as Dieter Semmelmann from Bayreuth. Dieter was the owner of a small local agency for pop songs and folk music but he was convinced that there was still a lot of money to be made with us. He also had a father who enjoyed taking risks and was willing to use his money to back this venture, even if the outcome was uncertain. After Dieter and I had come to an agreement, Semmelmann Sr phoned me and said, 'Hansi, please make a success of this. Otherwise I'll have to stand on the street corner holding out my hat and begging for alms when I retire.'

The band with whom I would be facing my fans in Germany after such a long time had only changed slightly. Our piano man Günter Platzek, my companion of many years standing, had died in 1992, and John Pearson had taken his place at the grand piano. The two saxophonists, Karl-Hermann Lühr and Harald Ende, had retired, and in their place came first Stan Sulzman and later Andy Macintosh. Guitarist 'Big' Jim Sullivan had left the orchestra in 1987 and for a while Peter Hesslein was the only guitarist in the band, until Erlend Krauser joined us in 1992.

In 1996 we started our first tour of Germany after so many years with bookings for 16 concerts. The first one was to be held in Suhl, a small town 40 kilometres south of Erfurt. Everyone employed by Semmel Concerts was waiting nervously backstage when, on 24 October, we opened with the 'Fanfare for the Common Man'. Two and a half hours later it was clear this gamble had turned out to be a success for all of us. The audience of 2,500 went wild, and indeed every concert hall during the tour was completely sold out. For Semmelmann it was the start of an international career in concert promotion. For me it was a great comeback in my home country and a wonderful reunion with my fans. 'Why on earth has James Last been away so long?!' asked the press and public in amazement.

That tour was so incredibly successful that we did another one the following year. However, 1997 was to be the most terrible tour of my life.

Fifteen Cranes

After my affair with Christine, my life with Waltraud had undergone a complete change. Our relationship became better than ever before. A totally new feeling, deep and full of understanding, developed between us. It's probably the same in many marriages: there are phases when the man wants to break out, and other times when the woman is fed up, and often they fail to find each other again. We must accept that emotions cannot be synchronised, and there's no rhythm track. Sometimes you need more closeness and sometimes less. But Waltraud and I were lucky. We suddenly felt a kind of love for each other that we had never experienced before, at least not in this form. We had grown together, and all of a sudden everything was right.

But then disaster struck.

My wife had cancer of the uterus. The diagnosis had been made five years earlier, but, after our negative experiences with the press when I'd had skin cancer, we did everything in our power to keep it a secret. The cancer had grown in the dark and that's how we wanted it to stay.

It almost seemed as if she'd made it through the critical period – but almost wasn't good enough. When you are confronted with such a fate it is very important to learn how to *live* with this illness. You shouldn't just give up. I am very proud of the way Waltraud handled having cancer, especially because of the inner strength and power she developed. When she was operated on the first time – in the autumn of 1992 – the doctors told her she would probably not live to see Christmas. In spite of this, they recommended chemotherapy – which Waltraud declined, thank you. Nevertheless, she was able to enjoy several more Christmases.

I didn't even attempt to persuade her to have the conventional treatment. In Florida we happened to have some friends who had become intensively involved with alternative methods of healing. Ronnie's ex-wife, Cheryl, was also very knowledgeable in this area. We were given the name of a Greek doctor who had developed a special injection therapy for cancer patients, and I flew to Athens with Waltraud. There this doctor applied his method of treatment to Waltraud – and me too – for several weeks.

Whatever people might think about so-called 'faith-healers', the facts of the matter were that we both had a really wonderful time in Greece and that this visit gave us incredible self-confidence. Among the patients that we got to know there was one who had an open tumour on his tongue. After being treated for a week, the tumour had healed over. This convinced us we were on the right track. Back in Florida, Waltraud had a series of tests done at a very famous hospital, and all the results pertinent to a cancer diagnosis were the equivalent of those of a five-year-old child. In plain English: the cancer had disappeared and all that remained was an unpleasant thrombosis.

We had planned to go back to Athens some time to freshen up this extraordinary therapy, but then it turned out that the clinic had closed down. And Waltraud grew weaker and weaker…

My wife's illness showed me in a very drastic way all the things I had missed out on in the 42 years of our marriage. I now realised how much I owed this truly wonderful woman. I remembered the many long absences, the huge amount of work that so often took first place in my life, my various affairs and Waltraud's unwavering loyalty. All of this went through my head and contributed to the fact that towards the end of her life we were even more closely united. Our time together was incredibly intense.

Shortly before the start of the German tour in 1997, Waltraud was so ill that I seriously considered cancelling the tour. But typically my wife wouldn't hear of it. So, when we flew from Florida to Hamburg to begin rehearsing, Waltraud boarded the plane knowing that this would probably be her last flight.

During the tour she stayed in Hamburg and, regardless of where we were playing, I returned to her every night after the concert, travelling home by bus, helicopter, plane, or whatever. I wanted so much to make up for everything, to show her how terribly important she was to me. Night after night during the concerts the tears ran down my face, above all when we played the song 'The Living Years' – 'I just wish I could have told you in the living years...'

About halfway through the tour we played in Hamburg. Although Waltraud was by now very sick, she refused to be robbed of the chance to come to the concert to say goodbye to the musicians who had been a part of her family for so long.

The tour ended in November and it was Waltraud's most heartfelt wish not to die in Hamburg with its damp, grey, rainy weather, but to go back to the warm Florida sun. As her condition was by now very bad, a normal flight was out of the question. I therefore chartered a medical jet in Switzerland and so she was able to spend the last days of her life in our house at Palm Beach. She lay outside on the terrace, Ron, Rina and I constantly with her. She could hear the birds singing, the gentle murmur of the palms and delighted in the warm air of the south. I know that in these last days she was happy.

rollercoaster rides

At the very moment that Waltraud left us, we saw 15 cranes rise into the air simultaneously at the front of the house. They rose above the trees in a wide arc and then flew away – as if they were carrying her soul up to heaven.

It was 1 December 1997.

After the death of my wife, my world stopped turning: everything was darker than ever, black. During the tour I had hardly got any sleep because of constantly having to travel back and forth. I was completely exhausted physically and mentally and my life suddenly seemed devoid of meaning. For a while I had the feeling that Waltraud and I had had no life with each other at all, as if everything had passed by us so fast. Herbert Grönemeyer described this feeling in his song 'Der Weg' (The Way): 'I can no longer see, don't trust my eyes, can hardly believe the way my feelings have turned round...' I had done my work; she had stayed home to raise our children. What else had there been?

Only many weeks later did I start remembering: our holidays together on Sylt, the trips to Tunisia, Guadeloupe or Florida, our many games of golf and our parties. But in my grief I only saw a picture of my wife and thought, That was it then, that was a life.

An abyss opened up before me; I fell into an endlessly deep hole. You fall and fall... and wait for the impact. But it doesn't come. So you fall even deeper... until suddenly you reach the bottom and have to pick yourself up again, and realise there is a way out of this blackness that leads upwards again. But that can take a very long time.

Rina was a great help to me in this situation. We talked again and again; even when she had returned to Hamburg I would call her, sometimes without even saying anything, just so that I could be silent with her.

It was Rina, too, who spoke the words that in the end were to give my life a new meaning. She remembered a young woman I had met many years ago who had meant a great deal to me. 'Dad, there was that woman, Christine from Munich. Do you remember her? Why don't you give her a call? It might help you...'

Of course I remembered her. Christine, my affair... But I knew that she'd had a partner for many years; she was – and still is – a very attractive woman, perhaps married by now, perhaps with children. My phone call might come at an inconvenient time...

part nine:
They Call Me Hansi

A Love Story

Christine and I had never completely lost touch, in spite of living our separate lives, but we had only heard from one another at very long intervals – particularly as we both lived in totally different worlds. But there was always something that connected us, something intimate, a mutual attraction – something Christine later described as 'amicable love'.

So I dialled Christine's number. I heard her familiar voice say 'Grundner' from the other side of the Atlantic. Grundner was Christine's maiden name, so I guessed she was not married...

I can't have been very entertaining in this first telephone conversation after such a long time. What she heard was a bundle of misery, broken, weeping, lost. I told her about Waltraud dying and the extraordinary thing was that Christine understood completely. Her father had died three months earlier, also of cancer, within just three weeks, so she'd hardly had time to say goodbye to him. She knew how I felt – the pain of losing a partner, the woman who had been at my side all my life – because she felt something very similar. Her father had always been there for her, and now he was suddenly gone.

From this time on, I phoned her every day. I was grateful for every opportunity to talk and I asked her if she would help me, if she could imagine coming to Florida to visit me. The marvellous thing about all this was that Christine was completely free. There were no problems of relationships that she would have to deal with. It was true she had lived with a steady partner for some years and that several times he'd asked her to marry him, but an inner voice had told her he wasn't really the right man. In the end she'd broken off the relationship. It seemed like a miracle that a woman like Christine was still unattached, and since then I have believed more firmly than ever in 'Him up there'.

When Christine arrived in Florida, we didn't fall into each other's arms immediately. At that time neither of us had the slightest intention of reviving our affair. But very soon that special feeling that had existed 15 years earlier returned. This time, however, it developed on a quite different level: we were both older, the situation was totally different and our relationship was moving forward on an as yet unfamiliar track.

After two or three weeks Christine had to go back to Munich. She had her flat there, her job in the financial sector, her various commitments. So, the next time we met, I went to see her and stayed with her in her little two-room nest with a view of the mountains. I delighted in this closeness, in our intimacy. On one occasion I stayed with her for two weeks and we went on outings to the Allgäu area where Christine had grown up.

Another time I only stayed a few days because I had some important appointments.

Gradually, my life took on more colour. I started to take an interest in many things. Music became *the* big topic for me once more and we started planning the next projects. Slowly, my world began to take on normal proportions again, and new prospects presented themselves.

In those weeks we talked together endlessly and bit by bit the direction in which we were heading became clear to us. Shall we give ourselves a chance at a life together? In fact, there was no real need for us to think things over for long. There was no alternative because our hearts could not have chosen any other course. It made sense to me that we would marry. It was important that everything should be done properly.

In June 1998, on Christine's 40th birthday, we became engaged. On 24 July 1999 she became my wife. We got married without any fuss at the registry office in Hamburg and afterwards went out for a good meal – that was our wedding. Instead of a wedding ring, I now wear a small diamond earring.

At some point the press heard about our wedding and reporters rang begging me to say something about my new wife – if she had any children, whether she had been married, or if there was at least some small piece of scandal to be had. Luckily, Christine's past was too ordinary for the media so the interest died down very quickly.

Nobody has ever commented unkindly on the big difference in age between us. Even Christine's family and friends accepted her decision immediately. Of course, seen biologically, I have lived a good many years, but in my head and in my attitudes I have remained fairly young – or so I believe. Not for a second do I feel like a man on the 'wrong' side of 75. I don't subscribe to the view that 'at my age I can't do this or that any more' and I don't just laze around in the sun reading the paper. That isn't me at all. As always, I still look for challenges in my life. When I am in company, I am sometimes surprised to find that I'm by far the oldest, although I always feel as if I'm the youngest. This may be because when I was a child I was always the baby, no matter where I was.

Christine and I do everything together, and we share an important hobby – golf. Everything is running along as it always did with my musicians, the invitations and the concerts – the one exception being that Christine attends every concert. Waltraud never accompanied me on my tours: the noise and excitement and the mad parties were too much of a strain for her. Now Christine puts fresh flowers in front of Waltraud's picture every day. She knows she's not in second place but rather Waltraud's successor.

Our relationship today is much stronger than it would have been if I had chosen Christine back then in 1982. We would both have been weighed down with guilt. Above all, I'm sure I would have always reproached myself dreadfully over Waltraud's illness.

My daughter Rina accepted Christine straightaway, as did most of my friends. It took Ron a little longer, but today they are like brother and sister. Christine has been accepted by everyone, including those in the music business. I'm proud of my wife. In the street I say to her, 'You can walk in front. I'll walk in your shadow – that's enough for me. Nobody could be happier than I am.' The fulfilment I feel with her is a fairy tale come true. It's beyond anything someone of my age could have expected.

Christine is not just my wife: she has become an important support in my work as well. When she came to live with me in America, she said, 'What am I supposed to do here in Florida? Sit in the sun all day long?' But there's no question of it being like that. She's always busy and looks after all my affairs, such as taxes, financial matters and appointments. She is with me when

TV appearances are being recorded, in the studio and for business negotiations. Sharing our observations and impressions after an important meeting has been imperative – and natural – for me for a long time now.

The paths of destiny are sometimes strange. If Christine had not come into my life, I probably wouldn't be here any more. Waltraud's death would have torn me apart. God must have protected me, perhaps because He knows that I want to make people happy with my music.

I have also managed to get my own cancer problems under control. Since the first diagnosis back in 1982, I have been going to Professor Breitbart of Buxtehude for a check-up every six months. My skin is systematically checked with a magnifying glass under a special light for any changes, and if there's anything wrong it can quickly be removed. I would recommend this examination to anyone who enjoys lying in the sun. Most important, you shouldn't sunbathe when you are exhausted, because the skin is an organ like any other and the effect of the sun is particularly bad when it is very tired.

My problem at the moment is that cancers always keep recurring in the same places on my face, but there is no tissue left there that could be cut away. We're down to the bone now. Because of this I had to undergo radiotherapy every day for five weeks and then again for four weeks until the wounds had healed. As I had not realised that this would be such a time-consuming process, the press conferences for the autumn tour of 2005 were held far too early. I was still in the middle of my treatment so my face looked a proper mess. Naturally, it didn't take long for the press to comment: the newspaper *Bild* published an enlarged photo of the part of my nose that was being treated, with the heading: 'JAMES LAST'S NOSE IS FALLING OFF!'

Nevertheless, I don't feel afraid any more. I have sorted out my life and feel positive about the future. I have my medical check-ups regularly, the diseased parts are removed and that's that. And if they ever really did have to cut off a bit of my nose, we'd just leave the first three rows of the concert hall empty, so nobody would get a close-up view. I would even perform without a nose!

A few years ago I had to have a knee replacement. While undergoing rehabilitation treatment, I realised how important it was never to give up on yourself. In order to liven up the boring but necessary exercises with the other patients, I started to sing 'Auf der Lüneburger Heide' (On the Heath at Lüneburg) – a well-known folk song – at the top of my voice. Suddenly, all of these recently operated-on people looked more cheerful and started to sing along. The nurses just shook their heads in amusement, thinking, What a nutcase! I only notice my new knee at the airport, because it's made of metal and always makes the detectors start bleeping. Then I have to show my scar so everyone can see that this old gentleman is not a terrorist but simply walks around with a built-in spare part.

Apart from that, I'm in fairly good health. Although my life was anything but healthy in the past, the doctors have always found to their surprise that my liver results were comparable to those of a baby – I must have good genes. And my mind still functions more or less OK – at least well enough to enable me to drag out my memories from the furthest corners of my consciousness to write this book!

2000 x Live

In 1999, the year of my 70th birthday and my marriage to Christine, we gave close to 50 concerts – from London to Vienna and from Zurich to Rostock. We didn't even have time to go on a real honeymoon. After celebrating my 70th in London, we had four days off in which we had planned to play golf. We drove up to Scotland to the famous links at St Andrews, but it just snowed and snowed without stopping. The snow came from all directions and the caddies went home, but Christine and I held out till the 17th hole. That was the first day of our improvised, pre-wedding honeymoon.

Back in the hotel we dried our things and then drove to Gleneagles. We played on Jack Nicklaus's new course, but even there the water was up to our ankles. So again we dried our things and drove on, this time to Turnberry. The forecast for the following day was sunny and we were looking forward to having a really good game, but in the evening the phone rang. Céline Dion was on the line, and she wanted to record some songs in our studio in Florida. We had no choice but to pack our suitcases that same evening. We set off at four o'clock the next morning and flew from Glasgow to Miami via London to record Céline's voice. It wasn't until after this that we got married in Hamburg.

The following year we gave performances in Germany, and in 2001 it was Britain again. Then in 2002 we toured Germany, Austria, Switzerland, Belgium, Holland and Denmark, both in the spring and the autumn. Journalists and fans are always asking me, 'Why are you doing this to yourself, at your age?!' And my answer is always the same: 'Others go to a health resort, I go on tour.'

Planning this kind of tour is a complicated and lengthy matter. The first preparations begin more than a year before the tour is due to start. Concert halls have to be contacted and booked, the route has to be fixed and schedules decided. Later on, the ideas for the stage and lighting for the show are worked out. The venue of our first concert is also where we hold our rehearsals – for financial reasons this always takes place in a smaller town. Roughly one week before the first performance, the production and technical staff begin building the stage set, lighting and cameras are installed, and the sound equipment is set up. After four days everything is ready, then the musicians arrive and for two days we rehearse the new programme. The fixed costs of such a concert tour come to about 70,000 euros per day. Local costs such as renting the hall, the preparations and advertising are a separate cost.

But a concert tour is like a fountain of youth to me. It's my life. When Barbara Freiberger of Semmel Concerts rang me in autumn 2003 to let me know the tour plan for 2004, she suggested 25 concerts over a period of four weeks. But I just said, 'Let's make it twice as long. I want to be on the road for at least eight weeks.' At my age it's a really fantastic thing to be able to stand on stage, give people something positive and sweep them away for a few hours. I actually see it as my job to prove to people that they don't belong on the scrap heap yet, that we can enjoy ourselves together.

My old friend from the jazz days, Max Greger, still comes to my concerts regularly. A while ago, after he'd been to one of my concerts, his wife said to him, 'Look, Max, if that old guy up there can still manage all that, surely you've still got it in you too!' And, lo and behold, it wasn't long before Max was back on tour. Joined by Hugo Strasser and Paul Kuhn, he had a successful Legends tour in 2002/03.

After our jazz time together early in our careers, both of us have played at various events like the opening of the Berlin Radio Broadcasting Exhibition, but our two bands have never actually played a concert together. Just recently, though, Max said, 'Hansi, we should record a CD together. With my saxophone and your ladies on the strings, it would really be something!'

If one day people don't want to see me any more, then I'll just have to face the fact that my time is over. But so far it doesn't look as if I will be forced to lead the life of a pensioner. Both the preparations for our big 2006 tour and of course the writing of this book have kept me very busy. And in 2007 I started on my farewell tour of the UK.

Nowadays when we go on tour there are close to a hundred people involved. There are 40 musicians, the whole of the technical department – sound, lighting, stage building, pyrotechnics, the video team – plus the tour managers, wardrobe attendants, management, bus drivers, catering people – it's like a real circus when we travel around. The orchestra and I usually spend the night in the town where the concert has taken place, but the technicians have to dismantle the whole stage in three hours straight after the show, load the whole lot on to trucks and travel to the next destination by sleeping coach – and then immediately begin reassembling everything for the next concert. It's an incredible achievement.

We have our own kitchen that provides us with healthy food at all hours of the day, and every day there are three menus to choose from. Never have my concert tours been so perfectly organised – it's a real joy. I have the feeling I am now experiencing the best and most successful tours ever. In the past many people came to my concerts simply because it was the in thing; today they come because they want to hear our music.

Some clever person worked out that the concert on 24 November 2002 – in Hamburg's Color Line Arena with 9,000 people – was the 2,000th of my career. Imagine, 2,000 times live on stage, 2,000 times stage fright and 2,000 times the feeling of joy that always comes over me when I sense I can make people happy with my music. What an incredible privilege!

On Stage – Backstage

During our 1999 tour, our tour manager Barbara Freiberger got the scare of her life. She was backstage at a concert in Erfurt, it was dark, and she was chatting to our tailor Charly Cisek. Every now and then, Barbara would look towards the stage to check that everything was OK. Of course, everything was fine as always: the musicians were playing and I was conducting. But, when she looked again, I had suddenly disappeared. Barbara thought something terrible had happened, that I had collapsed and left the stage forever. I wasn't getting any younger, after all. Charly noticed her shock, but stayed calm. 'Don't worry, he'll be right back.'

In fact, I had simply climbed down from the stage to waltz with some ladies from the audience. Charly almost died laughing!

Fans often ask me how the band can play on perfectly while I waltz in the stalls. The answer is quite simple. When on stage, I am not really conducting. Every musician has to know his part off pat. Once the show has started, there must be no more uncertainties: everybody has to know what to do. You could say the show has to be pre-conducted. I can detect immediately if one of my musicians is slacking. No grand gestures are necessary: a quick glance from me is sufficient.

Conducting is, primarily, a matter of personality. An episode from my time with the NDR Orchestra illustrates this best. The renowned conductor Wilhelm Schüchter, who had recorded many classical LPs, was rehearsing a piece with the NDR Symphony Orchestra that was to be performed later with Herbert von Karajan as conductor. Finally, Karajan came, went up to the conductor's desk, closed the score, raised his hand and began conducting: the orchestra had never played so beautifully. His charisma made the musicians perform at the top of their game.

I had a very different experience when I went to a benefit concert that some of my musicians had organised for the children of a choir singer who had passed away. The band, which was made up largely of my musicians, used my arrangements; Derek Watkins conducted and he played his solo in 'MacArthur Park' – but still the song did not click: it just sounded different.

On the other hand, sometimes the audience deceives itself. We almost always played live in the *Starparade* shows but one time I was in hospital with appendicitis, so it was clear that I could not appear. We had just finished working on a new album with folk songs, so we decided to have the band perform to pre-recorded music. To convey the impression of playing 'live', my brother Werner took my place as conductor.

Many 'expert' viewers called while the show was still being broadcast, saying, 'Kai Warner does a good job, but we can tell James Last is not there. With him the music just sounds much better…'

I think one reason for the success of our live performances is that I face my audience with total honesty. No matter how big the venue is, or how many people are there, I put my heart on stage each night. Mick Jagger has always been a great example for me. With him you always have the feeling of total commitment. I owe it to the audience to give my best at every concert, with every song, and to get the best out of my band. That's why I'm tense before each concert, even if it is the 20th night of a tour. I need my usual rituals to concentrate fully.

My preparation starts with the sound check: most of the time we play two or three numbers for the engineers and the sound people – and for the fans, many of whom are already in the hall during this fine-tuning. It's a good opportunity for me to talk to them, get some photos taken, sign some autographs. Many of my fans have known our music for such a long time that they know more about me and my records than I do.

Next there is dinner for the band – I'll only have a small bite to eat because I don't like to perform on a full stomach. When I'm finally in my dressing room, I like it to be quiet. Only Christine, Liz Pretty, my personal tour manager of many years, and sometimes Ronnie will be around. I will freshen up, take a shower and shave, put my stage clothes on, and then we're off.

The difficult part for my musicians is the many different styles they have to switch to and from every night: there's swing, rock, classical music, a waltz with lovely *ritardandi*, a polka – each with its own rhythm. Today, the audience listen with much greater attention than they used to. In the studio, the band's timing is impeccable. I don't like it if we sound different on stage. Such a disparity might arise from one musician playing too lazily, too jazzy or too far behind the rhythm while all others stay on the beat. The audience can't work out why a part doesn't sound as it should, but they feel something is wrong. That's why live performances have to become ever more perfect – and that's a huge challenge for all of us.

After a concert I feel drained and empty. I have given everything – I am mentally tired and physically exhausted. At the same time I am also extremely high from the applause, the happy people and the beaming faces. Adrenaline is running through the body, so it's impossible to go to bed. Since musicians reportedly have a penchant for the fast life, every now and then we used to end up in a 'sleazy' bar or club. That was pure high spirits – you don't go to a club like that looking for love, you go just for fun. When we turned up at such a place with the whole band, the girls would phone some of their girlfriends, tell them to come and we'd drink, dance and laugh.

After one concert in Innsbruck we ended up boozing the night away in a real Tyrolean Alpine brothel – it's amazing there even was such a place in religious Tyrol. Anyway, we skidded into the joint, the concert music still in our ears. And what did we see in a corner? Drums! Our drummer, an Englishman, couldn't be stopped. He played those drums for the rest of the night, but all he'd play was 'Wien bleibt Wien' (Vienna Remains Vienna) while singing along loudly. Any thought of fooling around with the girls soon went out of the window, but nevertheless we had a blast – '*a echte Gaudi*' as they say in this corner of the world.

One of our most stylish concerts took place in Vienna, as it happens – at the dignified ball of the even more dignified Vienna Philharmonic. A Viennese ball is a very traditional matter and the Vienna Philharmonic Ball is one of the society highlights in that beautiful city on the Danube. It takes place in the magnificent Golden Hall of the Viennese Musikverein, where the famous New Year's concert is performed. The Austrian Federal President presides, there is a reception committee, and the opening music is conducted by a high-calibre conductor: Abbado, Bernstein, Karajan, Muti, Solti – many world-famous conductors have shown their brilliance at this ball. And in the early 1970s I and my band were hired for one of these events! Of course, we played in one of the smaller halls – the Golden Hall was reserved for the Philharmonic Orchestra. It didn't take long, however, before things got riotous in our corner of the Musikverein. The whole dance floor was littered with shoes as girls danced barefoot in their expensive ball gowns – the band had literally blown away all the formal ritual!

In August 1985 we were invited to another event in Austria that was almost as traditional: the Bregenz Festival, where we gave two open-air concerts on the huge floating stage on Lake Constance. While we were performing 'Biscaya' – which is played without the wind section – a small boat suddenly glided across the water nearby. In it was our choir girl Madeline Bell, with Bob Lanese and Bob Coassin rowing, and Derek Watkins fanning her with a palm frond. It was a gag the band had thought up and it caught me completely by surprise: I was on stage, but had to stop conducting because I was laughing so much. As if that wasn't enough, during the second half of the concert, a huge full moon rose into the night sky to my left. One of the musicians started howling at it and the whole band joined in. The audience had no idea what was happening because they were facing in the opposite direction and couldn't see the moon – but I had a pack of moonstruck wolves on stage instead of an orchestra.

Even hotels and their guests could not always escape our pranks. In Munich's Hilton hotel we told the groupies – oh yes, we had them too – that all the girls in Hamburg went topless at our parties. The bubbly Munich girls didn't want to play second fiddle to anyone, and the result was a hotel staircase decorated with Bavarian bras. We partied on in our flautist Harald Ende's room until six in the morning, when the band had the idea of bellowing out 'Granada' at the tops of their voices. Fortunately, we had a neighbour with a great sense of humour – when he phoned the room he simply said tersely, 'You're singing a semitone too low!'

Our records always sold well in the Netherlands, so we were often guests on their big TV show *Grand Gala Du Disque*. We usually stayed in the same hotel when we went to Amsterdam – the one where John Lennon and Yoko Ono held their famous bed-in of 1969 – and a lot of pretty girls worked in its restaurant and bar. When the girls' shift was over, we took them to one of our rooms and partied on. Somehow this news got around, because the hotel manager's office called and asked if the girls were in our room.

'Why, no, no way!'

Then, presumably, we wouldn't mind if the hotel manager stopped by. So we had to hide the girls. Now, most Dutch girls are not exactly petite, so it was difficult to hide them in the closet or under the bed. When the strict manager came to collect his staff, the wardrobe swayed and the beds wobbled in mysterious ways while we – giggling like little school boys – acted like innocent angels.

Today everything is much quieter and more civilised. After the show we have a light meal – soup and a sandwich – in the hotel. It's a time for conversation with the band, our friends and acquaintances. It helps us to wind down, to relax and to get our normal pulse rates back. Often, one of the musicians will sit down at the piano, Chuck and Bob will get their trumpets, a singer will join in – and a great jam session will go on until way past midnight.

Sometimes some of my fans are among the friends and acquaintances at our post-show buffet. They are my best friends. Only with their help could I have become who I am today. They alone are to blame for my good luck! What could be more wonderful than being in touch with people who understand and love my work? All over the world!

I have known many of my fans for 30 years – that's how long they have been coming to our shows and showing their interest in our music. Of course, an amicable bond has developed; they tell me about their worries and their happiness, about their kids, their partners and their jobs. Often they write letters, send photos or bring small gifts.

They know each other, too – whole networks have developed over the years. British fans visit German fans, Japanese fans visit Chinese fans: they travel far afield. Take Peter, for example, a Swiss postal clerk. For years he has been coming to all our concerts. I don't know how he does it, where he sleeps, how he can afford it, but he spends all his money on these trips. He never asks for anything, and, when we sometimes invite him to our post-show get-together, he is overjoyed.

I think I'm the only artist who invites his fans into the hall for the sound check – which is against the law in Great Britain, by the way. They want to talk to me and the musicians, exchange views, hear what's new and meet other fans. Today, many of them are in my age group, but there are always some young people. One girl, who would always stand alone in front of the stage, wrote to me, 'Unfortunately, I can't come to your next tour: I'm spending a year as an exchange student in the USA. But I'll be back in 2004.' That year I welcomed her back from the stage.

I am especially happy about all the letters I receive from all over the world. I just got a letter from a Japanese fan who sent me photographs of his newborn baby girl. Or there is this letter from England: 'Ever since we've been listening to your records, our living room has lost its corners.'

To give you an idea of the diversity of letters I get, I'd like to quote from two very different ones.

A professor of philosophy from the University of Regensburg in Bavaria wrote: '...the concert on 12 November 2000 was an absolute delight for me. I heard your orchestra twice in the early 1970s in Ulm when I still went to school, and I have to say it wasn't any less thrilling this time.' Then the professor tries to explain in many, very perceptive sentences why he likes my music so much. His final, very simple comment? 'You could say it's the sound of joie de vivre and harmony. And harmony stands as much for being at peace with oneself as an exciting rhythm.'

Frank the railwayman from Chemnitz, on the other hand, writes about East German times:

I only knew Hansi as a successful double bass player so I was very curious to hear that this Hansi had now been re-named James and had his own orchestra. In between times, however, the Wall had been erected and information from the Western world was scarce. ... Slowly the first Last albums turned up among those railwaymen who had connections to the Federal Republic of Germany. The band with the party sound was a real smash, and we danced and rocked to your music. It was exhilarating when tunes by the James Last Orchestra were piped into the assembly shop and into the canteen. First we had to get a permit from the plant party executive, though.

In August 2003 Christine and I were invited to Bristol for the anniversary of our English fan club. It was a wonderful evening at a large hotel: several hundred fans came and danced to my old records, and many of those songs I had not heard in decades. The fans were over the moon: they were happy that I was in their midst, giving autographs and answering questions by the thousand. These gatherings can sometimes be quite exhausting, but they are fantastic all the same.

The Sound of the 21st Century

These days some of my older friends grumble a bit because they find some of my productions too modern. *James Last Plays ABBA* (2001) and *New Party Classics* (2002) have caused the most controversial reactions among German fans – perhaps some people expected the arrangements to be mellower. But I wanted the *ABBA* CD to have exactly this modern style, without any echo, the sound coming directly from the instruments. In my opinion, this is musically my best album in recent years and I'm sure *James Last Plays ABBA* will still sound modern in ten years' time. Those who like it really like it – they have understood what I wanted to do. It may take a few years for the others to come to terms with it.

The same thing applies to *New Party Classics*. In my opinion, there isn't a single weak track on it, but it was produced in a very aggressive style. We had a sensational brass session with five world-class trumpet players, including Chuck Findley *and* Derek Watkins. Ten days after the band had rehearsed in London, we went to the Café Schöne Aussichten in Hamburg, where we recorded the party atmosphere live.

For the first time in 15 years we had a real *Non Stop Dancing* party. The place was packed with musicians, friends and fans – everyone was there. And we served bread rolls with delicious toppings and a great deal of alcohol to loosen up the atmosphere. But there wasn't really any need for alcohol, because the people were much more relaxed about it all than in the past. No sooner had the band begun to play *New Party Classics* than the whole place burst into life: the café was rocking and the party really got under way. I had written, among other things, brand-new modern arrangements of two tunes we had recorded for our very first *Non Stop Dancing* album: 'Downtown' and 'Pretty Woman' – I almost felt like I was in a time machine!

Unfortunately, a couple of the people in charge at our record company were not so pleased with the modern style, so the album was among the also-rans and not marketed with much effort. But, if we play a song or two from this CD at a concert, the audience really gets into it – only the really weary can't get up out of their seats.

Of course, there are those fans who only ever want to hear 'Traumschiff' or 'Biscaya', but I would be deceiving myself if I tried to arrange things as I did 30 years ago, or just played 'At Seven in the Morning All's Well With the World When the Love Boat Sails Through the Biscaya...' until my dying breath.

Discussions about style are certainly nothing new to me. There was also a hullabaloo after my first Christmas LP, *Christmas Dancing*, was released in 1966. Although the record had been arranged in quite a gentle fashion, with a lot of strings and very little rhythm, an outraged listener wrote to the *Bild* newspaper, saying, 'What have you done to our beautiful Christmas carols! If I could, I would punch you in the face with my remaining intact fist!' Today this recording sounds as tame as a purring kitten. I'm sure the same will apply to those recordings that are too 'wild' for many today, simply because the sound doesn't fit in with what they imagine James Last should be.

Just for the record, I stand by my past. I am still as thrilled as ever with our 'old' sound. Recently a friend of mine played me a recording from 1970, from the album that had been intended for the US market but never released. The last time I'd heard it had been more than 30 years earlier, and I couldn't remember some of the tunes at all. Rediscovering this music after such a long time triggered an indescribable feeling in me: I was really moved by the recording. I can really stand behind what I did, and I certainly don't need to hide my face because of it.

On the other hand, I have always made an effort to take an active interest in new ideas, new styles and new techniques and technologies. Musicians who take pride in saying they have played like Glenn Miller for 40 years and still want to play like that today are a little behind the times – that is no longer the kind of precision I need. Now something else is required. Productions these days are so incredibly good and perfectly made that you have to keep up with the latest recording techniques – after all, the audience has already subconsciously adjusted to these sounds.

For years now I have been writing my arrangements and compositions on a computer – you can outline everything, every tiny nuance. But it takes time: it takes me longer to write now than it used to. Before we go into the studio, the entire playback is recorded using sound devices and then, instrument for instrument, replaced by real musicians. That has a number of advantages: the band members don't have to be at the same place all at the same time, the rhythmic timing is tighter and errors can be corrected more easily. The big disadvantage is the lack of 'us' feeling. When each musician records his part alone in the studio the shared fun is gone, along with the mutual inspiration.

The Bass Player of Fettes Brot

I am fully aware that not all my fans like the style that I am arranging and recording in at the moment. But for me and for my life it is the right thing to do. People used to react to a painting by Picasso with shock: 'What the hell is that supposed to be? That's got nothing to do with art!' Today no one is bothered by his paintings. The same applies to music. The first record I ever bought was a recording of the violin concerto by Bela Bartók with Tibor Varga as the soloist. Back then, at the end of the 1940s, those sounds were literally unheard of. And today? Bartók is a classic like Schubert or Brahms and no one thinks of his music as jarring.

Michael Jackson, Madonna, Prince, R. Kelly, the rappers – they have all advanced our musical world, and my music has to keep evolving, otherwise the work is not satisfying.

A few years ago, in 1999, I had the opportunity to experience first-hand how young people get down to business in the studio when I was working with the Hamburg hip-hop trio Fettes Brot. These boys are enormously consistent – other musicians could learn a thing or two from them. The precision of their performance is really remarkable.

'Ruf mich an' (Call Me) was the result of our efforts, and it all began with a phone call from them. Perhaps we could meet up? They had bought so many old records of mine at flea markets and had sampled my music – what about doing a project together? Of course! Why not? So we met in Hamburg on a cold, rainy, autumn day, had a bite to eat and something to drink – the lads only drank juice, by the way – and agreed we would record a song together.

I now have my own studio next to my new house in Palm Beach, and not only is it technically well equipped but, in contrast to most of the studio bunkers in Germany, it's flooded with light and has a magnificent view of the marshland. That is why it's called Paradise Sounds. So I said, 'Hey, it's so cold here. Why don't we do it in Florida? The sun is shining and it's so much more pleasant working there.'

The three of them were thrilled, so the 'where' was settled. What we hadn't decided on, though, was the 'what' – what we actually wanted to record.

'We have a couple of ideas,' was all they said.

'OK, when you've got that sorted out, just let me know so that I can be prepared.'

So I flew back to Palm Beach and waited – and waited – but nothing happened.

A few weeks later I got a phone call. 'When can we come?'

'Whenever you want, but first I'd like to know what you're planning to do.'

'What we'd really like is a kind of jam session, to try out a few things and see where they lead us…'

It was March when they finally arrived. I had been expecting four people: the Brots – Boris, Martin and Björn – and perhaps someone accompanying them. But no, a *dozen* people got out of the plane! A whole horde of them were standing there at Palm Beach airport. The Brots had brought not only their own sound people, but also a photographer and even a camera team because they were going to make a video of the whole thing. We had to hire a bus to cart the whole crew back to our place.

They had already fully prepared the lyrics, but the musical side of things was still open. So we sat down together and chewed over a few ideas. Finally, we got down to business. First a bass riff, which was sampled and repeated for a few bars; OK, that sounded pretty cool. Then the drums – a few beats were put together. Then one of them rapped to try it out, but they weren't so happy with that – it wasn't the right tempo, so the whole thing started all over again. This went on for days. Every morning they were in the studio at 11am, refining and reworking their material with such dedication, until the entire song sounded exactly as they had imagined it. For relaxation I took them for an occasional round of golf, and Christine and I cooked for them, since at this stage I was merely an interested onlooker.

When the Brots were finished with their bit, I said, 'Now clear out while I write the brass and the strings for it.'

After that we mixed their world with mine and released our generational crossover – 'Ruf mich an' – as a single, two mixes with lyrics and one purely instrumental version. At the beginning none of those involved was really sure how things would work out between the youngsters and the old fellow – but before long it was obvious it was working without a hitch.

'Ruf mich an' caused a big stir in Germany, and we even took Fettes Brot with us to a concert at the Royal Albert Hall. Of course, the English audience didn't understand a word of the German lyrics and they were probably surprised I'd turned up with a group of rappers, but in the end the fans found the experiment quite fun. We also did a TV performance in Mainz that only the three Brots were invited to, but since the song was by 'Fettes Brot with James Last' I had to come too. I slung an electric bass over my shoulder and trotted along behind the three lads through the crowd of teenagers.

In the middle of it all, I heard one girl ask her friend, 'Hey, who's that old bloke at the back?'

'Oh, he's the bass player for Fettes Brot.'

I nearly cracked up laughing!

I also experienced the precision and perfectionist detail with which Céline Dion and her producer David Foster work. They were both in our studio to record Céline's voice for her album *All the Way*, the backing tapes having been mixed already. She would start singing at nine in the evening and would work through until four in the morning, almost without a break. After all that, they would have one song in the bag.

Ron told me that usually the first version would have been good enough, yet they would still polish and refine it. David would say, 'Sing a third above, a fourth below,' and she'd do it. First voice, second voice, third voice – she pulled it all out of the hat. And all the while she was singing so loudly that from outside you'd have thought trumpets were being played in the studio – unbelievable! This naturally affected her vocal cords considerably, so every now and then Céline had to take a break – but even then she wouldn't have said 'ouch!' if you'd pinched her.

This all shows how hard the stars of today work, which is why I think the shallow criticisms you so often hear bandied about are usually unjustified. Whether it's Céline Dion, Britney Spears or Robbie Williams, all of them give their very best. If someone like Britney puts on a little weight, this is immediately jumped on – 'God, look at her! She looks *awful*!' But they should try standing and singing and dancing for an hour... I'd be out of breath in 20 seconds.

The days when I used to have to put up with a lot of – rather clueless – criticism are long behind me. The older you get, the more polite the press becomes. In the days when I was notching up one gold record after another and being showered with awards, the ladies and gentlemen of the trade didn't mince their words. Often very young critics, who were not my intended audience, would be in the audience at my concerts and more than happy to be able to inflate their egos by writing a damning review, even though they'd left after only ten minutes.

Thirty years ago Michael Naura, a former co-worker and the head of NDR jazz editorial for many years, coined a phrase that has been regurgitated by many unimaginative journalists in numerous variations: 'James Last music is like pulp for the toothless.' Even the *Spiegel* news journal adopted this metaphor: 'Beethoven and Blues, Haydn and *Hair* are all reduced to the lowest common denominator by James Last's orchestra machinery. ... He sands off the corners and edges and floods the melodies with opulent string and brass chords, thus making the music digestible even for the toothless sound lovers who can only feast on acoustic baby food.'

My response to these not-so-friendly critiques was simple: even the toothless have a right to live.

More recently, however, their estimation of me and my work has taken a positive turn. You only have to manage to get old enough and suddenly you become a 'cult star' and a 'legend'. Since our German comeback tour in 1996, most of the reviews have been positive. The press has spoken of the 'world's best band' and a 'unique sound experience', of 'fireworks of music' and 'feel-good sound'. Even the stern *Spiegel* has changed its position. In 1999, they published a long interview with the title 'I am a rocker', in which they designated me the Germans' tutor in matters of pop.

What really pleases me is that more and more young people are discovering my music – and not just the lads from Fettes Brot. For instance the techno group M.A.S. did a dance-floor version of 'Biscaya' called 'I Remember the Summer of '82'. German-based US singer Lamar and later Wu-Tang-Clan lead singer RZA rapped to 'The Lonely Shepherd'. P. Diddy, godfather of the American rap scene, made use of my composition 'Fantasy' from the *Seduction* album for one of his numerous remixes. DJ George Evelyn, alias Nightmares on Wax, sampled 'Washington Square' from 1970's *Beachparty I* for the cool tune 'Ethnic Minority'. And DJ Paolo Scotti made a six-minute-long 'Mojo-Club Remix' out of 'Happy Brasilia' which landed in the House charts in 1994. That makes me a little bit proud.

But whether I am labelled the 'Party King' or 'Gentleman of Music', a 'soft option' or 'cult star', I have never had much use for such labels. My life is simple, and for me my music is also simple, because I can express myself in it. I don't know how to describe my style: I am simply lucky enough to be one of the few people in the world who can hear one kind of music and immediately be able to translate it into another without having to think too much about it. Whether it's a piece by Earth, Wind & Fire or a composition by Mozart, I write it down how *I* feel it and a little bit of Last remains clinging to it. Even if I really wanted to, I wouldn't be able to change. I live in my world, and I enjoy the great privilege that this world has been understood by millions of people for more than four decades. Most of all I am glad to see that the grandchildren are following on from the grandparents and their children in finding their way to my world. And of course I consider it rather satisfying that my old records are being traded – sometimes at incredible prices – on various Internet exchanges. Who would have thought that the album *Well Kept Secret*, so unloved by Polydor Germany, would one day become a sought-after collector's item in the USA?

In 2002 I was a guest on the TV show of the German comedian and show host Stefan Raab. Stefan is not only a witty person but is also very convincing as a one-man orchestra. During the show he sang my composition 'Happy Luxemburg' for me – the entire song, including drums, trumpets and trombones. I was astounded to discover what wide appeal his programme had. For my appearance I wore a rather offbeat pair of trousers, rather tight with faded zebra stripes – not exactly what gentlemen over 70 usually care to wear. It was amazing how many people came up and mentioned them in the next few days: 'Oh! You're wearing your Stefan Raab trousers!'

A week later, in Lübeck, a couple of teenage girls with painted-on love bites appeared in front of me and asked for my autograph. I was genuinely surprised. 'What gave you *that i*dea?'

'We saw you on Raab,' they told me.

'What are you doing this evening?' I asked.

'Dunno – just hanging around and stuff, I guess.'

'Would you like to come to our concert?'

'Oh, yeah! You're sure that's OK?'

'Of course.'

'What are you playing, then?'

I listed a few songs from our programme and they asked, 'Could we come up on stage for "Hey Baby" and dance?'

'Of course,' I said. 'Then a lot more people will sing along!'

That evening the girls came to the concert, dressed to the nines, and reported excitedly, 'We told everyone at home we're going on stage for James Last and singing "Hey Baby"!' I must admit that was amusing.

But the youngest audience by far we have ever had was on our Chinese tour in 2002. But, before that happened and I could fulfil my long-held wish of a concert tour in the Middle Kingdom, I had to pass through one of the blackest hours of my whole career – a mutiny by my band.

The China Rebellion

It took years for talks with the Chinese concert agencies to reach our goal. A tour had been in the offing once already but it had to be cancelled at the last minute. But then at last the dates were confirmed. We were signed up to leave in September 2002.

But before that, at the end of our successful spring tour in 2002 in Zwickau, we recorded the show *A World of Music* for the US TV station PBS. Since the whole band was there, it seemed a good time to sign the contracts for the Chinese tour.

Without my knowledge, however, the musicians had secretly set up a kind of trade union before the two Zwickau concerts. This now became active – in the interval of the second concert. When tour organiser Dieter Semmelmann wanted to discuss the details of the tour with the band, everything suddenly came to a standstill. Almost all the band members refused to go on the Chinese trip on the terms that had been arranged. I had no idea this was going on when I came on stage, relaxed and totally focused, for the second half of the concert. However, during the first bars of the opening song 'Dancing Queen', I had an uneasy feeling that something was not quite right. The band wasn't 100 per cent focused – something must have happened.

Immediately after the concert I was confronted with the bitter truth in the dressing rooms: I now had practically no musicians. I simply could not take it in. We had just finished the last evening of an extremely successful tour, I was looking forward to a fun last-night party... and then *that*!

To this day, I don't know how the mutiny took hold so quickly. There were probably various reasons. One lot of musicians found the fees too low. Another group thought China was not safe enough to travel in – they couldn't have caught on to the enormous development that had taken place in China in the previous ten years. A third set wanted to know – four months before the tour was due to begin – the exact details of hotels, airlines and the itinerary. Anyone who has ever been to China will know that that is almost impossible. It is part of the ritual of the old and complicated Chinese civil service hierarchy to leave applicants in the dark about the decisions of these modern Mandarins for as long as possible.

Whatever, the band had perhaps already drunk a few too many to give themselves courage and had presumably reinforced each other in their respective opinions. Angered and shocked, I asked every one of them in the bus on the way back to the hotel, 'Are you coming?' – 'No.' – 'Are *you* coming with us?' – 'No.'

It was the worst moment of my career. Throughout our many years together, all of them had always had the best I could possibly give. Each had had his opportunity to present himself musically, all of them had received their fees without any fuss – and these certainly weren't a pittance – and all of them had eaten and drunk whatever they wanted. Hansi always saw to everything. Had I just been fooling myself all those years? Was that family feeling that I had always felt towards my band just one-sided? Was that wonderful sense of togetherness that I conjured up on stage night after night just an illusion?

Now, with the hindsight of a few years, I think that – on top of the reasons just mentioned, plus the uncertainty of the Chinese situation – it was simply the normal wear-and-tear of the years. Many of the band members had become sick of touring life over many years, and after spending so much time together – and with such intensity – perhaps some personal animosity may have developed between individual musicians. All in all, I suppose, this rebellion kind of cleared the air.

But at the time it was a very dramatic moment for me and not surprisingly bitter thoughts raced through my head. I thought of the money that I had spent on countless invitations which I could better have spent on my family or my grandchildren – easily several million marks over 30 years. But suddenly all of that was forgotten. Now it was just, 'We aren't going to China, and that's that.'

However, I had already signed the tour contract, so I had to go. It was a gigantic shock. I had never been hit so hard in my entire career and I was completely shaken. Back at the hotel I went straight to my room, because I knew that I couldn't have spoken to them at that moment. If I had done, certainly nothing good would have come of it. Christine cancelled our usual order of soup and sandwich, ordering a couple of drinks to be sent up to our room instead. We sat down and talked everything over once again. Finally, she said, 'What at first might seem to be a disadvantage can often hold the seed of a far greater advantage. Now you have the chance to make a new, fresh start. You'll see, things haven't come to an end by any means.'

That seemed to me to be a very optimistic view, since it was anything but simple to get together a new orchestra at such short notice. Would it even be possible at all?

The story of the rebellion soon made the circuit in the trade, of course, and immediately people started prophesying: That's it. Last is out the door. He won't survive that. There's no way he'll take on the responsibility of a new band.

But they would be proven very wide of the mark. After I'd overcome my initial frustration, I threw myself into the task. Who was I going to ring? Which orchestra positions need rejuvenating anyway? What should the optimal mixture of young and old look like?

The first person I wanted to call was Chuck Findley in the USA. For two weeks his number lay on my desk. For two weeks I kept going to dial it, but I couldn't bring myself to do it: if Chuck refused, I would have had difficulty taking it. Finally, I overcame my doubts and dialled, and, to my great astonishment, he agreed. Not only that, he also said he could bring his brother, Bob, a former second trumpeter for Herb Alpert! That was the first light at the end of the tunnel and there were more to come in the form of Ole Holmquist, Detlev Surmann and Bob Coassin. Erlend Krauser also helped me a great deal by bringing along musicians from his own band, who formed the new rhythm section: Joe Dorff on piano, Stefan 'Stoppel' Eggert on drums, Thomas Zurmühlen on bass and Pablo Escayola on percussion. The choir and the strings had never been involved in the revolt, so they signed up, too.

Christine's prognosis proved to be right. The new band fulfils my present-day expectations even better. The lads are in it with renewed enthusiasm and enjoy playing. The life of the band is blossoming – there is young blood amongst us and music is once again one of the main topics of conversation. A short while ago Stoppel Eggert rang me to say that the rhythm section can't wait to get on the road again!

China: The Middle Kingdom

Although all the 'newcomers' were fantastic musicians, it wasn't at all easy to set off on such a big journey with an orchestra that had never performed together. How would the younger ones fit into the band? How would it work with an entirely new rhythm section? I had good reason to be uptight when Christine and I left for the Far East.

We set off a couple of days early, as I wanted to show Christine Hong Kong, which I knew from earlier tours. From there we flew on to Beijing, where a big press conference and Internet chat took place. After that, the German ambassador invited us to dinner. The tour promoter was the son of a Chinese university professor of physics who had grown up in Vienna. His father, Professor Wu, is a man of high standing in China. He had the idea of bringing European acts to the country – the son organised, the father pulled the strings. To get a concert tour like this up and going in China you need to have incredible contacts – to all the local, regional and national cultural authorities, to the governments of every individual province, the mayors, the regional bigwigs in the party, the tourist offices, and so on. It all required a great deal of finesse but Professor Wu knew all the important people and all the tricks.

The first stop on our tour was the city of Canton – or Guangzhou, as it is known today – in the south of China, about 150 kilometres north of Hong Kong. Christine and I were already there as the band arrived, one by one, from Germany, Sweden, Australia and the USA. 'My' lads came to this land so foreign to us to make music together to transcend all borders – that was a truly elevating feeling.

After two days of settling in we had our first rehearsal – the moment of truth. But it worked – and how! The load that fell off my mind must have caused a medium-sized earthquake... my new musicians were simply wonderful! But a number of instruments were still missing, along with a lot of lighting and stage equipment. Professor Wu and the German Consul chased it up and in the end we could start our first concert on time.

That evening I had even more stage fright than usual. We had been warned: Don't expect too much from the Chinese, they are very reserved.

But what a surprise – the audience was really young and many families had come with their children. They all joined in with great enthusiasm and again and again people managed to break through the security barriers and come up to us on stage. Luckily, the security people didn't task their task too seriously in southern China. 'Heaven is high and the Emperor is far away' is the relaxed motto of the region.

These scenes were repeated at our other performances in southern China, the most moving taking place during the concert in Nanjing. Suddenly around 30 or 40 little Chinese children were on stage, all in their nifty Nike shirts, and they danced as if they had invented the music themselves. That was really cute. The kids had such a sense of rhythm – no one could have done it better, not even in Harlem. They were all thoroughly enjoying themselves. I had one of the little ones in my arms, as did the trumpeter, and the choir was joking around with them – I could shed tears of joy just thinking about it.

We were very impressed by the giant metropolis of Shanghai with its ten million inhabitants. New construction is going up so fast you can't keep count of the skyscrapers. We performed at the Grand Stage, the only genuine concert hall of the whole tour. Even fans from Japan travelled to be at this concert: they knew some of the 'old' band members from our previous tours of Japan and greeted them with a big hello.

The morning after the performance we were sitting at breakfast in the hotel – I was rummaging in a bowl of roast caterpillars – when Chuck Findley returned from one of his late-night excursions. He had spent all night in a jazz club, playing music with a few American friends he'd run into. He sat down with us, completely worn out... and took out his trumpet and played some more!

In Beijing we played to 10,000 people in a full stadium. The problem was, though, that the stage was a long way from the audience and the people weren't allowed into the actual arena part. The Emperor was a lot closer there and the security were therefore more strict. So we turned the tables – if the fans couldn't come to us, we would just have to go to them. Without any warning, the musicians swarmed out into the audience. Right up in the gallery we could see the two white shirts that were Chuck and Bob – since they had wireless mikes on their trumpets, they could play from anywhere in the hall. Admittedly it's technically difficult to play so far apart, but even so they were both always on beat! The choir, too, spread out through the hall. One of the singers, Tracy, even planted herself directly in front of one of the security guards and teased him with her rhythmic moves.

Strangely enough, our CDs had been on sale in communist China for many years – thanks to Mao's Cultural Revolution in the 1960s. At that time everything of Western influence was banned – only 'harmless' instrumental music was allowed. Consequently, a lot of Chinese people turned up with their old records. At one reception an excited fan thrust 70 CDs into my hand, asking if I would autograph them. The Chinese people standing nearby broke out in embarrassed laughter at this ambush, but I asked him if he was coming to the concert the following day. 'Give me your bag and tomorrow you will get them all back, signed.' That was something special – 70 albums in China!

The tour had been planned so we also had the chance to go sightseeing. We visited the idyllic West Lake of Hang Zhou, the hypermodern skyscrapers of Shanghai, Tian An Men Square in Beijing and the Great Wall of China. Who should we bump into there but 20 of our British fans, who had come to China specifically to be at our concerts in Shanghai and Beijing.

We were all impressed by the friendliness of the Chinese people and the perfect hotels we stayed in. Everywhere they treated us with the greatest hospitality – breakfast buffets until three in the afternoon, flowers upon flowers, giant receptions... The management went to great lengths on our behalf: our every wish was their command, 24 hours a day. In Beijing we stayed at the Hotel Kempinski which, bizarrely, even had a Paulanerbräu beer house complete with liver sausage, pretzels and home brew – all served by Chinese girls in Lederhosen.

When I consider these things today – a German band leader performing in a far-away country like China, accompanied by fans from Europe and Japan – I can only come to one conclusion: this is the good side of globalisation. We all live in one world: we need no borders. Borders are mostly created by wars and battles. Music, on the other hand, and culture in general, has grown out of all of us in all its different forms and breaks through all barriers and transcends them.

'Play a little bit more purple…'

In honour of my 75th birthday, my record company wanted to release a very special album. They wanted it to unite many different styles and performers – string sounds and hip-hop, pop hits and jazz, artists of my generation and fledgling new stars – but definitely performers that you wouldn't normally associate with the music of James Last. In a way, I was returning to my beginnings, when I used to arrange and produce music for many diverse singers.

I was thrilled with the idea, but the project soon turned out to be difficult and complicated. Early on, in 2003, Universal sent me a huge package of CDs so I could listen to them and decide whom I wanted to work with. Elton John and Sting were being bandied about, but that came to nothing for legal reasons. Some, like sophisticated German pop acts Orange Blue or Laith Al-Deen, wanted to be involved, but were rejected by the company. Others, like Luciano Pavarotti, did collaborate but their contributions couldn't be released in every country. The entire legal situation was extremely tedious.

they call me hansi

That wasn't an easy situation for me. As soon as I heard that a particular group or a certain singer was going to be involved, the usual flood of music would pour through my mind and I'd sit at the computer and start to write. Then some problem would pop up and the collaboration would fizzle out – and my ideas would land in the waste-paper basket. Even when it was clear which artists would be working on the project, the same thing would happen. I'd compose something – for the singer Xavier Naidoo, for example – that I really liked; the man in charge from Universal would listen to it and after a few of bars he'd say, 'That's boring,' even though the song had hardly got going! Ah well, bin it and start again...

Finally we found just the right mix: the German singer Herbert Grönemeyer, who had just had an enormous success with his album *Mensch* (Human), the German hip-hop star Jan Delay, US rapper RZA, Tom Jones, the opera-trained punk-rock eccentric Nina Hagen, the young New Zealand soprano Hayley Westenra, Luciano Pavarotti and the German jazz trumpeter Till Brönner.

What was particularly remarkable about this combination was that many of the young artists knew James Last from their childhood. Hayley Westenra, for instance, was not even a twinkle in her father's eye when we set out on our stormy flight through wind and rain to get to her hometown of Christchurch. But her grandma owned our records, and I was a familiar figure to her. Till Brönner and Xavier Naidoo had had almost the same childhood experience. Xavier recalled that as a young boy he had often stood in front of an imaginary orchestra and imitated my style of conducting. And now we all wanted to make music together. What an adventure!

The album was recorded in Hamburg, at my place in Florida, in Berlin and in London. The record company had chosen an English producer, Alex Silva, who had made his name in Germany with the Grönemeyer album *Mensch*. Working with him was for me the most exciting and at the same time difficult part of the production. Alex had learned his trade with Dave Stewart of Eurythmics, and his background was entirely different to mine. His world is the world of technoid sounds and fast video-clip aesthetics.

My first shock came when I heard what Alex had done to my 'Lonely Shepherd'. He had totally taken apart my melody lines, dissected the tune into its individual components and demolished my musical structure. 'This bit is boring. Out it comes! We'll take this bit out of here and put it back in further towards the end where it fits better...' And so it went on – and on. I was completely shell-shocked – what is this guy doing to my music! I grew pale and quiet, then even paler and quieter. Alex looked over at me: 'Everything OK, Hansi?'

'Yes, yes,' I'd say, full of turmoil inside. 'Just go ahead...'

But in the evening in my tiny London hotel room I was at rock bottom. I began to doubt whether the way in which I write music is still relevant at all. All I saw was a great big question mark. What on earth was I still doing in this music world? I couldn't recognise what was actually going on. Yet I had always had my own very clear sound concept when I was writing a song – and he had changed it all!

I was utterly miserable and felt like bursting into tears. I had to struggle with myself to grant Alex what I otherwise granted my musicians: his own way.

That was incredibly difficult for me. It went completely against the grain. For weeks I struggled with myself over whether I should see the album through at all. We must have visited London ten times while Alex made my musical world fall to pieces. Thank goodness Christine was with me in the studio. She was a great support in this time of doubt, because she could see things from the outside, with perspective, and calm me down. That was good for me, especially as she'd bolster me again and again up with her positive attitude. If she hadn't been there, I probably would have drowned my sorrows with vodka every evening.

It wasn't much better for my musicians either. Alex didn't allow them the slightest freedom. They had to play exactly according to his concept. They weren't used to that at all, since I give them more than ample leeway.

Guitarist Erlend Krauser and Thomas Zurmühlen on bass really had to sweat: they gave it all they had and were completely shattered every evening. It was really hard work. They virtually had to play against their instincts as Alex laid down exactly how it should sound. This also meant that individual strengths were lost. Thomas, for instance, is not a studio musician and almost gave up. What made the situation even more difficult was that Alex had his own personal terminology for what he wanted. It was an additional challenge to understand him straight away and be able to put this into practice.

Derek Watkins, and Chuck and Bob Findley also had to play exactly as Alex required. Initially, I asked myself whether such top musicians would put up with some computer guy – even if he was a good one – telling them how they were supposed to play. But easy-going Bob just said, 'Don't worry, we're used to that in Los Angeles. There are dozens of producers there who work like that – "Play a little bit more purple and now add a bit of green to it…" You just have to find your way into it.'

The strings had to adjust as well. 'You have to rasp more, rasp again, really scrape it!' Alex would call out. Stefan Pintev, who comes from a classical background, reacted with consternation at first. He, too, couldn't quite imagine what he was supposed to be playing. There was a constant tension in the air, but it was never mean-spirited or personal, and it had a certain creative side to it. Alex had me write four or five different arrangements for the Pavarotti piece – 'Caruso' by Lucio Dalla – before he was finally satisfied. He wasn't meaning to put me down, but it had to be exactly as he imagined it. But – and this was what was so wonderful – once everything was finished, the whole thing made sense. Many things sounded so much more modern and were really good. In the end, working with Alex opened up a new, contemporary horizon for me.

The weakest piece in my opinion is the purely instrumental 'Windmills of Your Mind', with Derek Watkins and Till Brönner as soloists. I think the version we played at our concerts in 2004 is better. Our version sounds completely rounded, whereas Alex's sounds to me somehow tacked together, bitty. Unfortunately, one recording – 'Mama' with Zucchero – didn't make it on to the album. The song was finished but Zucchero and Alex fell out because they couldn't agree on how it should sound. Perhaps I should have intervened more. Zucchero rang me to apologise for what had gone wrong, but by then it was too late. What a shame –'Mama' is a great song.

But Alex's incredible assertiveness had an advantage – he remained just as stubborn with the record company. He had to go through a real battle of wills with Universal. Those in charge wanted to cut off the finance because production costs had gone way over budget. Most of all, when Universal wanted to produce one of their usual cheap covers, he stuck to his guns and insisted, 'No one else will do but Anton Corbijn!' In doing so, he gave me a greater gift than he could ever have imagined.

Anton Corbijn is an absolute star. His photos are almost as famous as the music idols he has photographed: U2, Tom Waits, David Bowie, Johnny Cash, Miles Davis... Usually a five-figure sum (in British pounds) has to land in his bank account before Corbijn reaches for his camera, so he seemed out of reach for our CD cover. But Anton is Dutch and my music had always been popular in Holland. During our first conversation he told me his parents had loved James Last and he had more or less grown up listening to our records. So, yes, he would do it – it would be a great honour for him. And so Anton came to Florida with an assistant, a bag of equipment and a black hat in his hand.

Anton is great. There was a chemistry between us from the first moment.

'Hello, Anton. So what are we going to do?'

'Oh, well, nothing in particular. Let's just drive around the golf course in the cart for a while.'

Then, of all places, he stopped at the ugliest spot for miles around. 'Hansi, stand over there.'

'What? You mean *there*?' I asked in disbelief. He was pointing towards an uncared-for wall in a corner for rubbish.

'Yes, right there!'

'And what am I supposed to do?'

'Do? Nothing at all. If you want, just grab the hat and be you.'

Now that was certainly different to all my previous experiences with photographers: move this way, do this or that, cross your legs, Hansi in the lift, look up, Hansi in hussar costume, blue wall – white suit, white wall – blue suit, and so on.

With Anton there was none of that. No additional light, no props, no artificial poses. He just let me be and took photographs. It was entirely casual and relaxed. Anton had recognised who I was. All the others had imposed their idea of 'James Last' on me, but Anton captured me as I am. Half a day's work and we were finished. In the evening we went out for dinner and the next morning he was gone. The incredible thing about his pictures is that he made me see myself in a different light. The photos have actually changed me. I have discovered myself again – after 75 years.

Recently an agency that imitates the work of Anton Corbijn approached me, wanting to take photos of me with a black hat. I refused.

The CD we went to all this trouble for is called *They Call Me Hansi* and it was released at around the time our 2004 tour started. Despite a good PR campaign, it was not a great success. For many there wasn't enough 'James Last' on it, while others wanted more Naidoo, Grönemeyer, Delay, whatever. I felt really bad about it, especially for Alex Silva. Alex is a great guy. He was immensely dedicated to the project and had naturally hoped it would come to more.

The disappointment was great for me too. It is quite possible that *They Call Me Hansi* marks the end of my recording career. Now, when so many youngsters come along with something they've put together themselves, the labels shy away from the enormous costs of an orchestra. Although I have a contract with my record company that lasts until I'm 80, at the moment Universal doesn't seem to want to produce anything – and all the while thousands of ideas are running through my mind.

Maybe they think of me as an old codger who has no place in the contemporary music business, but I have fans all over the world who see things differently. If a CD production really is no longer lucrative, we will just have to hold great concerts instead. They are running fantastically. We have as much success with them as Elton John. By the way, the record companies have picked up on that too – now their contracts with new artists guarantee them a share of the tour takings.

One of my many ideas is doing a TV show with my band where famous singers could sing whatever they liked, which would sometimes be completely different from what people are used to hearing from them. Imagine what a party that would be!

epilogue
In Hamburg

Hamburg, my old home, in September 2006. Almost six months have passed since I began working on this book, six months of memories. But our latest tour is set to start and there are a thousand things to do, so there is no more time for nostalgia.

I can hardly wait to be on stage again and to really get down to business with my marvellous musicians. It is simply wonderful to see how the audience gets into the spirit of things, not just the tried and true fans but also the new concert audiences, how people get rocking who you would never have expected to. The enthusiasm and the applause are my nourishment. The older I get, the more I approach my limits. Today we play much more sophisticated compositions than we used to, such as 'The Tapestry of Nations'. Now that I only play what I want to, I am also understood by those who once only saw me as the Party or Polka King. The questions that the journalists ask clearly reflect that, since they now have more depth and reveal more genuine interest. Now the ladies and gentlemen of the press even arrive on time, whereas they used to trickle in when it suited them.

Well, soon we set off again and I hope this tour will be as perfect as the one in 2004. That was our cosy tour. The atmosphere in the band was incredibly harmonious, so positive. Everyone felt we could go on like this for weeks on end. Everything fitted and was free of stress for me. No one complained, there were no niggling disputes between the different instrument groups and there was wonderful discipline. Two top trumpeters like Chuck Findley and Derek Watkins could easily have envied each other the applause and been at each other's throat like divas but there was nothing of the kind. They supported each other, cheered each other on and enriched each other's performance.

I feel fit and up to the exertions of the coming tour. The worst part is the end of a concert evening: leaving the stage is not easy. I see people standing and cheering, their happy faces radiating joy, I wave to the people up in the galleries – and then it is over. Everyday routine takes over again and the party is over. I have to be very careful that tears don't come to my eyes. Every time is after all a farewell, and every farewell is a kind of dying. Will we ever see each other again? Will we get together again? Sometimes that really gets the better of me. It is so difficult for me to see myself as a 77-year-old. I don't feel old – in fact it seems to me as if I'm only halfway through the programme.

There is a lot of music waiting for me out there. At nine in the morning I turn on the computer and start to write, and that will never change. Even if there are no more CDs, at least there will be arrangements for concerts. I feel sorry for young people in the music trade who are so full of big plans and cannot realise them. Or for those who have lost themselves through money and fame. The pop-song business is the worst. Someone wins a contest, becomes a star for a short time and imagines their life will always go on like that. But it doesn't, and it is difficult to come to terms with this knowledge.

I don't believe I have distanced myself from my origins or the roots of my childhood. I may have travelled around the world many times, earned a lot of money, fulfilled all my wishes and had a great deal of success, but I have always acted in the framework of my own personality. As a child I learned music, then I was a student of music and today I am still a musician – I have never left myself behind and I still take pleasure in every lovely chord. If you know why the phrasing should sound just so and why this semitone should be in this particular position, you can live from that forever.

This kind of work provides nourishment for body *and* soul. That's why composers and conductors can never stop. They can always see and hear the good in the music and just keep going. I could think of enough to do for the next 20 years: arranging Puccini melodies, film music conveying deep emotions, an album with the cellist Yo Yo Ma... the last chapter of this book is a long way from finished! Recently when we moved from our place on the Outer Alster in Hamburg to our new address, we discovered a whole pile of unpublished scores I had written. Who knows what I can make of them? After all, I am only 77 – an old hat that can still be worn by many!

I am sitting in my study in my new home in Poppenbüttel and there's the score of a romantic melody on the computer monitor. The image of a small church in the Allgäu region springs to mind. We were recording in Kempten for a TV show and Christine's family were there, but she had to be in Munich and couldn't make it. I was disappointed and sad. I really missed her. So in the middle of the night I got in a taxi and went to a nearby golf course where there's a chapel at the eighth hole. I had my Discman with me, so I put on our Bach CD and – at half past two in the morning – wandered over the course for two hours in deep reflection. After that I felt a lot better.

Christine, my family and Waltraud have been the most important people in my life, along with a handful of musical friends. But real friends? I have often thought that one person or another would go through thick and thin with me, but things turned out quite differently. The chance of finding friends who have nothing to do with music was very low in my life – after all, everything revolved around music.

My gaze falls through the window on to the lawn in front of our home. There are children running about, shouting, laughing, completely at ease. I really enjoy that. These children show me that life always goes on. About a year ago I was at the funeral of Benny Bendorff's younger son, Florian. He, like his father, had been a guitarist. He had played for the Schürzenjäger – The Danglers – and had committed suicide. During the ceremony, from the back of the church, came the restless whimpering of a new baby and I thought, such is life – one life passes and another begins. A few months ago I became a grandfather for the third time. This time it was Ron and his wife Silke who had become parents. Clara Estella is the name of this tiny mortal. So Clara will also get to know her Opa, and who knows, perhaps she will see me on stage on my 80th birthday.

I have come to terms with my life. I know what I have done wrong and what I have done right. When 'Him up there' says it's time, then I will go – without sadness or regret. I consider myself one of the lucky ones who can say, 'That was it.' There is no panic that I might have missed out on anything, no urge to catch up on missed opportunities. I feel quite free, without the slightest degree of fear. What could happen anyway? Everything has already happened...

appendix
by Thomas Macho

The Last Family

James Last has always emphasised that there's a large family working on stage as well as backstage. This book would not be complete without giving some of these family members, on behalf of everyone, the chance to have their say.

The Brothers: Robert and Werner

Robert Last (1921–1985) recorded several LPs for Decca/Teldec in the early 1970s. Called *Happy Dancing*, they were trying to capitalise on the success of the *Non Stop Dancing* series but the sales figures were very modest. Layout, graphics and title showed clearly that these albums were typical 'me too' products.

'The fact that Robert became estranged from his brother Hans was definitely the biggest mistake of his life,' says Marianne Last of her husband. 'He knew this. But he was a very gullible man, weak and unable to assert himself, and he believed the declarations of some unreliable managers with their promises to make him a star. They produced four or five albums with him and that was it – then they dropped him like a hot potato. He never recovered from this disappointment. Our whole family suffered from this situation, our children as well as I. He was just sitting at home and didn't know what to do. He didn't have the heart to go to Hansi and say, "I'm sorry, what I did was wrong." Robert was never a star, and he would never have become one. He was just a good musician.'

The couple had two sons, Lutz and Roy, who was ten years younger than his brother. Roy was a musician, too, and sadly passed away in 2004.

Werner Last (1923–1982) was signed by Polydor in 1966 as Kai Warner as a musical arranger and bandleader, and became an important figure in the German entertainment industry. 'We decided that Kai Warner can do anything he likes, except be a "Last",' says Werner Klose, who was responsible for Werner's productions at Polydor. 'There was to be a clear distinction between his image and that of his brother: his was to be younger, more modern, more sophisticated. The slogan was "The fresh sound of Kai Warner". He was a very good musician and each of his albums sold between 18,000 and 20,000 units. That wasn't bad, but compared to Hansi's sales of course very little.'

Ossi Drechsler explains Polydor's strategy: 'It was important for us that Werner did not sign with a rival firm under his real name Last. I've got to admit, though, that our selection of his pseudonym Kai Warner was not very clever. You never knew how to pronounce Kai Warner right, if it was an English or a German name. Werner was very introverted, never talked about his records and did no promotion – which didn't exactly help the product. He was always in Hansi's shadow and brooded over why he was less successful, instead of standing up for himself and saying, "Look at me – I am Kai Warner and I'm producing great music."'

Werner was highly respected by his fellow musicians, but he was never pleased with himself. His range stretched from the *Non Stop Dancing*-like *Go In* series through folk songs (*Wer recht in Freuden tanzen will*) and vocal albums (*Poppa Joe's Party*) to classical music (*Warner plays Wagner*). At the end of the 1970s he signed with Philips, got a new image and switched to a mix of disco and the Philadelphia sound, but he never again came close to his sales figures at Polydor.

Werner also discovered and produced the pop singer Renate Kern, and composed several hits for her – 'Lass den dummen Kummer' (No More Stupid Heartache), 'Du musst mit den Wimpern klimpern' (You've Got to Flutter Your Eyelashes).

At the Controls: Ossi Drechsler and Werner Klose

The Viennese Drechsler, responsible for A & R, and the northerner Klose, head of marketing, soared to new heights at Polydor at the same time as James Last: the band leader was their first big success.

This is how Drechsler recalls the situation in 1965: 'When Hansi entered the music scene with his *Non Stop Dancing* concept, there were a lot of dance orchestras in Germany: Max Greger, Hugo Strasser, Alfred Hause or Kurt Edelhagen, for example. But they had dance orchestras in the traditional sense, evoking suits, ties and dancing close together. For them the term "band" would have been an unacceptable disparagement. Then there was Bert Kaempfert, who was hardly noticed in his home country and whose true value was not recognised there – he experienced his big successes as a composer in the USA. None of these musicians was in the least bit interested in the newest pop hits. There was a clear allocation of responsibilities: the long-haired youngsters were responsible for noise, and the orchestra leaders responsible for refined dance entertainment in tango, foxtrot or cha-cha rhythm.

'It's easy to see why, in conditions like these, an album like *Non Stop Dancing* came as a real bombshell. Suddenly this very neat, middle-class man in his mid-thirties came along and played Beatles and Rolling Stones songs, and suddenly all those hits which stood for youth revolution and nonconformist behaviour became listenable and danceable for their parents' generation. The reason for the enormous success of *Non Stop Dancing* was the fact that Hansi cut the hair off long-haired music and straightened the generation gap.'

In July 1965 *Non Stop Dancing* entered the German Top 40 album charts and remained there an incredible 60 weeks alongside albums like *Beatles For Sale* or *The Rolling Stones No.2*. Werner Klose remembers, 'We had a sales manager in Hamburg, Herr von Albedill, and sales managers were important people then. When Albedill listened to the album before it was released, he immediately said, "Now we've got our Beatles!" Then it was discussed in detail what to call this thing. Coining the phrase *Non Stop Dancing* was certainly of great importance, because, had we called the record *Hits for Dancing* or something like that, success would not have come so quickly.'

'For us the tremendous success of *Non Stop Dancing* was a blessing,' says Drechsler, 'because the record company had been struggling with a considerable drop in turnover. The hit market was saturated and there was a dramatic slump in singles sales, so

Last came to us just at the right moment. So we didn't waste any time – in the same year we released *Non Stop Dancing '66* with even greater success – internationally as well as at home. It was obvious we had a potential series of productions that could make the cash till ring twice a year. With one exception, every *Non Stop Dancing* album between 1965 and 1979 entered the German album charts, and many of them reached number one. In all, there were 33 albums in 23 years, making the *Non Stop Dancing* albums the longest and most successful series in the history of popular music.'

The workload Drechsler, Klose and especially the artist took on was enormous. Between mid-1965 and the end of 1969, the first four and a half years of his career, James Last produced an incredible 40 albums, two-thirds of which went gold.

Werner Klose: 'He made records that went down well with all the experts and raised Hansi's profile. They really expanded the horizon. People were surprised and said, 'Hansi can do that too!' Offbeat and unusual recordings like *The Threepenny Opera* or *Hair* were milestones, even if they were outside the mainstream of popular music.'

Because of Last's potential as a cash cow, Polydor increased his output: 12 new albums were released in 1971 alone. Klose pushed his artist to work more and more: 'The production line we demanded from him was downright inhuman: ten, eleven, twelve LPs a year. But one success creates a demand for more, and almost all the LPs entered the charts. In some weeks there were seven or eight albums in the sales charts.

'How tolerant is the market? Today you would say: one album every two years, or we've got one Udo – a second won't work. At that time, we at Polydor had signed 28 orchestras, dozens of pop stars, and almost all the German singer-songwriters. And everyone sold well. We *created* markets.

'With this vast number of new albums and musical styles, Polydor did not want to ask too much of the consumers, so we divided the productions into different sections, using the motto "Last times four".

'There was the party Last, the elegant Last, the folksy Last and the international Last. Each segment was aimed at a different type of customer. We were actually a firm within a firm, but with very few employees.'

This intensive work brought Last an abundant harvest. In 1972 alone he received 51 gold records. For each 'gold coin' you had to sell at least 250,000 LPs in Germany. After just eight years of 'James Last', Hansi received his 100th gold record – a true world record. At that time Elvis had notched up 76 gold records and the Beatles had 58.

In Cannes Last was awarded the MIDEM trophy, he won every audience and jury poll for 'best' or 'most popular' orchestra, Radio Luxemburg's Honorary Lion, the Silver Seagull, the Golden Gramophone, Star of the Year, the Golden Clef, etc. etc. etc... And according to GEMA in the 1970s Last was in third place for sales in the classical music division, surpassed only by Richard Strauss and Richard Wagner!

At the end of the 1970s two notable national accolades were added to the many honours and awards Hansi had already received. In 1979 he received the Golden Camera (then given solely for achievements in TV) and – a year earlier – one of the highest honours the Federal Republic of Germany can bestow, the Order of Merit. Federal President Walter Scheel awarded the medal in Bonn, then the capital, 'for his outstanding merit as composer, arranger, and orchestra leader, who gave fresh impetus to German popular music and who gained exceptional recognition at home and abroad.'

Klose puts it in a nutshell: 'Hansi was the only artist who had his own office with a secretary at Polydor in Hamburg. And rightly so: in his heyday, he made more money for the record company than any other artist worldwide, with the possible exception of the Beatles.'

Keen Ears: Peter Klemt, sound

It is no exaggeration to say that Peter Klemt was the most successful German sound engineer of the 1960s and 1970s. With his work for James Last and Bert Kaempfert, he set the tone for two of the most popular orchestras worldwide.

Munich-born Klemt began his career at the Bavarian Broadcasting studios before deciding to switch to Deutsche Grammophon in Hamburg 'for a year or two'. That was in 1959; Klemt still lives near the city.

No sooner had he arrived in Hamburg than he was entrusted with the production of a largely unknown musician, Bert Kaempfert. 'We made our recordings in the Hamburg Concert Hall, which had wonderful, natural acoustics,' he recalls. 'We had a mobile recording unit that we set up at night, once the audience had left. We would start recording just before midnight.'

Klemt's very first collaboration with Kaempfert, 'Wonderland by Night' became a mega-seller in the USA. This was followed a short time later by the world hit 'Strangers in the Night'.

After that the company sent Klemt to Paris to re-equip the Polydor studio from mono to stereo. 'I relished the task and I really felt at home in Paris. But I had to cope with an enormous difference in mindset. If recording was set for 10am, I'd be at the studio at 9.30, but the first musician wouldn't arrive until 10.15. He'd set down his instrument then disappear for a Pernod in the nearest bistro. You could bet on nothing happening before 11.

Back then singles might still have four songs on them, which all had to be done in a session of about three hours. But the musicians deliberately dragged overtime out of it – a little coughing fit here, an off note there and, in next to no time, we'd gone over time.'

When Klemt returned to Hamburg, the orchestra leaders were scrambling to secure his services. 'An 80-hour week was not unusual. I didn't have a weekend. At that time I took on anything and everything – Roberto Delgado (alias Horst Wende), Alfred Hause, Kai Warner, Helmut Zacharias, Max Greger, Günther Norisone – but I always tried to make something special out of every production. It was never something run-of-the-mill for me.'

Klemt supervised all Kaempfert's recordings, and when Last signed with Polydor, Klemt was top of the future Party King's list. From the very first production, he became Last's ever-present sound engineer, a collaboration that was to last almost 30 years.

The Long-Distance Runner:
Detlef Surmann, trombone

There is only one position in the Last band that has been held by one person since the 1960s – trombone, played by Detlef Surmann. His father, Willi, a saxophonist, and Hans Last had been colleagues at NDR, and that was how the young musician discovered Last was looking for a trombonist for his tour with Freddy Quinn. That year, 1968, 26-year-old Surmann became the youngest member of the band. Today he is the longest-serving member of the orchestra.

Shortly after his debut, Surmann took over the tiresome task of music copyist for his boss. 'The days when Hansi made an LP per month were fantastic for us from a financial point of view, but for

Hansi it was hell. As copyist I experienced first-hand what his writing routine was like. On average he managed a number per day. I was writing non-stop. His productivity was incredible – and he rarely made a mistake.'

Surmann, who lives in Hamburg and has a daughter who's also in the music business, knows his long-time employer like no one else. 'Hansi is a fantastic boss. He is generous and good-humoured and he always allowed us the leeway we needed. But there is a side to him that few people would suspect – he shies away from conflict and is often so caught up in his musical train of thought that it is sometimes difficult to get a decision out of him. If someone wanted something from him and it didn't suit him, he would simply turn on his heel and leave. He wouldn't even listen.

'I remember one time when Inge Schierholz, his assistant at Polydor, needed a decision from him: "So, Hansi, what are we going to do?"

'"We'll talk about it later."

'"You only need to say yes or no."

'"Later."

'Inge couldn't take it upon herself to accept the offer, so she had to pass on a negative answer. Three days later, when the topic was old hat, Hansi comes up to her and says, "So, what about this thing?"

'"I had to refuse."

'"But why?"

'"You wouldn't decide."

'"But you could have said something!"

'"But, Hansi, I chased you for three days about it!"'

Surmann has also worked for Kai Warner, Bert Kaempfert and Sammy Davis Jr, among others, as a freelance musician, so he knows how difficult it can be to engage the audience. 'From my position on stage you can only see the first two or three rows. The rest of the auditorium disappears into darkness or you can't see them for the lights. And there are always some who simply never, and I mean never, let themselves be drawn in. Then you think they aren't enjoying anything, but they are the ones you fix on as a musician. Sometimes it can make you despair.'

Although the millions of notes that Surmann has copied for Last haven't made him a millionaire, they have given him an insight into some of the 'secrets' of the Last sound and today he arranges music himself. 'I have learned a lot from Hansi, above all, to write simply. Of course, I sat down and asked myself how he does it, and sometimes I have thought that here or there another note could be added. Wrong. The art is in leaving things out. People think you have to keep adding and adding, even if it is just to keep everyone in the orchestra busy. But that is nonsense. Leave it out! That's how he works!'

The Last Beatle: Benny Bendorff, bass

Before Joachim 'Benny' Bendorff joined the band, Fiete Wacker was the man on bass. He played everything with a plectrum – much the same as Ladi Geisler did for Bert Kaempfert – and you could hear it clearly. For every stroke there is an identifiable 'click' in the 'upwards' sound before the actual tone is heard 'downwards'.

Bendorff (b. 1946 in Hamburg) brought to the band a strong bass sound in the rock and pop vein. He actually learned trumpet before he finally switched to the bass – a move inspired by Cliff Richard & the Shadows. In the mid-1960s Beatles fan Benny started to work as a studio musician – until a phone call from Waltraud Last changed his life: 'My husband is looking for a bassist for his new album – would you have time?'

'You must have dialled the wrong number. This is Benny Bendorff, I play rock 'n' roll.'

'No, no, you're exactly the man I'm after.'

Bendorff survived his baptism of fire – the production of *Hair* – with bravura, and since then he has been a fixture in the Last universe. And let's not forget, as a bass player he is something of an alter ego for his boss.

Occasionally, Last has recorded some of Bendorff's own compositions, but above all he gave him the chance to perform solo as a singer on songs like 'Live and Let Die', 'Silly Love Songs' and 'Mull of Kintyre' – Bendorff's enthusiasm for Paul McCartney is unmistakable. He has also released some albums of his own, one of which is called *Flowers of Liverpool* and is – surprise, surprise – dedicated to the Beatles.

Today he runs a sound studio, where he has recorded, among others, the bestselling Schürzenjäger (The Danglers).

The Man with the Broken Bell: Bob Lanese, trumpet

Bob, from Cleveland, Ohio, is the tall, striking former lead trumpeter in the Last band, the man with the famous dent in his instrument.

Cleveland seems to be fertile ground for brass players in the higher echelons – Rick Kiefer and the brothers Chuck and Bob Findley (who have worked with the Last band since 2002) also come from the university town on Lake Erie. Bob, born in 1941, has been playing trumpet since he was eight. He gained a degree in music education and was working in different bands when a letter from the army arrived. 'It said: either you volunteer for three years for a military band, which means you can stay in

Cleveland, or you will be called up, which means you go to Vietnam. So I volunteered to join the Norad-Commanders Big Band – but it didn't help. I still had to go to Vietnam for a year.'

After surviving the nightmare in Southeast Asia, Bob became a research assistant at Texas State University and did his Master of Performance in classical music. In 1970 he came to Europe as a member of the Glenn Miller Band. 'During a concert in Hamburg, the NDR people heard me and hired me. Besides, I met a very attractive girl, so I stayed.'

The bent bell of Lanese's trumpet has become his trademark. What many fans think is an ingenious variant of construction – or a homage to Dizzy Gillespie – actually has a rather mundane story behind it. 'My trumpet broke during a tour and I took it to Harald Wetzl, an instrument master builder in Hamburg, and he knew that I always hold my trumpet downwards when I play. That often caused a problem with the height of the microphone, because in those days we played two to a mike. If the man with me played straight ahead, he blew in a completely different direction. That's why Master Wetzl attached the broken bell – so I could play downwards, but the tone would still come out at the right height to the microphone because of the upwards kink. That's the secret.'

Since Bob Lanese plays for many other orchestras he is in a position to judge their different working methods. 'In the 1970s there were many band leaders in Hamburg who tried to sound like James Last – Les Humphries, Robert Last, Jo Ment. They played the same pieces and the same medleys and above all they had the same musicians. But they never succeeded in copying the Last sound. That was also due to the brilliance of our sound engineer Peter Klemt. With his great experience and intuition he knew how to get the right sound out of Hansi's arrangements.'

In Bob's view, albums like *In the Mood for Trumpets* or *World Hits* are milestones. 'They were super recordings. The car is running on all 12 cylinders and everyone is on the same emotional level. Even in terms of concentration, everyone is giving his all. That's luck. You can't plan it.'

In summer 2002, the working relationship between Lanese and Last came to an end in the controversy surrounding the China tour. (Even now, you can't mistake the tear in Bob's eye.) Today, Bob is out on the golf range at seven in the morning and afterwards he gives trumpet lessons to children. He conducts a state-sponsored youth big band and the swinging jazz Down Town Big Band in Hamburg.

But the greatest challenge for him is still the profession of studio musician. 'You get a phone call: "Be there at ten!" And that's it. No other info. So you pack all your instruments together and take different mutes with you – you don't have any idea of what you are going to play. It could be anything – classical, a solo, a ballad, Miles Davis, Dixieland, Happy Sound – and, whatever they demand of you, you have to deliver it as quickly and as well as possible. That's the challenge!'

The Choirboy: Simon Bell & Company

Simon Bell is the longest-serving member of the Last Choir. A Scot, he started his singing career in 1965, and four years later Madeline Bell (no relation) arranged his first studio jobs. Over the years Simon sang for stars like Julio Iglesias, Marvin Gaye, Hot Chocolate, Adam & the Ants and Dusty Springfield.

He first recorded with James Last in 1978, for the album *Non Stop Dancing '78*. He met Last at a benefit for the children of Joanne Stone, a singer who used to sing in Last's choir and who had died from a malignant brain tumour. Bell admired and was a close friend of Dusty Springfield. He spent many months at her side when she was stricken with cancer, and stayed with her until she passed away in 1999.

Over the course of 30 years, faces (and voices) in the choir have changed. Madeline Bell started a solo career (with her future husband Barry Reeves on drums) when she left in the late 1970s. Sunny and Sue Glover had a huge hit in 1975 with 'Doctor's Orders'. Russell and Joanne (R&J) Stone had a worldwide hit in 1976 with 'We Do It'. Tony Burrows, Kay Garner, Lynn Cornell, Irene Chanter, Stevie Lange, P.P. Arnold, Jimmy Helms, George Chandler, Jimmy Chambers and David Martin – many of these singers had very successful careers beyond the Last gigs. Helms, Chandler and Chambers, for example, formed Londonbeat and had a big hit with 'I've Been Thinking About You', while Martin is a well-known songwriter: his 'Can't Smile Without You' was a favourite for Barry Manilow.

The Soloist: Derek Watkins, trumpet

Derek Watkins (born 1945) comes from a highly musical family. Both his father and his grandfather played trumpet, and he was just five years old when he squeaked out his first notes on his horn. At 13 he was playing in his father's dance band. The list of stars he has worked with is endless, ranging from Henry Mancini to Robbie Williams, from Barbra Streisand to Tom Jones – there usually with two other members of the Last band, drummer Terry Jenkins and Big Jim Sullivan on guitar.

Last soon recognised what a jewel he had in his orchestra and entrusted Watkins with spectacular solo parts in the concerts. 'Exodus', 'MacArthur Park', 'Summertime', 'Rhapsody in Blue',

'My Way' and 'Windmills of My Mind' are just a few of the highlights he has contributed with his trumpet and flugelhorn.

'I have never felt as comfortable in any ensemble as I do with Hansi,' says Watkins. 'Playing for him is pure pleasure.'

The Storyteller: Conny Güntensperger, tour manager

'On his 50th birthday Hansi gave us a brief speech: "One thing I promise you, I will keep going for another ten years!" Well, we thought, he's probably just saying that. But now he is almost 77, and almost all our fellow musos who were with us back then have long since retired and he is the only one still on stage. Fantastic! I once tallied up all of our concert tours: we have performed in a total of 50 countries!'

Conny Güntensperger should know, since he has been responsible for the organisation of the Last tours since 1970. 'Before I joined Hansi, I was working for a Hamburg concert management organisation, where I dealt with everyone from the Rolling Stones to Roy Black. One day I was told we were doing a concert with James Last. James Last? Isn't that the Yank who modernises folk songs? I didn't really feel like doing it. But, when you are working for someone else, you don't get to choose. You've just got to do it. I went to the event in Travemünde, which had been organised by the *Stern* magazine, and I liked the "Yank" on the spot. That was in 1969, and since 1970 I have been his constant tour companion.'

Today Güntensperger's job is comparable to that of a theatre stage manager. 'I make sure that people stick to the schedule, that everyone appears on stage on time, that the choir comes on at the right moment. I also deal with the musicians' problems, like if they forget something or can't find their music, Sometimes they are like little children and I am their nanny.'

Güntensperger's area of responsibility used to be much wider. It started with working out the tour plan and booking the halls and extended to enormous financial responsibility. 'After every concert I had to cash up the box office with the local organisers. However, it would have been difficult to diddle us, since the halls were usually sold out, so we knew exactly how high the takings should be. Each evening I would get about 200,000 marks cash in my hand. Hansi and his band only got 30,000 marks and the rest went to the concert agency. I once broached the subject of how little he was getting out of it but Hansi only said, "That's OK. The concert agent is carrying the risk and I signed. That's perfectly in order."'

Güntensperger, one year younger than Last, is one of the great storytellers in the band, and after more than 30 years he knows his boss inside out. 'Hansi knows everything, even if a spotlight is hanging crooked. At the same time he is the most generous boss you can imagine. He has always showered us with presents. We're sitting at breakfast in London and Hansi asks, "What have you got planned this morning?"

'"Nothing in particular."

'"Do you feel like going shopping with me?"

'"Sure, let's go."

'We go into the best stores and my eyes are popping out of my head. I pick up something nice here and there, like a silk shirt with a crazy pattern, priced about £100.

'"Do you like that?"

'"Yes, it's great."

'"Then take five of them."

'Then Harald Ende happened to come by, so he gave him the same thing. I got two suits and a beautiful leather coat with fur trimming. On that morning alone Hansi must have spent about 10,000 marks on me.

'Hansi was always very generous to his audiences as well. During a concert in Duisburg there was a power failure, a total blackout. To while away the time the people had to spend waiting, Hansi made an announcement: "Anyone who wants to go home can go out on the left, and everyone else can go right, where there is free schnapps for all!" He paid for schnapps for 3,000 people. Even today I have no idea how he managed to organise so much spirits for so many people!

'We have all learned a lot from Hansi, most of all tolerance,' he muses, before adding with a grin, 'and how to crack open mussels and slurp oysters!'

Lord of the Threads: Charly Cisek, wardrobe

Charly Cisek, the tailor for the Last band, has been in charge of well-fitting suits and ironed shirts since the early years. He originally wanted to be a costume interpreter at the opera, but then decided to go freelance and, after a recommendation from Detlef Surmann's father, entered the circle of NDR musicians.

'I have known Hansi since 1962, when I made his first stage suit. He was still playing in Alfred Hause's and Franz Thon's orchestras at the time. Waltraud came to my workshop in her little VW with the kids on the back seat to pick up the things. Later he never had time, he was always working. I would come at all times of the day and night to his place so he could try things on. I don't know how many suits I have made for him.'

Proudly, Cisek recounts the following story: 'For his performance in the Royal Albert Hall I sewed him a white suit, a white tie and a white shirt, topped off with white shoes. The stage was entirely in darkness and the auditorium was black as night. As the strings played softly behind a black curtain, a spotlight went on and Hansi came down the stairs all in white in front of a black background. That was a bit of a risk for him going down the narrow stairs in the darkness – he could easily have tripped. But he looked so fantastic and the applause was enormous. When he reached the bottom, he opened his jacket and pointed to the label with my name on it. After the concert he said to me, "Charly, did you hear that? That was your applause." And sure enough the critics wrote that Last has the best-dressed band.'

Cisek has accompanied the band on its tours since the beginning of the 1980s. 'When Hansi comes into the dressing room, everything is hanging in the order that he likes to put it on: trousers, shirt, long shoehorn, shoes, and so on. Finally, I stand at the stage door and check that everyone is wearing the right thing. During the first part of the concert I iron the suits for the second part, and during the second part I prepare the wardrobe for the next day. I used to also have the schnapps in my care, just to make sure that no one had one too many!'

Even though Charly is now enjoying his retirement on the golf course, Last remains timeless for him. 'Whether Hansi is 40 or 60 or 75, when he is on stage he is the Music Man. He no longer feels any frailty. That is his elixir of life – he is young.'

First Fiddle: Stefan Pintev, violin

'When I joined Hansi at the age of 17, I was the youngest by far. The second youngest was 30 years older than me. And add on 20 and that was the average age of the remaining strings. It was a sort of pensioner string band.'

Stefan Pintev was born in Bulgaria, his family moving to

Germany while he was still a baby. After completing his classical violin studies, he went on tour with Bert Kaempfert at the tender age of 16. Afterwards he joined Last.

'My first Last album was *Russland Erinnerungen* (Russian Memories) and this music is in my blood anyway. Hansi thought it was great that such a young fellow played with the group. Bit by bit it dawned on him that it wasn't just old string players who could play well, but young ones too, and they would perhaps enjoy it more.'

So Last continued to choose younger string players. Most of the 'newcomers' are students of classical music who have been able to gain an entirely new experience in this type of orchestra. 'The unfamiliar motivates and liberates us. We gain a great deal of pleasure that would not be possible in this form at a classical concert. We can have fun on stage, and Hansi even encourages us to.'

Life on tour opens up new perspectives for the youngsters. 'For me it was a whole new world. I was a goodie-goodie violin student. Benny Bendorff and some of the women in the choir were the first people I met and they introduced me to sounds I had never heard: jazz, rock, Gino Vannelli, Tower of Power, Deodato – music I had never heard until then. And of course the old-timers wanted to show me *everything* they had learned in ten years in three weeks! Benny and I were sitting at the bar in Tokyo talking about life and perhaps about music when Hansi joined us, saying, "Benny, don't ruin the boy completely!"'

Last's relaxed and non-dogmatic way of dealing with all sorts of music was a revelation for Pintev. 'Hansi opened my eyes. You can be a good musician without having to be inhibited. That is the problem of classical training. There are strict rules that allow you very little freedom to approach the music playfully or to interact with the audience. And it is exactly this interaction between the band and the audience that is constantly taking place with Hansi. That is why so many fans come again and again. They draw a breath of life from it.'

Last understands human nature and to ensure the right artistic quality he places his faith in the carrot and not the stick. 'Hansi's authority arises among other things from his attempt to make his musicians feel good, whether it is a matter of the hotels, the restaurants, the buses or his caring way of asking whether you'd like something to drink and then pouring it for you himself. He always travels with us, he eats with us, he drinks with us – that forges a bond. And he also allows us great musical freedom. He doesn't dictate a particular variation, but simply says, "Play it how you feel it." Hansi is not the boss but your counterpart, and through that he achieves the greatest possible homogeneity and performance. Performance that grows from motivation, not pressure.'

Apart from Last, Pintev also plays for the NDR Symphony Orchestra, is a sought-after studio musician and has his own string quintet, The G-Strings.

The Technology Fan: Tommy Eggert, synthesiser

By the time Tommy Eggert was 13, amplifier cables, microphone stands and loudspeakers – not to mention clouds of nicotine and alcohol fumes – were nothing out of the ordinary for him. A trained bass player, he had already performed – armed with a special permit from the Hamburg youth protection authority – in various jazz clubs in the city with the Mac Thomson Jazz Brothers.

In 1972 Ronnie Last joined Tommy's class at the Albert-Schweitzer grammar school and the two of them soon founded their first band, Bierfass (Beer Keg). They played loud, hard rock and Ronnie would regularly lug over his father's unwanted instruments from Studio Hamburg.

Eggert was mostly interested in anything that made electronic noises and one day when Last needed a specific sound effect for his new *Non Stop Dancing* LP, Eggert's hour had come. 'Hansi rang me at home. My mother came to get me, all excited. "Come quickly, James Last is on the line!" I thought it was a joke. Why would he ring me? I only knew him from my friend's birthday parties. But it really was him. "Tell me, Tommy, Ron says that you are really good on the synthesiser. Is that right?"

'"Yeah, well, a bit."

'"Would you like to play a few sounds on it for our new LP?"

'My first reaction was: Wow, I'd have to practise really hard! But I was sure it would take about six months to record an LP like that – by the time the music was ready, the musicians had practised, weeks of rehearsals… there's plenty of time. So I said yes. "Good. Then get yourself a taxi, pack your Mini Moog and come to the studio." My heart sank like a stone. What have I let myself in for!? But now that I'd said yes, I had to go. So I arrived at the studio, knees weak, and in front of me stood Hansi, the megastar…

'They were playing that typical 1970s pop, and it was the first time I had heard a sound like that out of those giant loudspeakers. It sounded fantastic. Super horns. I was really impressed. Then Hansi played me a couple of tracks and said, "I need these two or three sound effects – do you think you can manage it?" My luck was really in: I could do exactly what he needed! I rode home full of pride and Hansi was happy, too. I was quick and I knew how to do it. That was 1977 and since then I have been his synth man.'

Eggert has been a fixture in the production team ever since *Biscaya* – Last's first accordion and synthesiser album. 'We developed a very intense working atmosphere together. We didn't just do electronic things – we also formed quite a good rhythm group, for the *Jahrhundertmelodien* (Melodies of the Century) album, for example. Hansi played piano, Ronnie drums and I was on bass.'

Many of the albums were done under extreme time pressure. 'One Sunday evening in 1987 Hansi rang me: "Hi, Tommy, what are you up to tomorrow?"

'"Not much."

'"Good, then could you be at the studio at 10? Polydor has just rung. They want an LP by Friday and I can't manage it alone."

'There was nothing there, not even a choice of songs, nothing. But they wanted the master on Friday! I sat down and wrote a couple of songs and at two in the morning I rang a couple of girls I know: "Help! I need some nonsense lyrics urgently – they want a jokey LP." On Monday morning Hansi also had a couple of songs, so we started recording.

'We were more or less alone in the studio – Hansi, me, the choir and Peter Hesslein, who played a few different guitar parts, and that was it. We managed to get the deadline postponed a bit, making it ten days rather than five, but I delivered the master the following Wednesday. That was a mistake, because the record was no highlight. It was called *Alles hat ein Ende nur die Wurst hat zwei* (Everything Has an End, Only a Sausage Has Two) and was the last carnival production we did. But of course they didn't say on it that it had been made in ten days. No one would have cared anyway.'

The Professor of Sound:
Ron Last, mixing console

Ron took over as Peter Klemt's successor during the 1990s, becoming the sole sound engineer for all his father's productions. 'Working with Peter Klemt taught me a great deal. I sat next to him with eyes and ears wide open, held my tongue and learned an incredible amount. I honestly have to say that I am very grateful to him for broadening my horizon into the past, so to speak. He is my link to acoustic recording. But there is a clear distinction in our philosophies. Peter recorded entire orchestras, whereas I record individual instruments and only put them together as an orchestra when I am mixing.'

When Ron Last speaks of his work, it turns into a seminar for apprentices. 'Klemt mixed more spatially, in particular for rhythm. When I mix it is drier. But this allows for considerably more range in terms of frequency response, and the mix is thought through differently in three-dimensional terms. I make a spatial distinction in the frequency spectrum. Each instrument is assigned a particular bandwidth and the next one follows on directly from that. That way I can achieve greater clarity because the instruments don't overlap.

'Also I mix them like a stereo image: at the "front" is the rhythm, which is relatively dry, and at the "back" the strings with the appropriate reverberation. Today only three or four instruments at most are recorded at one time – apart from the strings. If one musician makes a mistake, we simply redo the take. In the past, 20 people used to be in the studio at the same time. If 19 musicians had played well and one had been off, you simply accepted it. That made the music more human. But of course for a man with such fine hearing as Hansi, it's better if he can re-record any part that's not perfect.'

All the same, Ron regrets the passing of the big-studio sound. 'I am constantly searching for suitable rooms for our string recordings. We have even recorded in a school assembly hall. That was for three songs by the legendary Chinese singer Teresa Tang, for an album especially for the Asian market. The entire studio was transported into this school. It was an enormous effort, but the acoustic results made it well worth the trouble. There was one problem, though. The school lies in the flight path of Hamburg airport, so every few minutes a jet would thunder overhead and we had to wait. That was a bit too much of a pain.'

Working in small studios has had an effect on Last's writing style – the strings, for instance. 'We generally consider the strings as a single instrument, which means 24 string players sit in a semicircle in front of one microphone. As you can imagine, for all the players to be the same distance from the microphone, it has to be quite a distance away, which means a large room. The technique didn't work in smaller studios, so Hansi said, "Look, in this room, the strings sound a little sharp on the high notes. When we record here next time, I'll arrange the strings a bit lower." So he doesn't just do his arranging to suit the capabilities of the individual musicians, but also the qualities of the recording studio. I don't know of any other arranger who thinks so much about the means at his disposal as Hansi.'

The Man in the Hollowed-Out
Speaker: Erlend Krauser, guitar

'In 1992 I joined the band in the middle of a tour of Great Britain. I thought I was entering the top flight, but far from it. It was such a shock to hear what this orchestra sounded like live: very imprecise. From my point of view the entire rhythm section was totally disorganised. It was like dragging sacks of potatoes.'

That is pure Erlend Krauser: a man of gentle guitar tones but not gentle words. The rhythm section that bore the brunt of this criticism was made up of Last veterans like Benny Bendorff, Terry Jenkins and Herbert Bornholdt, musicians who had experienced and helped to shape Last's most successful times. But Krauser lives in his own special world of sound and his demands tread the fine line between passion and arrogance. He is completely in his element on this subject, pontificating on micro-timing and groove, on freestyle music and exact beats, and he does it with an enthusiasm that proves he's a heart-and-soul musician.

Krauser is a Banat Swabian, born near Timisoara, Romania, in 1958. His father was a violin teacher and played in a Romanian symphony orchestra, so junior was expected to become a violinist, too. But the youngster never really warmed to the instrument: 'My salvation was the guitar combined with noise. Jimi Hendrix, Led Zeppelin – that's how I regained my joy for music.'

Krauser became a member of the band Phoenix, which had to camouflage its songs with elements of folklore to avoid being banned from performing in communist Romania under Ceaucescu. The 19-year-old finally smuggled his way out of the country in a hollowed-out bass speaker on the back of a lorry, thus making his way to Germany.

'I am still looking for *my* sounds, the sounds that belong to my soul. My style is 10 per cent jazzy, a little Pink Floyd, a little rounded, a little Balkan – in any event, calming. Some would call it New Age or esoteric. I try to draw images with my sound. The same applies for my solos for Hansi.

'My wish for him is that he could take his great talent – the ability to write for strings, bass and rhythm – to places no one else can reach. But Polydor/Universal won't put up the money, so all the albums have to be produced at high speed. I once suggested to him, "You've got that super studio in Florida – why don't we make an LP that's really cool, like *Well Kept Secret*?" That's one of his best productions. A lot of people would like to hear more of that: modern, but with elements of improvisation. It doesn't get enough attention. I want to be able to spend ten days on an album, even if I only get paid for five.'

Krauser sees his task in the band as twofold. 'I can totally subordinate myself in a piece and be a humble little worker bee, and in the next piece I am the soloist, as on "Always on My Mind". I need these three or four minutes per evening to show people my soul. Luckily Hansi likes that. We really fire each other up on stage, like Mick Jagger and Keith Richards. We both get something out of it, but it also has its price. I like being the frontman, and these sounds – not just mine – are important for all of our spiritual lives.'

Band Genealogy

In the course of four decades many musicians have played in the James Last band – so many that it would be impossible to list all their names here. There are many, for example, who have worked on numerous recordings but never, or only rarely, appeared live. It's the public appearances that are the key, so the timeline of the band begins with the first tour, with Freddy Quinn, in 1968. There were often 'stand-ins' who are not mentioned here, which is no reflection on their musicianship. Despite the changing line-up, there was always something of a core team that shaped the James Last family. The number in brackets indicates the year they joined the band.

Trumpets:
1) Adam Weckerle/GER (68) – Leif Uvemark/SWE (70) – Rick Kiefer/USA (72) – Derek Watkins/UK (76)

2) Kuddl Pohle/GER (68) – Dieter Kock/GER (70) – Hakan Nyquist/SWE (76) – Chuck Findley/USA (01)

3) Manfred Moch/GER (68) – Bob Lanese/USA (72) –
   Bob Findley/USA (02)

4) Heinz Habermann/GER (68) – Lennart Axelsson/SWE (72)
   – Jan Kohlin/SWE (80) – Bob Coassin/AUS (81)

Trombones:
1) Manfred Grossmann/GER (68) – Wolfgang Ahlers/GER (70)
   – Georges Delagaye/BEL (72) – Ole Holmquist/SWE (78),
   also Pete Beachill/UK (91)
2) Detlef Surmann/GER (68)
3) Egon Christmann/GER (68) – Conny Bogdan/GER (69) –
   Nick Hauk/SWE (77) – Björn Haengsel/SWE (84) –
   Mats Lundberg/SWE (91) – Anders Wiborg/SWE (02)

Drums:
Robert Last/GER (65) – Barry Reeves/UK (72) –
Terry Jenkins/UK (78) – Stefan Eggert/GER (02)

Guitar:
Heinz Schulze/GER (68) – Bernd Steffanowski/GER (68) –
Helmuth Franke/GER (69) – Peter Hesslein/GER (71) –
Jim Sullivan/UK (78) – Peter Hesslein/GER (85) –
Erlend Krauser/ROM (92)
Bass:
Fiete Wacker/GER (68) – Benny Bendorff/GER (69) –
Thomas Zurmühlen/D (02)

Saxophone and Flute:
Willi Surmann/GER (68–69)
Karl-Hermann Lüer/GER (66–91)

Emil Wurster/GER (68) – Harald Ende/GER (69) –
Stan Sulzman/UK (79) – Andy Macintosh/UK (88) –
Matthias Clasen/GER (99)

Piano, Organ and Keyboard:
Günter Platzek/GER (65) – John Pearce/UK (91) –
Joe Dorff/USA (02)

Percussion:
Barry Reeves/UK (71) – Herbert Bornholdt/GER (72) –
Pablo Escayola/ECU (01)

Synthesiser:
Peter Hecht, Tommy Eggert, Ron Last/all GER,
Hans Gardemar/SWE

Accordion:
Jochen Ment/GER

Oboe:
Manfred Zeh/GER

First Violin:
Erich Kunisch/GER – Eugen Raabe/GER – Stefan Pintev/GER

The James Last Appreciation Society

In 1974 Polydor decided that a fan club was needed. Up to this
point Hansi had never been happy about this kind of fan mania:
he feared an endless array of competing provincial organisations
that might be too demanding even for his apparently bottomless

resources when it came to dealing with the press and fans. So Germany was out of the question for a fan club, but an international club based in Great Britain sounded much better and so he agreed.

When Polydor decided to found the club, they already had the right man for the job in mind: Peter Boosey, an amateur DJ and a Last fan right from the beginning.

You could say Boosey was the first victim of a Polydor PR campaign to make Last known in Britain. 'In 1966 a series of *This Is ...* LPs were released here,' Boosey recalls. 'The British market was supposed to be opened up to German orchestras. Max Greger, Bert Kaempfert, Roberto Delgado – and James Last. In contrast to the normal price of £2, these albums only cost 65 pence. But the only thing on the cover was *This Is James Last*. You couldn't tell if it was a singer or an orchestra, and I had never heard of James Last. Oh well, 65p wasn't such a big loss, so I risked it – and I liked the music straight away.'

Boosey began collecting Last LPs, and when the first Last concert in England was held in 1971 he went along. 'It was in the old Victoria venue in London, a former cinema that could hold up to 2,000 people. The entire audience was of my age then, between 30 and 40. Oddly enough, the curtain was open even before the show began. The auditorium light went out and the musicians came on stage. As an introduction they began with a slow piece, "Once on a Sunday Morning". But suddenly this slow number transformed into a wild "Sabre Dance" by Khachaturian, and it was like I'd been struck by lightning. I'd never heard such loud music before. There were speakers galore to the left and right of me, and it took 20 minutes for me to get used to it. A pop band might play like that, but an orchestra?!'

That made Boosey curious. He was always writing to the record company for more information and that had its consequences. One afternoon Peter's telephone rang. It was Polydor asking if he felt like setting up a James Last fan club. Boosey didn't need to think twice: after all, it was his big chance to meet his idol. After several discussions, everything was agreed.

'I certainly wasn't the greatest James Last fan since I only had 20 albums,' Boosey says, 'but I was obviously the most inquisitive consumer. After a brief period of preparation we started the fan club in 1974. I don't receive any form of payment for it, but there is an account that I can use to sell any Last LPs before they are officially released, and that's what I live on. Only LPs that sound more international are released in Britain, but in Germany and Holland I discovered a completely new James Last world. So I imported these recordings for all the British fans. One day my financial adviser at the bank rang me to let me know that several thousand pounds had now been paid into my account and that was far beyond the usual income. In his view this was now a full-time job, so I founded Boosey Records and then Boosey Travel for group fan trips. Suddenly my hobby had become my profession.'

The fan club is called the James Last Appreciation Society (JLAS). Honorary members number one and two are Andy Williams and Kai Warner. JLAS is still as active as ever: there are James Last dance evenings, a fan magazine and group summer and winter holidays. The fans follow their idol to all his performances around the world by the busload. Whether it's to a show in Holland, a TV recording in Germany or even the concerts in China, many of the fans have experienced dozens of events with Hansi. In the meantime, with their colourful umbrellas, printed T-shirts and club flags, they have become part and parcel of a Last show. Whenever Last has the feeling that one event or another needs a bit of pepping up, he calls on his faithful British fans for help.

The JLAS also organises bus trips to the famous *Sing mit* (Sing Along) parties in Hamburg, and the number of British fans who travel there grows from year to year. Every year Last thinks of something special for this group. Once he invited them to the studio, once to his office, once to the Rathauskeller (a traditional restaurant in the cellar of the Hamburg town hall), but he always takes care of their creature comforts. The biggest surprise for Peter Boosey was in 1979 when they arrived at the railway station in Hamburg: waiting for them on the platform was Last with a brass band, and afterwards he had them served soup, bread rolls and mulled wine on the steps of the Plaza Hotel.

When the British fans followed their favourite to the USA, Last really splashed out for such loyalty. 'When the TV recording for the programme *Beachparty '95* was being made, we were in Miami with a group of 50 fans. Hansi invited us all out to a restaurant every day. "Order what you like, wine, beer, one course, two, whatever you feel like." On the last day we partied all night – the fans, the choir, the musicians, the TV crew – there must have been around 200 people. Hansi paid for *everything*. It's always been like that. He is extraordinarily generous. You could write a whole book about the relationship between him and his fans.'

A particular highlight for Boosey was one special evening in Hamburg. 'Hansi's manager Bodo Eckmann and his wife Silke, my wife and I were waiting in a fantastic restaurant near St Michael's Church. Five minutes later Hansi storms in and says, "Drop everything and come with me!" He dragged us up to the church steeple of St Michael's and at the top some members of the tower brass ensemble played just for us. There was champagne and a brightly illuminated Hamburg stretched out before us below. He had organised it just for the fun of it, a madcap idea.

There we were, standing above the city, just the six of us – that was a magical moment for me.'

A special moment for the whole club was the day in August 1999 when Last flew from Florida to London especially to celebrate the 25th anniversary of JLAS with his fans in Bristol. As the fan magazine reported, 'Hansi was in top form ... he was simply enjoying being with his fans. Although the queue lining up for autographs at Hansi's table didn't seem to be getting any shorter, there was not an inch of room on the dance floor. Hansi noted attentively every song we played, many of which he had not heard for years. ... During the draw of the raffle Hansi spontaneously came on stage and donated an additional prize of two weeks' holiday in Florida.'

Boosey has been running the JLAS for more than 30 years now, making him one of Last's longest-serving co-workers. 'Shortly after we founded the club I went backstage after a concert to introduce myself to the musicians. Of all the people who were involved back then, including tour attendants, Polydor co-workers and so on, there are only four people still there: Hansi, Liz Pretty the British tour manager, trombonist Detlef Surmann and I.'

Boosey also believes he knows the secret of Last's continuing popularity. 'Orchestras are completely out at the moment. There's really only André Rieu, who has turned back the clock about a hundred years, and James Last, but he is modern. Hansi has survived all this time because he is constantly adapting. Conniff sounded exactly the same for 40 years, Kaempfert, too. Hansi might have lost some fans along the way because he was too progressive for them – if you ask him his favourite band he'll say Iron Maiden or Usher. I don't know how many 77-year-olds have heard of Usher, but Last has entertained two or three generations of people and is still at the forefront.'

Dancing the Night Away – A Fan Party

A light industrial area near Düsseldorf – plain factories and warehouses, broad streets on a grid plan. There is no suggestion of enjoying life – people come here to work. The area is almost empty after 6pm, particularly on a Saturday. Yet somewhere loud music is playing – *Beachparty*, *Non Stop Dancing*, *Happy Lehar* – and there's a distinct smell of lamb chops and sausages. On Saturday? In an industrial area?

Frank and Sybille run a wholesale photo business. They also like to listen to loud music in the evening, so to avoid the neighbours complaining, they simply built their house next to their business. After all, there's no one there in an industrial area on Saturdays – apart from the 35 people who have just descended on the generous buffet that Sybille has prepared. In fact, they've come especially because of the loud music: to the big Hansi Summer Party. They're from all parts of Germany, Switzerland and France, and they're real hardcore fans: most of them have known each other for years.

Frank and Sybille's house would pale any James Last museum. It's full of posters, concert programmes, thousands of photos, *all* the records, CDs and videos available (and some that aren't), newspaper cuttings, backstage passes, fan T-shirts, an oil painting of their favourite with a very personal autograph and – their crowning glory above the fireplace – a wooden carving of Hansi's profile. The two of them have been leading a 'James Last marriage' for the last 30 years. The bandleader is the focal point of their interest – and naturally their son is named Ron.

'Naturally, it all looks kind of crazy,' says Sybille with disarming frankness, 'but we feel so close to Hansi. We are grateful to him for so many wonderful experiences and he is a fixture in our lives. We were so relieved to find that we weren't the only nutters: there are loads of other people who feel the same way. That's why we have this party.'

Frank and Sybille's enthusiasm costs them around 15,000 euros a year. Other fans take out loans so they can follow their hero on tour. The keenest concert-goer is undoubtedly Peter, from Switzerland. He's a postal worker so he doesn't have a huge income, but he saves all his money to see as many concerts as he can. 'I probably hold the record,' he says proudly. 'My 300th James Last concert was in 2004 at the Color Line Arena in Hamburg.'

Each one of the guests can talk for hours about James Last, and they all know every record, every song, every note inside out – in fact, just about everything there is to know about him. They have all met him several times and can recount at least one very personal Last experience. Take another Peter, for instance, whose young son died a few years ago. 'Hansi really helped me through the situation,' he says. 'He reassured me again and again to keep going and not let my head down. Without him and the support of my friends here, I wouldn't have survived it.'

Peter was just a small boy the first time he met Last. 'I was visiting an aunt who lived in the same street as James Last. I was just on my way home when Hansi suddenly appeared in front of me. I was so excited I could only stutter, but I managed to ask him for his autograph. He said quite casually, "If you want to, why don't you come over for coffee?" And before I knew it I was over at James Last's house for coffee and cake! I thought I was dreaming! Twenty years later I asked Hansi if he could remember that afternoon, and he could still remember everything exactly as it was.'

In the meantime, the party has really got going. Frank is also a talented DJ. From now on in, it's non-stop dancing only. Charles, from France, provides the entertainment, mimicking James Last and his whole band, including a particularly good imitation of Bob Lanese. Then comes the highlight of the party: Frank sets off fireworks into the clear night sky and sparklers are distributed as a recording of a concert from 2000 plays. Gradually, the warm summer night takes on the atmosphere of an open-air concert: 70 arms stretch up into the air and wave in time to the music: 'You'll be in my heart…'

What more is there to be said?

♪

acknowledgements

My co-author and I would like to thank all those people who contributed to this book with their memories, archives and photos as well as their ideas and their work, in particular my wife Christine, my children Ron and Caterina, and Marianne Last, the widow of my brother Robert.

We would also like to thank in alphabetical order: Kats Aoyama, Simon Bell, Peter Boosey, Karl-Heinz "Charly" Cisek, Richard Clayderman, Anton Corbijn, Ossi Drechsler, Bodo Eckmann, Tommy Eggert, Barbara Freiberger, Peter Gertsch, Conny Güntensperger, Meinhart Heim, Ingeborg von Heynitz, Sybille and Frank-Michael Kammann, Peter Klemt, Werner Klose, Erlend Krauser, Angela Kuepper, Bob Lanese, Peter Lüken, Marc Le Maire, Milva, Wencke Myhre, Markus Naegele, Gabriela Nowotny, Stefan Pintev, Carla Platzek, Freddy Quinn, Heinz and Elfriede Reincke, Dieter Semmelmann, Roland Spiegel, Ingo Stein, Michael Surböck, Detlef Surmann, Olivier Toussaint,

Rainer Tratnig-Frankl, Werner Triepke, Martina Tuma, Harry van der Veen, Thomas Walentin, Michael von Winterfeldt.